'The new edition of *Postmodern Narrative Theory* stands out from its competitors because of its concision, clarity, and refreshingly lively style. Mark Currie achieves this while also presenting a highly nuanced and sophisticated account of this increasingly important field of study.'
—Dr Brendan Stone, University of Sheffield, UK

How have developments in literary and cultural theory transformed our understanding of narrative? What has happened to narrative in the wake of poststructuralism? What is the role and function of narrative in the contemporary world?

In this revised, updated and expanded new edition of an established text, Mark Currie explores these central questions and guides students through the complex theories that have shaped the study of narrative in recent decades. *Postmodern Narrative Theory*, Second Edition:

- establishes direct links between the workings of fictional narratives and those of the non-fictional world
- charts the transition in narrative theory from its formalist beginnings, through deconstruction, towards its current concerns with the social, cultural and cognitive uses of narrative
- explores the relationship between postmodern narrative and post-modern theory more closely
- presents detailed illustrative readings of known literary texts such as Stevenson's *Dr Jekyll and Mr Hyde* and Conrad's *Heart of Darkness*, and now features a new chapter on Coetzee's *Elizabeth Costello* and *Slow Man*.

Approachable and stimulating, this is an essential introduction for anyone studying postmodernism, the theory of narrative or contemporary fiction.

Mark Currie is Professor of Contemporary Literature at Queen Mary, University of London, UK.

Transitions critically explores movements in literary theory. Guiding the reader through the poetics and politics of interpretative paradigms and schools of thought, **Transitions** helps direct the student's own ical analysis. As well as transforming the critical development by interpreting them from the perspective of the present day enacts transitional readings of a number of well-known literar

transitions
General Editor: Julian Wolfreys

Published titles
TERRY EAGLETON David Alderson
JULIA KRISTEVA AND LITERARY THEORY Megan Becker-Leckrone
BATAILLE Fred Botting and Scott Wilson
NEW HISTORICISM AND CULTURAL MATERIALISM John Brannigan
HÉLÈNE CIXOUS Abigail Bray
HOMI K. BHABHA Eleanor Byrne
GENDER Claire Colebrook
POSTMODERN NARRATIVE THEORY 2nd edition Mark Currie
FORMALIST CRITICISM AND READER-RESPONSE THEORY Kenneth Womack and
  Todd F. Davis
IDEOLOGY James M. Decker
QUEER THEORY Donald E. Hall
MARXIST LITERARY AND CULTURAL THEORIES Moyra Haslett
ROLAND BARTHES Martin McQuillan
LOUIS ALTHUSSER Warren Montag
RACE Brian Niro
JACQUES LACAN Jean-Michel Rabaté
LITERARY FEMINISMS Ruth Robbins
SUBJECTIVITY Ruth Robbins
DECONSTRUCTION • DERRIDA Julian Wolfreys
TRANSGRESSION Julian Wolfreys

ORWELL TO THE PRESENT, 1945–1999 John Brannigan
CHAUCER TO SHAKESPEARE, 1337–1580 SunHee Kim Gertz
MODERNISM, 1910–1945 Jane Goldman
POPE TO BURNEY, 1714–1786 Moyra Haslett
PATER TO FORSTER, 1873–1924 Ruth Robbins
BURKE TO BYRON, BARBAULD TO BAILLIE, 1790–1830 Jane Stabler
MILTON TO POPE, 1650–1720 Kay Gilliland Stevenson
DICKENS TO HARDY, 1837–1884 Julian Wolfreys
SIDNEY TO MILTON, 1580–1660 Marion Wynne Davies

Forthcoming titles
NATIONAL IDENTITY John Brannigan
SPACE Christina Britzolakis
POSTMODERNISM • POSTMODERNITY Martin McQuillan
POSTCOLONIAL THEORIES Jenni Ramone

Transitions
Series Standing Order
ISBN 0-333-73634-6
(*outside North America only*)

You can receive future titles in this series as they are published. To place a standing order please contact your bookseller or, in case of difficulty, write to us at the address below with your name and address, the title of the series and the ISBN quoted above.

Customer Services Department, Macmillan Distribution Ltd, Houndmills, Basingstoke, Hampshire RG21 6XS, England

---

transitions

Postmodern Narrative Theory

Second edition

Mark Currie

palgrave
macmillan

First edition 1998
Second edition 2011 published by
PALGRAVE MACMILLAN

Palgrave Macmillan in the UK is an imprint of Macmillan Publishers Limited, registered in England, company number 785998, of Houndmills, Basingstoke, Hampshire RG21 6XS.

Palgrave Macmillan in the US is a division of St Martin's Press LLC, 175 Fifth Avenue, New York, NY 10010.

Palgrave Macmillan is the global academic imprint of the above companies and has companies and representatives throughout the world.

Palgrave® and Macmillan® are registered trademarks in the United States, the United Kingdom, Europe and other countries.

ISBN 978–0–230–24935–6 hardback
ISBN 978–0–230–24936–3 paperback

This book is printed on paper suitable for recycling and made from fully managed and sustained forest sources. Logging, pulping and manufacturing processes are expected to conform to the environmental regulations of the country of origin.

A catalogue record for this book is available from the British Library.

A catalog record for this book is available from the Library of Congress.

10   9   8   7   6   5   4   3   2   1
20   19   18   17   16   15   14   13   12   11

Printed in China

To Tory, my story without a beginning

Contents

General Editor's Preface

> Transitions: *transition-em,* n. of action. 1. A passing or passage from one condition, action or (rarely) place, to another. 2. Passage in thought, speech, or writing, from one subject to another. 3. **a.** The passing from one note to another **b.** The passing from one key to another, modulation. 4. The passage from an earlier to a later stage of development or formation . . . change from an earlier style to a later; a style of intermediate or mixed character . . . the historical passage of language from one well-defined stage to another.

The aim of *Transitions* is to explore passages and movements in critical thought, and in the development of literary and cultural interpretation. This series also seeks to examine the possibilities for reading, analysis and other critical engagements which the very idea of transition makes possible. The writers in this series unfold the movements and modulations of critical thinking over the last generation, from the first emergences of what is now recognised as literary theory. They examine as well how the transitional nature of theoretical and critical thinking is still very much in operation, guaranteed by the hybridity and heterogeneity of the field of literary studies. The authors in the series share the common understanding that, now more than ever, critical thought is both in a state of transition and can best be defined by developing for the student reader an understanding of this protean quality.

This series desires, then, to enable the reader to transform her/his own reading and writing transactions by comprehending past developments. Each book in the series offers a guide to the poetics and politics of interpretative paradigms, schools and bodies of thought, while transforming these, if not into tools or methodologies, then into conduits for directing and channelling thought. As well as transforming the critical past by interpreting it from the perspective of the present day, each study enacts transitional readings of a number of well-known literary texts, all of which are themselves conceivable as having been transitional texts at the moments of their first appearance. The readings offered in these books seek, through close critical reading and theoretical engagement, to demonstrate certain possibilities in critical thinking to the student reader.

It is hoped that the student will find this series liberating because rigid methodologies are not being put into place. As all the dictionary definitions of the idea of transition above suggest, what is important is the action, the passage: of thought, of analysis, of critical response. Rather than seeking to help you locate yourself in relation to any particular school or discipline, this series aims to put you into action, as readers and writers, travellers between positions, where the movement between poles comes to be seen as of more importance than the locations themselves.

Julian Wolfreys

Acknowledgements

The first edition of this book was written with the support of my colleagues in the English Department at the University of Dundee, and particularly with the encouragement and detailed comment of Julian Wolfreys. I owe thanks to the School of Literature and Creative Writing at the University of East Anglia for providing me with the time to produce this second edition, and to the students at UEA for their fascinating creative and critical responses to the issues of postmodernism. I would like to thank several attentive readers of the first edition of the book for comments and arguments that led to improvements for the second edition, most notably the participants in a British Council seminar in Sibiu, Romania, in 2000, whose discussions of the contents changed my thinking in very positive ways. Ken Newton at the University of Dundee deserves special mention for the precision and intelligence of his responses, and for being a formative influence on everything it contains. I would like to thank Margaret Bartley, the original commissioning editor, Sonya Barker and Felicity Noble for their enthusiasm for and help with this second edition, and David Joseph for many valuable editorial suggestions.

Abbreviations

EC   J.M. Coetzee. *Elizabeth Costello: Eight Lessons.* London: Vintage, 2004.

HD   Joseph Conrad. *Heart of Darkness* (1902). London: Penguin, 1983.

JH   Robert Louis Stevenson. *Dr Jekyll and Mr Hyde and Other Stories* (1886). London: Penguin, 1979.

SM   J.M. Coetzee. *Slow Man.* London: Vintage, 2006.

Introduction

Part 1: What is a postmodern narrative?

Postmodern narrative theory, as a phrase, presents an awesome trinity, a grouping of terms and relations that produces complex questions from the start. This is a book about three things that have to be thought about together: postmodern narrative, postmodern theories of narrative and the postmodern world. The awe is partly inspired by the sheer size of these things, these generalities the size of epochs, and the quantity of material they encompass. But from the start there is some uncertainty about the size of entity under consideration. The postmodern world sounds like the universal set, encompassing the other two as subsets, but how big are the subsets? Is a postmodern narrative one kind of contemporary narrative, or is it any contemporary narrative? The noun phrases *postmodern narrative* and *postmodern narrative theory* are inhabited by this basic tension between part and whole, or between the qualitative and the epochal description.

This is a tension that I propose to live with in the discussion that follows. We should dispense with the illusion, from the outset, that words like *postmodern* can be nailed down, even if that means tolerating an oscillation as severe as this, between a kind of writing and a universal condition, which is after all no different from the conceptual instability of a word like *modernist*. On the other hand, it would be unreasonable to begin by saying that this is a book about three things (postmodern narrative, postmodern theories of narrative and the postmodern world) none of which can be defined because the key term in each is wobbling around too much. In the second part of this introduction, the task will be to address the question of what postmodern narrative theory means, what contemporary theory has to say about narrative and whether there is non-postmodern contemporary narrative theory. In this first part, the project is to outline what critics and theorists tend to mean when they talk about postmodern narrative, and to point to some of the problems.

One of the lines of argument in this study is that the expertise we have acquired for the analysis of narrative in general owes its greatest debt to linguists and critics working with literary texts, and particularly with the novel. This may be because novels are the most elaborate narratives that we have, or it may be that, for whatever reasons, they are simply the narratives that have received the most analytical attention. There is an issue here that lies at the heart of postmodern thinking about narrative. When we think of narrative in general, we have to think of a lot of different, non-fictional domains of experience (representations, conversations, explanations, memories) alongside the plethora of fictional narratives that populate the contemporary world. If expertise in narrative has its origins in the analysis of the novel, we have to ask to what extent that expertise is adaptable to narrative in general, to what extent non-fictional narratives share properties and techniques with fictional ones, and therefore whether a literary critical understanding of narrative has anything to contribute to, or occupies any privileged position in, the project of understanding narrative in general. The question of the relation between fiction and reality is not only one that presides over the transferability of literary narratology to a more general narratology; it is also one that seems to preoccupy the postmodern novel itself. For these reasons, an enquiry into the question 'What is postmodern narrative?' finds a useful starting point in the question 'What is a postmodern novel?'. I would like to offer three answers to this question that aim to survey, at too great a speed, the most widespread uses of the word postmodern in relation to the novel, and go on to illustrate and complicate them through the book as a whole.

(1) A postmodern novel takes the issue of the relationship of fiction and reality as a central concern. Postmodern novels are often thought of as anti-realist. They construct fictional worlds only to expose them as artificial constructions. They like to thematise their own artificiality, often by constructing an internal boundary between fiction and reality, which allows for reflection on the relation between fiction and reality, as well as the irony that both the fiction and the reality are, in the end, fictional. They favour illusion-breaking devices, especially ones that highlight the presence of an author, such as the intrusive authorial narrator who steps in to declare the fictionality of a fiction,

or the surrogate author: a figure within the fictional world who occupies the role of an author, or a role analogous to the author. For many, a postmodern novel is, above all, one that involves metalepsis, which is usually defined as frame-breaking, a crossing of some uncrossable boundary between different orders of reality or being, as when a character steps out of a fiction, or an author steps into it to interact with characters. Postmodern novels are metafictions: fictions about fiction; self-conscious fictions; fictions that incorporate critical and theoretical reflection into their fictional worlds. They are, for a whole generation, historiographic metafictions: fictions that raise questions for the philosophy of history, or problems for the reality or the knowability of the past; fictions that draw attention to the artificiality of historical representations, or to the narrative devices that give shape to historical material.

(2) Postmodern novels are intertextual novels. They are highly aware of their condition in a world pervaded by representations, and of their place in a tradition, or a history of representations including other novels. They are citational, in the sense that they cite, allude to, refer to, borrow from or internalise other texts and representations, both real and fictional. They belong to a more general cultural condition in which cultural forms recycle, repeat, reshape and rewrite past forms. They use fictional intertexts as ways of incorporating the boundary between fiction and reality within a fiction, and therefore of dramatising their own relationship with the outside world. They celebrate intermediality, or the representation of relations between novels and other media, such as films, television programmes, images or works of history. They particularly favour the identification of a particular, usually well-known intertext, in the form of a novel, often for the purpose of rewriting it, especially from a point of view that was marginalised in, or not represented by, the original.

(3) Postmodern novels represent a contemporary state of global culture dominated by new technologies. The form and content of postmodern novels reflect aspects of globalisation, especially the metaphorical contraction of the world into a village, and the contradictory pressures of standardisation and diversification that characterise that contraction. At the level of content, the postmodern novel represents worlds of simulation, of the proliferation of representational technologies, and of personal and collective archiving that belong to the contemporary phase of capitalism. They reflect a world in which simulations are increasingly inseparable from the

things they copy, and that the condition of inseparability is inherent in the process of commodification. They represent, above all, issues of identity and cultural difference seen against a backdrop of global, cultural standardisation. At the level of form, new experiences of time and place that derive from globalisation and technological innovation produce experimental narrative forms, especially ones that reflect the simultaneity of a global village, the loss of linearity in temporal experience, or the tendency to experience, in technologically assisted ways, the present as a future representation or recollection.

In this barrage of usages, it is clear that the notion of the postmodern in the phrase *postmodern novel* designates a kind of writing, but one that points towards the most general, epochal tendencies. Some of these uses seem incompatible with each other. There is a claim in (2), for example, that a postmodern novel is often an historical novel, whereas the account given in (3) seems to depend on the novel's ability to represent the contemporary world; the characteristics advanced by (1) on the other hand could be deployed in any kind of novel, and seem concerned with questions inherent in all fictional discourse. Any word that purports to represent something so ungraspable and complex is bound to strain in this way to contain the diversity of its referents, and this one, as we will go on to explore, is under particular stress. We also need to ask, at this point, whether these answers to the question 'What is a postmodern novel?' help us in any way towards the broader question 'What is a postmodern narrative?'. Many of the characteristics listed above pertain to the fictionality of the novel, or operate intertextually within the universe of the novel, by evoking and rewriting, other novels. At first sight it would seem that these answers are absolutely non-transferable to a more general understanding of narrative. The question of a boundary, for example, between fiction and reality seems to offer little of use to what I am going to call the socionarratologist, or the person who aims to use the critical tools of narratology to understand narrative in its broadest contexts, beyond the boundaries of the novel, or of literature in general.

An understanding of the postmodern novel is in fact more productive for narrative theory than it initially appears, but it is not the whole story. It is productive for three reasons. (1) The contemporary novel has produced an enormous resource of complex narrative experimentation, the understanding and analysis of which has enhanced narrative theory's comprehension of the possibilities and problems of narrative. (2) The postmodern novel is highly self-conscious, engaged in its own analysis of these possibilities and problems, and is, as such, a narratological novel: it is, in other words, part of the enquiry into the nature and method of narrative in general. (3) With its concern for the relation between fiction and reality, the postmodern novel's own enquiry into narrative has at its core a belief that fiction, far from being some ghetto of the made-up, is woven into all: its contribution to understanding narrative is an exploration of the difficulty of dividing fiction from reality not only within the genre of the novel, but in discourse more generally, if not the entire discursive formation that constitutes our epoch. These reasons go some way towards indicating the importance of the novel in the analysis that follows, but there is another, equally important story to tell, which has little to do with the postmodern novel. If the question 'What is a postmodern novel?' puts down some co-ordinates for our enquiry, any attempt to address the broader questions of the nature and function of narrative in the contemporary world has to look to narrative theory itself, and to the spectacular accumulation of analytical power it has witnessed in the twentieth century and so far in the twenty-first.

Part 2: Narratology, death and afterlife

Diversification, deconstruction, politicisation

Narratology is the theory and systematic study of narrative. It has been with us in one form or another throughout the twentieth century, and it has evolved into one of the most tangible, coherent and precise areas of expertise in literary and cultural studies. It began as a science of narrative form and structure, acquired a formidable dominance as an approach to literary narrative, overshadowed historical perspective for several decades and then, somewhere in the middle of the 1980s, ran into problems. After years of protest from the historicist camps and after two decades of assault from poststructuralists on its scientific orientation and authority, people started to declare the death of narratology.

Something may have died. Something inside. A certain youthful spirit perhaps. But narratology at large underwent nothing more dramatic than a transition, and a very positive transition away from some of the limits and excesses of its youth. This book aims to describe the transition from the formalist and structuralist narratologies of the recent past, to set out the principles and procedures of the new narratologies, and to illustrate the extended scope and continuing vitality of a narratology in the process of transforming into something much bigger than it was: a narratology capable of bringing its expertise to bear on narratives wherever they can be found, which is everywhere.

If there is a contemporary narratological cliché it is exactly this claim that narratives are everywhere. Many recent studies begin by pointing out that narrative is not confined to literature. However often it has been repeated, it is a key characteristic of the recent change in narratology: a massive expansion in the narratological remit, in the scope of objects for narratological analysis. Commonly cited examples of narrative in everyday life are films, music videos, advertisements, television and newspaper journalism, myths, paintings, songs, comic strips, anecdotes, jokes, stories of our holidays and accounts of our day. In more academic contexts, there has been a recognition that narrative is central to the representation of identity, in personal memory and self-representation or in the collective identities of groups based in regions, nations, race or gender. There has been widespread interest in narrative in history, in the operations of legal systems, in psychoanalysis, in scientific analysis, in economics and in philosophy. Narrative is as inescapable as language in general, or as cause and effect, as a mode of thinking and being. After seminal studies such as Paul Ricoeur's *Time and Narrative* it does not seem at all exaggerated to view humans as narrative animals, as *homo fabulans* – the tellers and interpreters of narrative. In the light of these recognitions it is hard to see how narratology could die out. There may be a crisis of self-importance, requiring that narratology adapts its methods to these new demands, or an identity crisis caused by this diversification. But this is diversification, not death.

Diversification is the first of three principles that can be used to summarise the transition in contemporary narratology. The second principle, if it can be called that, is deconstruction. Deconstruction can be used as an umbrella term under which many of the most important changes in narratology can be described, especially those that depart from the very scientific emphasis of structuralist narratology. As an *-ology*, narratology declares the values of systematic and scientific analysis by which it operated before poststructuralist critiques impacted on literary studies. Much of this book will be devoted to the importance of these critiques and their narratological legacy. At this stage it might be useful to convey some of the general characteristics of this legacy.

From discovery to invention, from coherence to complexity, and from poetics to politics, this is the short summary of the transition that took place in narratological theory in the 1980s. The first change – from discovery to invention – reflects a broad shift in belief away from the scientific assumption that narratology could be an objective science which discovers inherent formal and structural properties in its object narratives. Poststructuralist narratology moved away from the assumed transparency of the narratological analysis towards a recognition that the reading, however objective and scientific, constructed its object. Structure became something that was projected onto the work by a reading rather than a property of a narrative discovered by the reading. Structure came to be seen as a metaphor used by readers of a structuralist bent to give the impression of stability in the object – narrative meaning. Terms like construction, construal, structuration and structuring were preferred by poststructuralists because they point to the active role of the reader in the construction of meaning. Other terms, like process, becoming, play, differance, slippage and dissemination, challenge the idea that a narrative is a stable structure by borrowing their metaphors from the semantic field of movement. In short, poststructuralists moved away from the treatment of narratives (and the language system in general) as buildings, as solid objects in the world, towards the view that narratives were narratological inventions construable in an almost infinite number of ways.

The shift from coherence to complexity was part of this broad departure from the view of narratives as stable structures. Most of the formal sciences of narrative were effectively sciences of unity and coherence. Like the physicist, the chemist or the microbiologist, the role of the narratologist was traditionally to uncover a hidden design which would render the object intelligible. For the traditional critic, the most profound hidden design in a narrative was its unity, the exposure of which would also be a revelation of the work's formal, thematic or even polemic coherence. In other words, in the critical quest for unity there was a desire to present a narrative as a coherent and stable project. In the view of the poststructuralist critic, this was just a way of reducing the complexity or heterogeneity of a narrative: by suppressing textual details that contradicted the scheme, the traditional narratologist could present a partial reading of the text which saw it as a stable and coherent project. It was a key characteristic of poststructuralist narratology that it sought to sustain contradictory aspects of narrative, preserving their complexity and refusing the impulse to reduce the narrative to a stable meaning or coherent project. This will be illustrated later.

The deconstruction of narratology then involved the destruction of its scientific authority and pointed to a less reductive kind of reading which was not underpinned by notions like the coherence of the authorial project or the stability of the language system in general. The deconstruction of narratology was also closely linked to what I called, a moment ago, the diversification of narratology, since deconstruction was no respecter of boundaries, least of all the boundary between literature and the real world. But deconstruction became notorious in the early 1980s for what politically engaged critics such as Marxists saw as its fundamentally conservative character, for a political quietism. Intent as it was on the discovery of doubt and the celebration of irreducible complexity, deconstruction was perceived as another formalism, as a kind of anti-historicism, lacking any basis in historical and political reality and without any programme for social change. How then is it possible to argue that part of the legacy of deconstruction was the transition from poetics to politics?

There are several ways of approaching this issue. The first argument begins from the fact that formalism and historicism had been at war within literary studies through most of the century. In the United States there had been a long period in which the formalist approaches of New Criticism were dominant in literary studies. This was not an unchallenged dominance: American literary journals in the period from 1910 to 1970 attest to a constant opposition to formalist approaches from the historicist camps. When poststructuralist perspectives arrived in the United States in 1966 after a very brief period of interest in structuralism, they were seen by historicists as continuations of the New Critical emphasis on form, and as the next incarnation of the anti-historicist approach. This was not an accurate perception, ignoring as it does the extent to which poststructuralist perspectives were founded on a critique of the synchronic and atemporal nature of structuralist analysis. Many poststructuralists were poststructuralists exactly because they sought to reintroduce historical perspectives into criticism. Even if some of the main deconstructors looked like new New Critics in their formalist orientation, there were important aspects of their theory, which will be described later in this book, which allowed for the convergence of historical and formal critical approaches. This is an important principle which I will do no more than state at the moment: that deconstruction allowed for the reintroduction of historical perspective into narratology, and that this acted as a bridge towards a more political criticism.

The transition from poetics to politics can also be seen as a deconstructive legacy because deconstruction introduced new methods for the unmasking of ideology. While the term 'ideology' had, in the period of polemic warfare between historicism and formalism, been part of the armoury of the Marxist critic and therefore had been broadly perceived as an anti-formalist weapon, it was a term that became a point of convergence for the interests of poststructuralist and Marxist criticism. It became common to hear critics such as Kenneth Burke, Mikhail Bakhtin, Louis Althusser, Pierre Macherey, Michel Foucault or Theodor Adorno invoked for a poststructuralist Marxism, reflecting the perception that there were common denominators between the two approaches traditionally viewed as polemic opponents. At a general level, there were common philosophical denominators. Poststructuralists and Marxists both demoted the individual or subject as an explanatory category and saw the individual as part of a larger social system. As a result, both camps viewed the production of language as the unknowing reproduction of ideological forms and values and not as an original act of undetermined creativity. Both therefore approached literature as an ideological form despite the individual intentions that authors may have held. Given these broad similarities, any new reading procedures from deconstruction which advanced the project of ideological unmasking were bound to be seen as critical resources by politically orientated critics.

A specific example of the way in which deconstruction advanced the unmasking of ideology was the approach it took to the binary opposition (further discussion of which can be found in Chapter 2 of Wolfreys' *Deconstruction • Derrida,* in this series). This was an area of critical procedure and theory which belonged specifically to the apolitical tradition of structuralism, but which took on a more political inflection in the hands of some poststructuralists. Structuralist linguists had perhaps overstated the importance of the binary opposition as a meaning-generating unit, and structuralist narratologists were sometimes obsessive about the structural role of the binary opposition in narrative. The poststructuralist critic often shares this obsession but tends to view the binary opposition as an unstable basis for meaning and as a place where the values and hidden ideologies of the text are inscribed. A deconstructive reading, for example, will characteristically view the binary opposition as a hierarchy in which one term of the opposition enjoys a privilege over the other, and the reading often proceeds to demonstrate that the text contains counter-suggestions which upturn the hierarchy.

These narratological procedures are analysed in more detail later in this book. My aim for now is to point to an emphasis in deconstructive reading on the uncovering of hidden values in a narrative – values which often subvert what might be called the conscious intention of the narrative.

Even if deconstruction did not always see these aporetic oppositions in obviously political terms, it was nevertheless part of the legacy of deconstruction to provide new approaches to the discovery of ideology in narrative. Since deconstruction, it is common to find overtly political narratologies articulated in an identifiably deconstructive vocabulary and bringing distinctly deconstructive approaches to bear on issues in the politics and ideology of narrative.

Diversification, deconstruction and politicisation then are three characteristics of the transition in contemporary narratology. It will already be apparent that the three terms are mutually implicated, forming a triangular menage. The transition they describe is a transition in the general assumptions and procedures of poststructural narratology, and the importance of each term varies in specific works of narratology and narratological theory. But it takes no more than a browse in the bookshop to confirm that a transition has taken place along these lines. Studies published before 1987 often use the word 'narratology' in the title. They have chapter headings like 'Events', 'Characterisation', 'Time' and 'Focalisation'. They are abstract grammars that declare their allegiance to linguistics at every turn, in their style and terminology. And they are focused on literary narrative. Studies after that date are more interdisciplinary, harder to shelve and to find. They don't use the -ology word in their titles, preferring narrative theory or even narrativity, and often link the question of narrative to particular identity groups (gender, race and nation) or types of discourse. They are less abstract, less scientific and more politically engaged. They often begin by declaring that narrative is everywhere, that it is a mode of thinking and being, and that it is not confined to literature.

Models for narratological change

In 1937, John Crowe Ransom wrote an influential essay titled 'Criticism Inc.'. It posed a very persuasive argument that in the new age of professionalism the literary critic had a weak academic identity. It argued that the critic had to develop an area of expertise which was distinct from that of the historian and the philosopher, and that departments of literature should no longer see themselves as branches of bigger trees: as the history of literature or the ethics of literature. For Ransom the identity crisis in literary studies was resolvable by the development of a distinct technical expertise which would enhance the critic's ability to describe the text itself without reference to historical context or philosophical ideas.

In 1983, Terry Eagleton published an enormously influential introduction to literary theory which argued the opposite: that the formalist
expertise that had been the dominant strain in literary studies through
most of the century was a restriction on the professional literary critic
because it excluded issues about the politics and ideology of literature
and prevented the critic from working in the service of social change.

These two arguments represent the poles of historicism and formalism
between which literary studies oscillated in the late twentieth century.
Whenever one camp seemed dominant, the other would declare a state
of crisis resolvable only by the displacement of one kind of criticism by
the other. In the 1970s and 1980s there was a new crisis every 20 min-
utes as textual and contextual critics sought to destroy each other in one
of the most absurd debates in intellectual history. Perhaps because of the
increased speed of the oscillation, the debate became increasingly about
nuances of difference in the politics of reading. The so-called 'theory wars'
of the 1970s and 1980s actually tore departments of literature apart in
debates organised around the narcissism of increasingly minor difference.

Perhaps a peak of absurdity was reached in 1989 when Paul de Man's
wartime journalism was discovered by a Belgian scholar. For the politically committed, de Man's readings of narrative represented the dangers
of a criticism with a formalist orientation, and in the 1980s his work
was the subject of a kind of witch hunt, where the witchery was characterised as the presentation of a right-wing politics in the costume of leftist
radicalism. The wartime journalism – mostly inoffensive reviews for a
collaborationist newspaper in Belgium – was widely viewed as confirmation of the latent fascism in deconstructive narratology. The case was no
doubt aggravated by de Man's apologists, who brought deconstructive
narratological perspectives to bear on the new narrative of de Man's
life. For many, the episode seemed to confirm the link between the
deconstructive celebration of doubt and indeterminacy in narrative and
the question of the critic's political responsibility, or, in stronger language,
the link between deconstruction and fascism.

Eagleton's argument was part of an evolving political rectitude in criticism which effaced the difference between a formalist orientation in
narratology and war crime. I would not want to understate the ideological power of narrative in areas such as the legitimation of nation, of
empire building, in attitudes to race and gender, or in the perpetuation of
inequality. I would however contest the importance of narratological orientation to social change on two grounds. The first is a profound doubt
about how much impact the unmasking of narrative ideology could ever

have on political culture in general. If the role of an intellectual is to speak the truth to power, as Gramsci formulated it, the evidence suggests that power is not listening. Recent debates on education in Britain, for example, illustrate the greater impact of recent thought on the importance of spelling at school level than the dissident narratologies of university English. The second ground for doubt is the dubious alignment of historicist narratological orientations with social change and of formalism with political quietism. It is now much more apparent than it used to be that historicist and ideologically orientated critics depend on formalist narratological terminology and models for analysis in order to be able to say anything precise about the history and the ideology of narrative. The strength of contemporary narratology lies in the wealth of descriptive resources that were developed by mainly formalist critics and could then be used by critics of a more historicist bent. In other words, the issue of social change is a red herring, and the understanding of how ideology operates in narrative is an important subset of a contemporary narratology that depends on the descriptive resources of its formalist history.

Part of the problem here lies in the absurdity of a debate that casts formalism as the polar opposite of historicism when the two camps have clearly forged a more co-operative relationship. But the problem also lies in the models that have been used to theorise critical change. One model, or metaphor, that has been widely used is that of fashion. According to this metaphor, no critical orientation is more capable than any other of conveying the truth about a text, but critical approaches have a built-in obsolescence. After a period of dominance they will give way to an approach whose main critical virtue is newness, even when that newness consists in the recovery and recontextualisation of the past. Criticism adhered to the value of newness to an embarrassing extent in the twentieth century, where the names of critical approaches functioned as flags of allegiance to modernity – New Criticism, New Historicism, Poststructuralism, Postmodernism, Postmarxism, Postfeminism and so on – and the terminology of each approach resorts to neologisms – the -ologies, -icities and others – which perform the same function. The fashion industry itself has started borrowing terminology back from the world of philosophy and criticism: deconstruction has become a designer clothes label and a record label, and postmodernism is widely used as a marketing term for items of clothing, decoration and style.

The metaphor of fashion, of course, carries negative connotations of superficiality, conformism and directionless change. As such it is often an accusation levelled against dominant critical approaches – that they are mere fashions. The more weighty version of the same model is the idea of the critical paradigm, a model borrowed from the philosophy of science. This model was originally used by Thomas Kuhn to describe revolutions in scientific procedure, which were brought about by a crisis in the ability of existing science to answer new questions. For Kuhn, a paradigm was a period of consensus in the scientific community about the questions asked and methods used by scientific investigation. At key moments in the history of science, such as in the transition from Newtonian to Einsteinian physics, this consensus would be broken by interpretative requirements not accommodated by the existing paradigm. After a period of crisis, the entire framework of ideas and methods through which the universe was interpreted would be forced to change to meet the demands of new interpretative requirements. Kuhn's model, then, defined scientific authority not as the authority of objective truth but as a consensually performed interpretation: that the authority of a science was derived from the simple fact that everyone in the scientific community was playing the same game by the same rules. An important function of the model of the Kuhnian paradigm when adapted to criticism was, therefore, to describe a principle for change in a similar way to the metaphor of fashion while at the same time adding the gravitas of an analogy with the evolution of scientific investigation.

The widespread influence of Kuhn's model in criticism brought with it some of the perspectives that led some to view narratology as a dead science. Despite a clear emphasis in Kuhn's own work on the incremental character of successive paradigms – that they did not simply break from the science of the past but modified past science to meet new requirements – many critics used the model as one of the linear displacement of one kind of criticism by another. An extremely reductive version of recent critical history resulted, where New Criticism was replaced by structuralism, which was in turn displaced by deconstruction, which was supplanted by New Historicism. For most narratologists, this is an unrecognisable account of recent events whose temporality was on the one hand much more confused and on the other much more continuous. Structuralist narratology, for example, could not have advanced the study of narrative in the spectacular way that it did if it had not been for its formalist progenitors in the European and Anglo-American traditions. Notably, the study of narrative point of view in American New Criticism, the critiques of realism in Russian Formalism or the analysis of speech and thought presentation in British stylistics were all places in which the systematic analysis of narrative was advanced either before or along-side structuralist approaches. It is also true to say that the most rigorous analytical concepts of structuralist narratology did not really impact on university literary studies until much later, and here I am thinking of certain key publications which synthesised narratological method for the Anglo-American tradition – works such as Leech and Short's *Style in Fiction* in 1981 and Rimmon-Kenan's *Narrative Fiction* in 1983. Whatever revolutionary moment structuralist narratology may have inhabited in its heyday in the 1960s, the impact of narratological method was certainly greater in literary studies at large in the 1980s, when it was operating alongside new critical developments from deconstruction and various new historicisms. Rather than a model of linear displacement, it would be more realistic to see the new criticisms of the 1980s and 1990s as approaches that were enabled and resourced by narratology – as the products and not the successors of narratology.

Kuhn's model was abused in other ways, particularly by critics claiming that a paradigm shift was underway and leading inexorably towards their own brand of critical approach. Hans Robert Jauss said this of Reception Theory in the late 1960s, and ever since there has been a queue of appli-cants for the status of paradigmatic dominance from deconstruction, New Historicism and cultural studies. In Kuhn's own work, a paradigm was a whole framework of analytical and interpretative procedures which could only be perceived in retrospect. The abuse here involved critics using the model of a paradigm not as a description of the past but as a prescription for the future, not for the purposes of critical history but in critical mani-festos. At a pinch it is possible to argue that a paradigm shift is describable in the present tense when there is a clear, unified, manifesto-led move-ment in criticism which seems to command a general agreement. As in literary modernism at the turn of the century, there have been moments of high historical self-consciousness in criticism – critical bandwagons – that theorise the need for change in advance rather than describe it his-torically. If it is possible to argue this about the origins of New Criticism, or the manifestos for structuralist linguistic approaches in the 1960s, it becomes more difficult in the 1970s and 1980s when criticism was no longer governed by systematically applicable rules.

The model of the paradigm shift becomes particularly difficult to apply after deconstruction for two reasons. The first is the fact that deconstruction and New Historicism strongly resisted the idea of a systematic method in criticism. In reaction to literary structuralism, deconstruction claimed that it was not a method at all, that there was no theoretical basis for reading, and that a reading always emerged from the specific complexities of the text itself. The commitment to historical specificity in the new historicisms similarly denied theory the status of a unifying, consensual method required by the paradigm model. Even if there were methodological implications in these new approaches, they were not prescribable in advance, and it may still be too early to abstract them in retrospect. The second problem for the paradigm model is the idea of the serene methodological consensus on which it depends. The recent proliferation of criticism into identity groups, the co-existence of incommensurate approaches known as pluralism and the widespread commitment to specificity and the irreducible difference of readings make it impossible to posit consensus or the dominance of any approach in the 1980s and 1990s.

Most historians of criticism acknowledge this: that there has been a breakdown in consensus in the second half of the century from which we, if that word still has meaning, may never recover. In doing so they (e.g. Christopher Norris, Jonathan Culler, Hans Robert Jauss, Frank Lentricchia) usually cite the relative serenity of New Criticism in the United States up to about the middle of the 1960s, after which the consensus yielded irreversibly to critical pluralism. There may be a few grains of truth in this account. It is certainly consistent with ideas such as Lyotard's notion that the postmodern age is characterised by the transition from grand narratives to little narratives, echoed in media studies as the transition in television from broadcasting to narrowcasting, the fashion for niche marketing rather than catch-all advertising, or perspectives from cultural geography on the growth of regionalism.

But to anyone literate in contemporary narrative theory, the story of a lost consensus in criticism also rings loud alarm bells. This is because it is clearly a version of a familiar narrative ideology itself, a kind of Golden Ageism, an Adamic myth which sees change as a fall from the stable conditions of the past into a state of crisis. Theorists such as Raymond Williams, Michel Foucault and Jacques Derrida have taught us to resist the charms of this narrative scheme that idealises the past from which we have fallen. Indeed it only takes a few hours in a library, among the principal journals of New Criticism in the United States, to recognise that the New Criticism never existed as a serene consensus or a unified methodology in quite the way that commentators of the 1970s and 1980s describe. The consensus of the New Criticism was a retrospective construct, one that had to exclude the constant assaults from historicist critics and efface the complex heterogeneity of ideas within the school to present the New

Criticism as a unified consensus. The New Critical consensus was, to use Foucault's words, a structure of exclusion of the kind that is necessary to present the singular character of a bygone age: like the exclusion of madness in the story of the age of reason. In Raymond Williams's words, the New Critical consensus can be seen as a myth functioning as a memory, words he used to describe the pastoral myth of a happier and more natural past.

This is a first brush with the ideological unmasking of narrative. As first brushes go, it is a particularly complicated one since it is not only the ideology of a narrative that is unmasked but the ideology of the narrative of narratology. Poststructuralism tends in this direction, not towards the interpretation of things but towards the interpretation of interpretations or towards the interpretation of metanarratives rather than narratives themselves. Poststructuralists have often argued that this is the only game in town because we have no access to things in themselves except through their interpretations, because all narratives are themselves interpretations, or because all narratives are ultimately metanarrative. These ideas will be unpacked later. For now they present the problem that can be described, to paraphrase Stephen Melville, as criticism beside itself.

How then do I tell the story of a transition in the study of telling a story without getting beside myself? Two things are clear. The first is that too much characteristically postmodern self-consciousness about one's own narrative values, assumptions about the transparency of language or historiographical ideology will be of no help to anybody, least of all me. The second is that a new model for critical change is required that will not so misleadingly construct the narratological past as a happy consensus only to contrast structurally with a complex present. What is required in the new model is an ability to describe the heterogeneity of contemporary narratology, its diverse applications and political uses, its respect for the particularity of narratives, while at the same time summarising this diversity and assembling a more general collection of principles and techniques.

There is a scene of comic banality at the beginning of Quentin Tarantino's *Pulp Fiction* in which Vincent explains to Jules that in Paris the McDonald's Quarter-Pounder with Cheese is known as a Cheese Royale. His account of this apparently meaningless difference bristles with unspoken and ungrasped importance. It is a recognisable modern platitude that delivers a cultural difference in the form of a sermon without moral intent. As a moment of lightness preceding a moment of unspeakable violence, it is part of the film's concern with the morality of filmic violence, contrasting with some of the film's more obtrusive and consequential ser-monising. There are two things that interest me about this scene. The first is the manner in which it encapsulates the essence of a film which constantly poses the question of how one assigns moral attitude to or defines the moral function of a narrative. There are some well-known ver-sions of the debate about the moral function of represented crime, such as the exchange between John Grisham and Oliver Stone over *Natural Born Killers* or the debate about the representation of drug use in *Trainspotting*, which highlights the importance of the question and the gaping need for a narratological basis for its answer. Very few participants in such debates understand anything about the way that narrative works at the ethical and ideological level. It is my conviction that academic narratology can significantly inform these debates, but only through communicable, applicable analytical techniques. The second reason is the complex rela-tions it conveys between cultural standardisation and difference. This is cultural difference perceived through one of the most powerful symbols of global standardisation we have. It is postmodern difference, discernible only against the background of standardisation. It reflects a decision made by the McDonald's corporation somewhere in the early 1980s to diversify menus in recognition of cultural diversity in the market. In this respect it signals the co-dependence of diversification and globalisation, or sameness and difference – the staging of difference against the scenery of standardisation and globalisation – which is as apparent in the mar-keting strategies of the transnational corporation or the unification of Europe as it is in the deconstruction of the literary canon.

Narratology now operates according to the laws of this dynamic. There is an abstract pool of resources drawn eclectically from differ-ent narratological histories – various formalisms, Marxism, Reception Theory, deconstruction, New Historicism, postcolonialism. But it is no longer possible to look upon narratology as a paradigm for critical prac-tice, a template that reduced the rich differences between narratives to a set of arid structural relationships. Narratology has changed exactly because the values of standardisation have been replaced in literary studies by the values of pluralism and irreducible difference: not only difference between texts but difference between readers. In this sense, Roman Jakobson's structuralist dream of a global science of literature has yielded to an uncontrolled fracturing of narratological method. Yet para-doxically, the particularity of texts or readers only becomes recognisable through a shared descriptive vocabulary which in itself constantly threat-ens to homogenise the heterogeneity it advances. It is this paradoxical model of change, the simultaneity of standardisation and diversification, which makes it still possible to write this book or to talk of narratology, if only provisionally, as if it were a unified entity.

Poststructuralist or postclassical narratology

The idea that the early achievements of narratology are still with us, and are still the basis of much of what we know about narrative is easily illustrated in contemporary narratology. Much of the summary that I have just offered describes a critique of scientific narratology and a turn towards identity, ideology and politics, but the idea of narratology as a neutral science has remained very much alive, and has flourished in the twenty-first century. One reason for this is that the projects set out in structuralist narratology had distinctly European origins. In the United States, structuralist narratology had not really taken hold in university literature departments before the poststructuralist critique arrived from Europe, whereas in Europe the situation was substantially the opposite: the structuralist project was well-established and there was little recognition of anything called poststructuralism that might demolish or displace it. It is broadly true to say that the structuralist narratological project has continued uninterrupted in Europe, with all the rigour of its initial scientific character but without the dramatic profile, the sense of an end to cherished literary critical values or the fear that traditional scholarship is in retreat. There have been areas of linguistics and philosophy, such as possible worlds semantics, and discourse theory, that have carried the narratological project forward in its most scientific form, or refurbished its basic concepts. The narratologies with the most influence in the present are still committed to Jakobson's vision of linguistics as a king of global science in literary studies, but have embedded that science inside something even more global: linguistics, for contemporary narratology, is understood as one of the cognitive sciences. In many ways cognitive narratology fulfils the objectives that I have been describing in relation to the diversification of narratology and the turn outwards from literature to broader contexts, to a wider conception of narrative. There is also, in cognitive narratology, an engagement with linguistics that is far more comprehensive, more rigorous and more satisfying than the sometimes dogmatic adherence to Saussurean precepts in literary structuralism. There is, for example, an attempt to overturn what David Herman, following Thomas Pavel, calls the 'structuralist moratorium on referential issues' (2002, p. 4), and a general call 'for updating and enriching narratological theories by incorporating models and tools from discourse analysis, linguistic pragmatics, and cognitive linguistics' (2002, p. 5). Cognitive narratology follows the incremental model of narratological change, in that it takes from structuralism the most important frameworks, terms and methods and incorporates them with perspectives drawn more widely from linguistics, from contextual studies of narrative, and from other approaches to cognition in psychology and philosophy on one hand to neuroscience on the other. There is, in cognitive approaches to narrative, a determined effort to take narratology out into the world, and to bring its insights to bear on narratives wherever they can be found, which as we know, is everywhere. But would we be right to think of it as postmodern? The dichotomy from which this introduction began identified an ambiguity in my title between the theory of postmodern narrative, which might have something to tell us about the postmodern novel, and narrative theory that is itself postmodern. It would be difficult to argue that cognitive narratology had anything particular to tell us about the postmodern novel, but there are interesting reasons for this. A brief detour into David Herman's concept of *storyworld* will help to set out some of the characteristics of the new projects and to highlight an important distinction between what might be thought of as the postclassical, as opposed to the poststructuralist, strands in contemporary narratology.

Storyworlds are, for Herman, 'mental models of who did what to and with whom, when, where, why, and in what fashion in the world to which recipients relocate – or make a diectic shift – as they comprehend a narrative' (2002, p. 5). They are not texts, or objective structures, but mental models produced by readers in response to worlds encoded in narratives. Herman is drawing here on the body of work that I referred to in the previous paragraph as possible worlds semantics, a body of thought about language adapted from philosophical logic, and particularly from ways of talking about necessity and contingency in philosophical statements. Possible worlds offer something to literary narratology that helps it to move beyond the impasse of its Saussurean linguistic premises, or perhaps more accurately, beyond the received idea of what Saussure's work meant for conceptions of linguistic reference (which is the subject of Chapter 2). There is, in Ruth Ronen's words, a 'legitimization of referential problems and issues that have to do with the relations fiction – reality in literary theory' (Ronen, 1994, p. 6). One of the key emphases of possible worlds theory, which finds its way into Herman's use of 'worlds' and 'storyworlds', is the conviction that fictional narrative should not be regarded a special case of narrative on the grounds that it is made up. In fact, discourses of all kinds refer to states of affairs that can be thought of, like fiction, as non-actual, and the concept of possible worlds aims therefore to rescue thought about fictional narrative from a certain kind of isolationism, a certain kind of literary theory that constantly insists on the special ontological properties of fiction. For Herman, the notion of 'worlds' in narrative theory comes as a long awaited thaw after the great referential freeze:

> Also motivating my terminological shift is the very productive use that narrative theorists have made of the idea of *worlds* in recent years. In this respect, I use *storyworld* to suggest something of the world-creating power of narrative, its ability to transport interpreters from the here and now of face-to-face interaction, or space-time coordinates of the encounter with a printed text or a cinematic narrative, to the here and now that constitute the deictic centre of the world being told about.　　(Herman, 2002, p. 14; original italics)

The interest that this notion holds for a conception of postmodern narrative theory lies in the terms of the dichotomy from which we began between a restricted and an inclusive notion of postmodernism: between a narratology concerned with the postmodern novel and a narratology capable of encompassing narratives wherever they are found. For Herman, the importance of the word *storyworld* is its suggestion that all narratives have world-creating power, and that 'storyworld applies to both fictional and non-fictional narratives' (2002, p. 16). The cognitive project seems to take, as its preliminary orientation, the aim of developing a narratology focused on narrative as a mode of cognition, and therefore of thinking about narrative far beyond the ghetto of postmodern novels.

This conception of narratology as a broad and neutral cognitive science, with its relaxation of the formalist rules on reference, offers a very positive direction for the future of narratology and for the possibilities of what might be called a socionarratology. But it does also revert to a traditional division of labour between the analyst and the object of analysis, to the notion of an objective science capable of transparent reference to its objects, and to a descriptive terminology that connotes the values of neutral analytical distance, of a kind that is somewhat at odds with the positions normally associated with poststructuralism. This is a kind of narratology that has decided to get on with its business in spite of the questions about the descriptive power of linguistic terminology that arise in the work of Derrida and de Man, or the issues about critical distance that are articulated by the postmodern novel. The sense of convergence between literary and critical writing that characterises Barthes's later writing is, in cognitive narratology, decisively rejected in favour of a return to the division between narrative and narratological writing, or between creativity and criticism. And we might add that, just as structuralist literary narratology made its name by exposing the structurality of realist narrative, there is, in the notion of storyworld, a marked preference for the kind of narrative that successfully and transparently creates a world, to which a reader unproblematically relocates, over the world-breaking deviations of the postmodern novel. To describe this dichotomy, we can borrow the terminology that has developed inside the cognitive tradition as a description of its own history. Herman, for example, points to a shift from *classical* to *postclassical* narratology: 'In short, postclassical narratology, which should not be confused with poststructuralist theories of narrative, contains classical narratology as one of its "moments" but also includes more recent perspectives on the forms and functions of narrative' (2009, p. 26). Herman is reluctant here, in a way that I have not been in the discussion that follows, to talk of a poststructuralist narratology at all, preferring the phrase 'theories of narrative'. There is undoubtedly a sound justification for this terminological nuance, and it will be apparent in the following discussion that the idea of a poststructuralist narratology as any kind of unified science is difficult, nay impossible, to establish. What is at stake, in my mind, in the dichotomy between poststructuralist and postclassical narratology is the logical status of linguistic descriptions, and the subject–object relations that these descriptions assume; these questions form the basis of the discussions that follow, especially in the first half of the book. There is also the question of what the new narratologies, under both banners, can say about what is distinctly postmodern in contemporary fictional narrative, and by extension, what might be thought of as postmodern in the field of narrative at large. It is my position throughout that postclassical and poststructuralist narratology are allies in this venture.

Part I

Lost Objects

1 The Manufacture of Identities

Is our identity inside us, like the kernel of a nut? Most of the perspectives presented in this book are implicitly dedicated to the proposition that personal identity is not inside us. There are two types of argument. The first is that identity is relational, meaning that it is not to be found inside a person but that it inheres in the relations between a person and others. According to this argument, the explanation of a person's identity must designate the difference between that person and others: it must refer not to the inner life of the person but to the system of differences through which individuality is constructed. In other words, personal identity is not really contained in the body at all; it is structured by, or constituted by, difference. The second type of argument is that identity is not within us because it exists only as narrative. Two things are meant by this: that the only way to explain who we are is to tell our own story, to select key events which characterise us and organise them according to the formal principles of narrative – to externalise ourselves as if talking of someone else, and for the purposes of self-representation; but also that we learn how to self-narrate from the outside, from other stories and particularly through the process of identification with other characters. This gives narration at large the potential to teach us how to conceive of ourselves, what to make of our inner life and how to organise it.

We perhaps automatically think that characters in novels have ready-made moral personalities. It is tempting to see our response to characters as individual and free judgements as the result of an encounter between our own moral values and those represented by the character. It is part of the referential illusion of fictional narrative, for example, that we make inferences about fictional characters no different from the inferences we make about real people. The purpose of this chapter is to illustrate the contribution narratology has made to understanding the technical control of such responses and inferences: to show how our responses are manufactured by the rhetoric of narrative. Chapter 2 deals in more general terms with the illusion of reference. This chapter is concerned in particular with the evolution of questions about sympathy for characters into questions about the ideological function of narrative.

It is not too gross an exaggeration to say that narratology spent the first 50 years of the twentieth century obsessed by the analysis of point of view in narrative. The phrase *point of view* is potentially misleading, suggesting as it does the idea of an opinion or stance on a topic. It is more accurate to understand the narratological meaning of the phrase as a visual metaphor – that in narrative there is a point from which a narrator views fictional events and characters as if visually. Like the camera in a film, the perspective of a narrative is always located somewhere, up above events, in among them or behind the eyes of one or more of the characters involved. Like the film camera, the narrative voice can move around from one point of view to another, often shifting undetectably from outside to inside views. Many of the terms that originated in the analysis of point of view are visual metaphors – like the concepts of narrative distance or focalisation – but they are metaphors in the sense that the only real vision involved in reading is the vision of printed words. In verbal narrative, vision is an illusion in a more obvious way than it is in film. We see a fictional world in verbal narrative in a less literal way than we do in film, however much the narrative aspires to conjure a picture.

The analysis of point of view is one of the great triumphs of twentieth-century criticism. Its power was partly the power of analytical terminology, to describe subtle shifts in the narrative voice, the movement into and out of other minds, or the modes of presenting the speech and thought of characters. But it was more than descriptive power. It was a new exploration in the rhetoric of fiction, the way that fiction can position us, can manipulate our sympathies and can pull our heartstrings, in the service of some moral aim. The analysis of point of view above all made critics aware that sympathy for characters was not a question of clear-cut moral judgement. It was manufactured and controlled by these newly describable techniques in fictional point of view. It was the beginning of a systematic narratology, one which seemed to assert that stories could control us, could manufacture our moral personalities in ways that had not previously been understood.

Despite a pronounced move away from authorial intention in New Criticism, there is always a sense that the analysis of point of view in fiction is the unveiling of authorial control. Sometimes the impression is that a work of fiction is a polemic wearing an elaborate disguise or, to change the metaphor slightly, an act of authorial ventriloquy where the ventriloquist's own polemic can be hidden among the fictional voices of puppets. Consider, for example, the opening of Wayne Booth's landmark study of point of view in *The Rhetoric of Fiction*: 'In writing about the rhetoric of fiction, I am not primarily interested in didactic fiction, fiction used for propaganda or instruction. My subject is the technique of non-didactic fiction, viewed as the art of communicating with readers' (1961, p. 1). Booth's work is an analysis of the art of persuasion in fiction which is not openly polemic. It tends to assume that aspects of point of view in fiction are marshalled by an author in the service of an argument, but an argument that operates through the manipulation of sympathy.

Voice, distance and judgement

How can techniques in narrative point of view control a reader's sympathy for characters? This question has never seemed to me very different from the question of why we feel sympathetic towards some people in life and not others. I'll begin with two basic propositions about sympathy which apply to narrative and life: (1) We are more likely to sympathise with people when we have a lot of information about their inner lives, motivations, fears and so on; and (2) We sympathise with people when we see other people who do not share our access to their inner lives judging them harshly or incorrectly. In life, we get this kind of information through intimacy, friendship or Oprah Winfrey. In fiction we get it through the narrator, either reliably reported by the narrator or through direct access to the minds of characters.

There is an obvious objection to these propositions: if our access to the inner lives of characters is access to a sick mind, to twisted motivations, evil or anything else that offends our ready-made moral values, the result will not be sympathy. And yet much contemporary fiction acquires its moral controversy exactly through the creation of sympathy for morally offensive characters. Truman Capote's *In Cold Blood*, Brett Easton Ellis's *American Psycho* and Irvine Welsh's *Trainspotting* are examples of places where access to the inner lives of characters can confront commonly held moral attitudes to murder or drugs through the creation of a strange sympathy for the devil. These are novels which create an intimacy between readers and moral monsters purely through access to their minds. Through this intimacy, readers often find themselves technically siding against their own moral prejudices as they witness the judgements of other characters in the fiction who are not in possession of this detailed background of psychological information.

Information alone cannot necessarily elicit a sympathetic response. Sometimes it is the careful control of the flow of information, of where it comes from and how it is presented, which controls a reader's judgement. To illustrate the role of point of view in the control of judgement it is worth summarising Booth's analysis of Jane Austen's *Emma* and the way that it creates sympathy for an unlikeable heroine. In a less extreme way than the examples above, Emma does not automatically inspire a reader's sympathy. She lacks generosity, self-knowledge and understanding. In the course of the narrative, her character reforms to become a more complete marriage prospect. Booth begins his analysis by stating this as a problem facing the artist: given that sympathy is necessary if we are to follow Emma on her moral journey to reform, how can Jane Austen create sympathy for a character with such unlikeable faults?

To restate the problem, how can Jane Austen, on the one hand, make us like Emma enough to desire her reform and, on the other hand, make us stand back from her in judgement and thus perceive her faults? His answer is a brilliant demonstration of the oscillation in *Emma* between closeness to and distance from a character. He argues first that Jane Austen avoids distancing us from Emma by using her as a kind of narrator. Though the story is narrated in the third person, events are often seen through Emma's eyes, reflected or focalised through her mind, so that the reader can see beyond the surface of Emma's selfish manipulations and perceive the qualities which might redeem her. For Booth, this redeeming evidence is much more persuasive when presented as an inside view than it would be if the same evidence were offered in authorial commentary. The inside view creates the illusion of unmediated access to Emma, so that judgement of her character appears direct and free from control. But even if the reader found nothing good in her thoughts, the inside view would create sympathy for Emma just by being an inside view: 'the sustained inside view leads the reader to hope for good fortune for the character with whom he travels, quite independently of the qualities revealed' (Booth, 1961, p. 246). Booth also points out that by focalising through Emma, we are withheld from other perspectives which might alienate us from her. If we were given sustained inside views of Jane Fairfax, for example, we might prefer her to Emma, see her as the narrative's positive value or become alienated from Emma's wrongheadedness about Jane. Control of the inside view, therefore, sustains our sympathy for Emma, prevents us from judging her over-harshly, at the same time as it allows us access to her faults. In so doing it relieves the third person narrative voice of the need to preach about or judge Emma's moral personality.

An author should never preach. Even in a tale with an obvious moral or philosophical purpose an author should never be seen to preach. Even a sermon acknowledges this, conventionally offering a narrative sequence up for judgement as a preamble to any explicit moral lesson. Like Aesop, the narrative preacher must ensure that readers have reached all the right moral judgements about the story before the revelation of the narrative's moral purpose. Authors who neglect this principle, like D.H. Lawrence, often find themselves reviled for using narrators or characters as doctrinal mouthpieces. Yet some authors, and Booth treats Jane Austen as one of them, do have clear moral purposes which have to be subsumed subtly in the fiction. In the case of *Emma*, Booth analyses the oscillation between the closeness of an inside view and the distance of the third person narrator standing back with the reader in moments of more explicit judgement of Emma as a technique for disguising, or creating co-operation for, doctrinal intent. At one pole of this oscillation there is the inside view. At the other there is explicit judgement from the narrator, like this one in the first paragraph: 'The real evils of Emma's situation were the power of having rather too much her own way, and a disposition to think a little too well of herself.' Moments like these, where the distance between Emma and the reader is greatest, then have to be corroborated by moments of direct access to Emma's mind and the witnessing of her actions.

Between the two poles are degrees of distance. The narrative voice distances itself from judgement of Emma by putting judgemental commentary into the mouth of Mr Knightley. The narrative voice adopts a tone of irony, often slipping into the recognisable voice of a character, creating what Booth calls 'sympathetic laughter'. The narrator reports a thought in isolation rather than sustaining focalisation through Emma's eyes. The narrator summarises a conversation or a line of thought without giving us access as direct speech or the inside view. In short, we find ourselves as readers yoked to the narrator, our distance, whether ocular or moral, controlled by the subtle shifts in point of view between layers of represented voices and thoughts, by the information we are given and that which is withheld from us.

This kind of analysis implies several things about the value of narratology and the nature of fictional narrative. Perhaps most important is the stance it takes on the production of sympathy: that it is technically produced and controlled by the devices of access, closeness and distance. Booth, for example, compares the function of access to the technique of dramatic irony on stage, where the audience has information not shared by all the characters on stage. Think of Volpone lying in his deathbed, tricking his suitors out of gifts and favours while the audience, knowing him to be healthy, laughs at their attempts. There is little to choose, morally speaking, between these characters. They are all equally motivated by greed. But the audience is technically placed on the side of Volpone because of the information it shares with him. The moral satire, though applicable to all, is directed away from Volpone and towards the suitors by this information pact between audience and hero which prevents dramatic irony from distancing us from his atrocious actions. As Booth constantly reminds us in *The Rhetoric of Fiction*, this is a principle that applies to life far beyond the boundaries of fiction, whether it is a carefully planted self-revelation among the complicated dynamics of friendship or a media event like Princess Diana's *Panorama* interview in which image management masquerades as a privileged inside view. In such cases, social power derives from moral sympathy which is controlled by techniques in information management and not by rectitude.

The analysis of point of view also implies the value of aesthetic distance in reading. Booth claims that 'only immature readers ever really identify with any character, losing all sense of distance and hence all chance of an artistic experience' (1961, p. 200). In other words, *distance* not only specifies a moral or quasi-visual gap between the reader and characters: it also characterises a mature, aesthetic experience of narrative. This is the kind of claim that critics dare not make any more. The idea of this kind of intellectual distance has come to be seen recently as a sham or a delusion. The argument is that a critic adopts a stance of disinterestedness, abandoning naive questions such as 'do I like Emma Woodhouse?' in favour of more technical ones such as 'how is my sympathy for Emma manufactured?'. Recent narratology tends to be more sceptical of the possibility that any reader can suspend his or her identity or climb to some Olympian height, some transcendental aesthetic realm which is no longer cluttered by the thorny issues of identity such as gender, race or class. The analysis of point of view tends to talk of the reader in the singular as if all readers respond in the same way, subject as they are to the same technical mechanisms in the rhetoric of narrative.

This is one of the key issues in the transition to a poststructuralist narratology. In effect it is an issue that walks hand in hand with another unmissable implication in the analysis of fictional point of view – that the author manipulates this ideal reader according to some intentional plan formulated in advance. Ruminating at length on whether Jane Austen's art was conscious or intuitive, Booth's reading of *Emma* gives the impression that the novel sprang from the need to find a solution to the problem of how to create sympathy for an unlikeable heroine because it was necessary for the moral plan – as if the novel were a moral–philosophical tract disguised as a story. But what happens if we analyse the story in a similar way, for its technical operations, for the structure of its multiple voices and for its control of access to the inner lives of characters, without reference to authorial intention? The answer is that we preserve all that is valuable about Booth's analysis of point of view while leaving behind some of its unsupportable assumptions about the communication between a single-minded author and a singular reader: or we move from the analysis of rhetoric to the analysis of ideology.

Formalism and ideology

Most commentators speak of American New Criticism as if it were incontrovertibly a formalist method of analysis. As I suggested in the Introduction, this is not a simple issue. While the concept of *form* is most easily definable in relation to that of *content*, the term *formalism* derives meaning largely in opposition to *historicism*. We would expect a formalist analysis, then, to ignore both the content and the historical context of the literary work. Perhaps because the content of a narrative is harder to ignore than, say, that of the modernist lyric poem, New Criticism tended towards rigorous formalism more obviously in its dealings with non-narrative poetry than in its narratology. Booth does declare a certain disinterest in history in *The Rhetoric of Fiction*, but his writing is engaged with literary history in the sense that he is deeply involved in characterising modern fiction in terms of formal developments which enable the modern writer to explore the representation of thought, consciousness and subjectivity. On the issue of content, it is impossible to argue that Booth's formal analyses bracket off or ignore the content of narrative. When he speaks of our access to Emma's mind, we are always conscious of the content of her thoughts, of her faults and redeeming qualities, of the fictional events in which these thoughts are embedded or of the moral personality of the narrative voice. These issues would not be in the foreground of a rigorously formalistic analysis. It might be more accurate to define Booth's position as an interest in the form of content, or the way in which narrative content is constructed and represented. If one puts on one's rigorously formalist hat, under which words are just sounds and graphic marks, and narrative techniques are techniques for their own sake, we find ourselves, on reading Booth, constantly taking it off again as we greet the content of his narratives at every turn.

What then would a rigorously formalistic narratology be like? If Booth is operating on the assumption that the content of a narrative is inseparable from form, packaged in it and not unpackable, is it possible to go further towards banishing content altogether? The history of narratology after the New Criticism might be seen in these terms as a quest for a more rigorous formalism. Booth was a formalist in the sense that he was interested in technique and rhetoric, but his study of form always reads like a study in the art of representational content. Fictional characters are perhaps the most apparent case in point. For Booth, they are representations of people, not mere constructs of verbal form. However much they are rhetorically controlled, our responses to fictional characters for Booth are fundamentally similar in nature to our responses to real people in the world.

The quest for a more rigorous formalism found new direction in the arid scientificity of linguistics. It was not that linguistics was formalist in itself, the realms of syntax and semantics roughly corresponding to the polarity of form and content in literary studies. But linguistics did have a vocabulary for the description of form, structure and grammar that was indifferent to the content of words or sentences. The critic in pursuit of an uncontaminated formalism could borrow terminology from the more form-orientated branches of linguistics and bracket or banish content in the process. But did this really work?

To answer this question, it might be worth beginning with an extreme example – computational stylistics. Computational stylistics does not ask questions like 'is Emma a likeable person?'. It asks questions like 'how many times does the word *like* occur in Conrad's *Heart of Darkness*?'. When the answer has been computed, a stylistic fact is established. On its own, however, this fact is no more than a number which might be comparable with the number of occurrences in another work of similar length. At a pinch, the computational stylistician might use the number to support a view that Conrad likes *like*, and content is not invoked. But if this theory were extended to assert that Conrad's style is characterised by similes, the analysis would cease to be purely formal, since the recognition of a simile depends on content and context at least as much as it does on the occurrence of *like*. The point here is that this purely formal analysis of verbal structure in literature seems to leave out all that is important and pleasurable about literature or literary style until the content of those words is allowed to re-enter the analysis.

It is quite common for the linguistic critic to theorise the relationship between the dry observation of verbal structure and the pleasure of reading. Leo Spitzer, for example, argues:

> I would maintain that to formulate observation by means of words is not to cause the artistic beauty to evaporate in vain intellectualities; rather, it makes for a widening and deepening of the aesthetic taste. It is only a frivolous love that cannot survive intellectual definition; great love prospers with understanding.   (Quoted in Leech and Short, 1981, p. 2)

Umberto Eco expresses the same sentiment with his adage 'even a gynaecologist can fall in love'. The idea of leaving one's feelings, one's pleasures, out of a scientific analysis was never a major source of controversy. While we obviously require it, in theory and practice, of the gynaecologist, we also accept that the botanist does not dissertate on the beauty of flowers in an academic context. It is arguable that the academic narratologist should leave pleasure and love at home for the sake of science, objectivity and understanding. It is less easy, however, to find explicit statements from formalist linguists or critics about the status of verbal content in relation to dry formal observation. Part of the problem here is that many of the most rigorously formalist critics of recent decades have operated under the influence of Saussurean linguistics, and it is not easy to decide, reading Saussure's *Course in General Linguistics*, where he stood on the question. The question of the status of verbal content in structuralist thought is considered in detail in Chapter 2, which addresses the issue in relation to realism in narrative. For now, my interest is in the structure of voices in narrative, and the way that critics moved from seeing this structure as part of the rhetoric of fiction to a more ideological interpretation of these techniques.

If Booth illustrated the importance of the representation of speech and thought in narrative from the point of view of the New Critic, his insights were certainly not destined to disappear with the end of New Criticism in the United States. Linguistics, particularly linguistic approaches to literary style, had an enormous input to make into the precise description of the structure of voices in narrative. Where Booth talked about the shift from telling to showing in the narrative voice, or from narrative distance to the inside view of character as a sympathy-securing technique, the linguistic stylistician evolved exact ways of distinguishing different layers of speech in the novel. New categories of speech and thought presentation appeared with names derived from linguistic terminology: direct and indirect speech, free indirect speech, narrative report of speech act, narrative report of thought act, free direct speech and so on.

The categories of speech and thought presentation might not seem, at first sight, the most exciting narratological concepts on the market. What is exciting is the way that narratology was gathering descriptive power by the time Leech and Short's *Style in Fiction* was published in 1981. In criticism, as in many other areas of cultural life, the 1980s was a decade in which different traditions of thought about narrative were encountering one another for the first time. So far we have touched on the analysis of point of view and the precision that linguists were able to add to that analysis. *Style in Fiction* was one of several synthetic guides to narratology which brought academic linguistics to the aid of the analysis of point of view. In this respect, one of its functions was to demonstrate to the world of literary studies that the analysis of point of view had been enhanced and not displaced by the arrival of linguistics in narratology.

There is something slightly repressed about *Style in Fiction* in that it is a book which presents itself as a 'linguistic guide to English fictional prose', yet it systematically ignores the contribution of structural linguistics and of literary structuralism to the understanding of prose fiction. Even Saussure hardly gets a look in. There may have been some resentment on the part of Leech and Short that in the preceding decade departments of English had fallen in love with the idea of linguistics without casting a glance towards non-structuralist stylisticians. Leech and Short's allegiances are pointedly anti-structuralist, elevating perspectives from New Criticism and Reception Theory above the then fashionable narratologists at work outside the Anglo-American tradition, their index reading like a who's who of the opponents of structuralist narratology.

But if *Style in Fiction* embraces the analysis of fictional point of view as a kind of origin for Anglo-American stylistics, there was nothing it could do to stop other guides from performing a similar synthesis between point of view and structuralist narratology. Rimmon-Kenan's index in *Narrative Fiction* is a directory and a lexicon of structuralist approaches to narrative fiction, where every chapter of the text foregrounds the continuity between Anglo-American New Criticism and structuralist perspectives. For Leech and Short the analysis of point of view leads inexorably towards the categories of speech and thought presentation as ways of describing the dynamics of narrators and characters, narrative distance and inside views. For Rimmon-Kenan it leads towards focalisation and other specifically structuralist terms. Two things are clear: (1) The analysis of point of view has not vanished like some redundant paradigm, and it was never replaced by new, fashionable linguistically orientated critical approaches. It was qualified and improved in different ways by literary stylistics and structuralism. (2) Narratological approaches from different schools came into collision in the 1980s in such a way that it was possible to see the formation of a single body of resources drawn from formerly disparate traditions. The affirmation of these two principles can certainly be found in recent work in cognitive narratology (Fludernik, 1996; Herman, 2002) where the interest in point of view is not only sustained, but productively developed by a concerted effort to draw the analytical resources of these traditions into a single narratological resource.

From point of view to positionality

Booth's analysis of *Emma* depends heavily on the thesis that the reader does not normally notice the rhetorical devices which control the position of that reader in relation to fictional characters. The mobility of the narrator between distance and closeness effectively determines the position from which the reader views fictional events, creating sympathetic bonds between the reader and particular characters by making that position one of intimacy and mental access. We might now compound the narratological pile-up by exploring the way in which the Marxist concept of ideology has interacted with the analysis of point of view so as to rescue it from the charge of apolitical formalism. If Booth's explanation of fictional rhetoric was a moral one, it can be argued that his principal legacy was to furnish an ideological explanation of fiction. The change in emphasis occurs between the idea of fictional point of view as the manufacture of sympathy and the idea of *interpellation* as the manufacture of identity.

In 1969, Louis Althusser's essay 'Ideology and Ideological State Apparatuses' (1977) toyed in a rather unspecific way with the idea that literature plays a role in the constitution of a subject. A subject in this context is a person, an individual who is, on the one hand, subject to some greater authority such as the nation-state and, on the other, whose inner life is constituted in part by the illusion that one is a free agent. This contradiction lies at the heart of Althusser's notion of ideology and forms the basis for his theory of the ideological function of literature. In fact, Althusser hardly mentions literature at all in this essay, but his naming of literature as one of the mechanisms by which the subject is constructed as a slave with delusions of freedom gave it a seminal place in narratological history. Althusserian Marxism flourished from the late 1980s to the end of the millennium mainly because of the synergy between this notion of subjectivity and what narratology already knew about fictional point of view.

This synergy can be explained quickly. If Booth shows that fiction controls the position of the reader and that this position determines issues of sympathy, Althusserian Marxism simply adds that, by controlling the reader's position, a fiction calls on a reader not only to sympathise but also to identify with, and therefore occupy, certain subject positions and social roles. Interpellation is the name Althusser gives to this process. Like subjectivity in general, it is a process which is controlled by the text, yet the reader is under the illusion that identification is freely entered into.

Earlier I cited Booth's disapproval of the idea of identification between a reader and a character in fiction. His preference for the idea of sympathy over identification is revealing. It implies that readers' own identities are untouched, no matter how friendly they have become with particular characters. Sympathy amounts to little more than a feeling of goodwill towards a character. Identification suggests self-recognition. One difference is that the manufacture of sympathy will not profoundly change the world. When I reach the end of *Emma*, I will resume normal life. Identification, on the other hand, touches my own subjectivity in a more profound way, because I have seen myself in the fiction, projected my identity into it, rather than just made a new friend. This gives fiction the potential to confirm, form or transform my sense of myself. As a result I cannot enter into identification casually, but must recognise myself in it, as if looking into a mirror. Does this mean that I can sympathise but not identify with Emma Woodhouse?

Suddenly, in this shift from sympathy to identification, my own identity has come into play. The category of sympathy allows Booth to speak of the reader as if all readers were alike, equally able to enter into the narratological pact with Emma. But is this true? I am a man. If I cannot identify with Emma for reasons of sexual difference, will I sympathise with her in the same way as the female reader will? Will all women enter equally into the sympathetic contract with Emma, regardless of background, sexual orientation, views on marriage or ability to play the piano? The answer is obviously no, and because it is no, that distinction between sympathy and identification begins to look pernicious. It allows Booth to speak of the singular reader and therefore to pin the text down to determinate and communal meanings in a way that ignores the diversity of the readership. It effectively divorces narratology from the phenomenology of reading – the way that reading actually takes place – and reduces its specific complexities to general idealities.

This is one direction in which Althusser's concept of interpellation has pointed – towards a less generalised, more interactive account of fictional meaning. The identity of the reader as an already constituted subject, the effect that identification has on sympathy and the consequent fracturing of the readership into irreducible difference – these are new emphases which derive not only from the Althusserian interest in the ideological constitution of a subject. In the narratological pile-up of the late 1980s it became increasingly difficult to attribute these new emphases or trace their roots in converging traditions such as Reception Theory, deconstruction, feminism, Queer Theory, psychoanalysis and postcolonial theory. The new narratological formations were places where the identity of the reader was at stake both in the way that particular readers construed particular fictions and in the way that particular fictions contributed to the formation of those identities.

A good example of the foundational importance of point of view and the way that it has been adapted to analyse the formation of subjectivity can be found in the branch of film narratology that begins in Laura Mulvey's seminal essay 'Visual Pleasure and Narrative Cinema' (1975). If this essay is a beginning in film studies, it might also be seen as a kind of outcome for the analysis of point of view – the moment at which it was extended and transformed by Marxist and psychoanalytic thought – 'psychoanalytic theory appropriated as a political weapon', as Mulvey puts it. And although there is no equally open acknowledgement of point-of-view-based narratology, its presence is apparent. I suggested earlier that point-of-view terminology is highly visual. Mulvey begins from the idea that cinema satisfies 'a primordial wish for pleasurable looking'. Using Lacan's account of the moment when a child recognises its own image in a mirror as a critical moment in the constitution of the ego, Mulvey characterises the pleasure of looking in cinema as a process driven by two contradictory desires: first, the pleasure of looking at another person as an object, and second, the narcissistic pleasure of identification with a person on screen. The first desire is that of the libido; the second, that of the ego. Whereas Booth was careful to exclude the idea of identification with a fictional character, seeing it as an obstacle to aesthetic pleasure, Mulvey reintroduces it as a way of viewing narrative as one of the places in which the constitution of subjectivity is at stake. In one step, Mulvey leaves behind two crucial values of Booth's type of narratology. First, she abandons the snobbish conviction that identification is an immature stage before aesthetic pleasure, which implies that the pleasure of a narrative is available only to those with the critical sophistication to stand at a distance from the mechanisms of that narrative. Second, she abandons the view of the readership/audience as a homogenous lump, since the relations of pleasurable looking and identification will vary according to the ways in which an individual is already constituted as a subject.

Many narratologists saw this fracturing of the readership as the solution to a problem in the 1980s. Teresa de Lauretis, for example, puts it like this:

> The problem, I believe, is that many of the current formulations of narrative process fail to see that subjectivity is engaged in the cogs of narrative and indeed constituted in the relation of narrative, meaning, and desire; so that the very work of narrativity is the engagement of the subject in certain positionalities of meaning and desire . . . Thus, finally, they fail to envisage a materially, historically, and experientially constituted subject, a subject engendered, we might say, precisely by the process of its engagement in the narrative genres.   (1984, p. 106)

For Mulvey and de Lauretis, the most significant aspect of this failure is its indifference to gender difference, and Mulvey proposes that 'an active/passive heterosexual division of labour has controlled narrative structure' (1975, p. 117). Thus, the subjectivity of the viewer is engaged in the sense that the viewer identifies with a particular gender position in the narrative. Most film narratives, says Mulvey, are split between the active role of the male protagonist and the passive erotic image of the female. A male protagonist is active in two senses: first, as the centre of narrative action, the person in the narrative who makes things happen, and second, as the active bearer of the gaze, actively looking upon the erotic image of a female character. Identification then, for the male viewer, is an identification with the narrative action itself as opposed to the passive image of the female icon, as well as being an identification with the bearer of the gaze. If Booth speaks of the ungendered surrogate reader as someone who positions the external reader in relation to fictional events, Mulvey speaks of the surrogate spectator as a narrative position with which the male heterosexual voyeur can easily identify, being hailed into the film to ogle the erotic image of a female character.

As a first step, this seems like a very reductive approach to the interaction of an already constituted gendered subject and the available subject positions of a given narrative. It suggests that a film, for a man, is a double pleasure, a visual and a narrative pleasure. For a woman it offers identification with a female figure who is framed by the camera as an image, an icon, the object of the male gaze, whose look is relayed by the look of a male character acting as surrogate spectator. It seems to offer little help with, for example, a narrative with a female protagonist, or one that objectifies a male character. It also posits identification as a simple, determined process in which men see themselves as subjects and women as objects. Mulvey's first version of the essay was open to these charges, concentrating as it did on the male viewer in relation to a cartoon version of the way in which film narratives are gendered. It characterised film identification as masculine, as identification with the male gaze, and implied that the female viewer was simply interpellated into a male fantasy in which she was objectified.

The role of narrative positionality in forming subjectivity needed a more complex articulation. In 1981 Mulvey returned to the question of the male gaze after 6 years of being heckled on the issue of the woman spectator and the possibilities of pleasurable identification with film narrative. Her answer lay in Freud and the possibility of transsexual identification. Freud had claimed that female subjectivity was characterised by an alternation between feminine and masculine modes of identification. In other words, identification was neither simple nor biological for a woman but involved a contradictory interplay between different subject positions, vying for, and achieving, supremacy at different stages of a woman's life. He had also claimed that, for a woman in the pre-Oedipal stage, masculinity dominates femininity so that identification with a masculine subjectivity becomes, in later life, a kind of nostalgia for a former mode of subjectivity. In cinematic terms, this alternation between masculine and feminine aspects of subjectivity comes into play as an oscillation between identification with the subject and the object of the narrative, with active and passive positionalities, with the look and the image or with narrative action and visual image. For the female spectator, the pleasure of identification becomes a two-sided process in which the identity positions of looking and being looked at are at war. In this respect, a woman's subjectivity is at stake in narrative in the sense that the narrative is a process which enacts the opposition in which her subjectivity is founded.

In what sense then is narrative positionality constitutive of subjectivity? If women arrive at the cinema as already constituted subjects, already oscillating between socialised femininity and the memory of masculine desire, won't they leave the cinema unchanged? The answer to this question is yes, and this characterises the ideological function of narrative – that it repeats and confirms the possibilities of identification that have already constituted our subjectivities. This is more than claiming that narrative reflects life. It is saying that narrative is one of the ways in which identity, the ideological subject, is manufactured. It is also saying that the manufacture of identity is not a single originary occurrence but a process of repetition in which the positionalities of cinema and the subject positions of extra-filmic social relations converge in an ongoing relation of mutual confirmation.

2 Terminologisation

The language of literary criticism and theory has become the ugliest private language in the world. Narratology has been one of the places where the most offensive terminology has taken hold, particularly in its structuralist and poststructuralist phases. Often the problem lies in a puerile overuse of abstract nouns like textuality, discursivity, narrativity, historicity, referentiality, intertextuality, supplementarity, iterability, synchronicity, subjectivity, specificity, directionality, positionality, apsectuality, modality, contiguity, multiplicity, intentionality, plurality, structurality, intelligibility, heterogeneity, homogeneity, polychronicity, temporality, post-modernity, linearity, specularity, canonicity, hyper-canonicity and hyperreality. Then there are all those new processes invented by criticism which also become abstract nouns: focalisation, reification, problematisation, characterisation, naturalisation, defamiliarisation, totalisation, structuration, identification, interpellation, contextualisation, recontextualisation, acceleration, duration, actualisation and historicisation. Narratology in particular raided the terminology of linguistics and classical rhetoric for formal descriptors too numerous to list, some of which will feature in the argument of this chapter.

The issue of critical terminology can appear superficial, especially when much of the terminology itself seems superficial. What, for example, is *positionality* in relation to *position?* One answer would be that it is position-*ness* – the abstract quality of having or being implicated in position, like historicity in relation to history. But how then can the word be made plural, as in the phrase *narrative positionalities?* The plural form specifies difference which contradicts the initial abstraction. Perhaps worse is a phrase which is ubiquitous in new historicism – *historical specificity.* If the phrase *to a certain extent* usually means *to a completely unknown extent,* the phrase *historical specificity* is similarly translatable into its own opposite. It is a gesture to the idea of precision and particularity which is rarely delivered upon. The blood of a thousand readers has boiled at the outright pretension of such neologisms and gestures – the pure superficiality of terms used as flags to declare a critic's allegiance to science, to history, or even just complexity for its own sake. Some, like Tom Paulin, have dismissed large swathes of critical writing on the grounds of its ugliness, and others, like Zadie Smith, have damned the discourse for its otherness to the domain of art.

There is an old assumption – associated with *belles-lettres* and an age before the division of labour between critical and literary writing – that criticism operates under an obligation to be aesthetically pleasing, or that one of its principal functions in the world is to enhance aesthetic pleasure. There is a more recent assumption that criticism has a scientific descriptive power to refer to its literary objects without theoretical difficulty or complication. If the first of these assumptions underlies the charge that criticism is ugly, the second underlies the objection to the superficiality of contemporary terminology. One way of assessing the impact of deconstruction on narratology is in relation to these two assumptions, both of which address the question of the logical relation between criticism and literature, the first aspiring to a relation of similarity and reciprocity, the second to a relation of otherness and distance. Chapter 3 is about the re-aestheticisation of criticism, or the convergence of literary narrative and narratological criticism. This one is about the transition from structuralist to poststructuralist narratology with particular reference to changing attitudes to linguistic terminology.

The accusation of superficiality in critical terminology carries with it a deep presupposition. Following Baudrillard, many commentators have characterised the postmodern age as one in which the traditional, dualist model of surface and depth in accounts of signification has been abandoned. As surface without depth, superficiality is only an accusation in a world conceived on the dualist model, according to which there is more to language than its material surfaces. For the dualist, language has content as well as form. If poststructuralist criticism conforms in the most general terms to a model of surface without depth, it is monistic not dualistic, meaning that it operates under the conviction that the form and content of language are categorically inseparable. To use the traditional metaphor, language would then no longer be seen as the dress of thought, but as the flesh of thought. Or to put it another way, language would be seen as pure externality, as form without content, and as surface without depth.

Can this possibly be true? It is about the most counter-intuitive thing that could be said about language – all the more so in relation to narrative. There are some modernist poems which might seem to conform to this monistic view, in which content cannot be abstracted from the unique form of their expression, or in which *what is said* is identical with *the way in which it is said*. But a realist novel? How can it be claimed that the language of narrative realism is pure externality? If nothing else there seem to be two different orders of vision involved in realistic narrative: we see the written word on the page and we see the fictional world of represented events, characters and places which constitute the content of the narrative. Any narratology that denies this spits in the face of common sense, but it was from this counter intuitive claim that structuralist narratology derived its radical force: that the ability of narrative to refer to something other than itself was an illusion.

Traditionally the idea of reference in language has been understood as a kind of transparency: language is like a window through which a pre-existing reality can be perceived. But in the world of linguistics there were places where this traditional view had been shaken and undermined. The clearest example is Saussure's *Course in General Linguistics,* in which it is argued that 'in language there are only differences without positive terms'. Saussure's account of difference is particularly challenging to the idea of language as a system of names for entities that have some pre-existing reality. There are no 'positive terms' in language for Saussure, in the sense that a sign generates its meaning not by pointing to an entity in the world, but rather by pointing to other words in the language system which it is not: the meaning of a sign is thus defined negatively, as difference from other signs which it is not. It was in this way that the binary opposition came to be seen as the basic meaning-generating unit in language. Signs were understood as having a significant other, an antonym against which any particular sign could define its meaning negatively. So the meaning of the sign 'night' is defined particularly by its negative relation to the sign 'day', as 'not day'. This simple idea was responsible for the thesis that reference in language was not properly understood as transparency to an underlying reality, but was an effect of difference: reference was a function of language, generated by language, meaning that 'reality' was an effect actively generated by language rather than a pre-existing state passively reflected by signs. A similar argument can be found in the work of the American linguists Sapir and Whorf who argued the case that perception of the 'real world' is determined by the particular language through which reality is being seen. Different languages encode the world in different ways, so that 'reality' can be seen as culturally relative, generated in different ways by languages with different systems of differential relations. In the wake of these hypotheses, lecturers in the arts and social sciences began to queue up to tell their students that the real world exists only as a language and that Eskimos have 26 words for 'snow'.

Stupid arguments broke out in university bars. If you die of exposure in a snowstorm, is it exposure to language? If you are attacked by a lion, are your wounds generated by the differential relations between signs? The cultural relativity argument could seem as unimportant as the difference between being killed by snow and being killed by the light tingly snow that falls on windless nights in February. Nor would the sense of the lion as 'not tiger' save the structuralist from a mauling by the real world. For many, the founding proposition of structuralism was an absurd exaggeration. It seemed to take the linguistic conditions which made reference possible – the systems of differences, conventions and codes – and elevate them to the status of referents, so that meaning was not only enabled but actually constituted by difference. Fredric Jameson, for example, argues in *The Prison House of Language* that structuralist criticism came to view the form and system of narrative as its only content:

> The most characteristic feature of structuralist criticism lies precisely in a kind of transformation of form into content, in which the form of structuralist research (stories are organised like sentences, like linguistic enunciations) turns into a proposition about content: literary works are about language, take the process of speech itself as their essential subject matter.   (1972, pp. 198–9)

According to this view, the linguistic conditions of a given narrative were viewed by structuralist narratologists as its true content. Anyone who thought otherwise was the dupe of language, distracted from its ineluctable self-referentiality by the referential illusion, and led into a kind of ideology that Paul de Man defined as the 'confusion of linguistic and natural reality' (1986, p. 11).

Throughout the evolution of structuralist narratology there was a slippage between two quite different attitudes to linguistic analysis. The first attitude amounts to no more than a modest claim that linguistic analysis is the science of form, structure and system, which merely brackets off the referential content of a narrative. The second attitude was a more radical claim: that linguistics had proved the self-referentiality of language, and that this proof had become a premise for the argument that narrative could only ever refer to itself. It is broadly accurate to say that this second, more radical attitude became dominant as structuralist narratology evolved. The hypotheses of Saussure, Sapir and Whorf became an underpinning authority for the thesis of self-referentiality that was evoked every time criticism used a technical term derived from linguistics. My point here is that this process, this slippage, left narratology with a shaky premise – an ambiguous attitude to reference which underpinned some of structuralism's most radical claims. This is worth dwelling on for a moment. It helps to explain how critics of narrative went from writing sentences like this: 'When Anne first meets Captain Wentworth after their years of separation that follow her refusal to marry him, she is convinced that he is indifferent', to sentences like this: 'The aporia between performative and constative language is merely a version of the aporia between trope and persuasion that both generates and paralyses rhetoric and thus gives it the appearance of a history.'

Somewhere between these two statements the linguistic model took hold in narratology. Roman Jakobson was probably first to call explicitly for the internalisation of literary studies within the field of general linguistics: 'Poetics deals primarily with problems of verbal structure... since linguistics is the global science of verbal structure, poetics may be regarded as an integral part of linguistics' (1960, p. 35). The resurrection of the term *poetics* designated a new structural science, but the idea of science itself was ambiguous: was poetics going to tell us something new about the self-referential nature of all language, something that linguists knew and critics so far did not; or was it just a kind of division of labour, an interpretative or methodological choice, whereby linguists would foreground the structure of language (because that is their thing) and implicitly leave the question of content to others without denying its existence.

Jakobson's own attitude to reference and self-reference is an interesting starting point. In 'Closing Statement' in 1960 he argued that any utterance or act of communication has at least six distinguishable aspects or *functions*. There are already many full accounts of Jakobson's model of communication. I want to look in particular at three of the functions he identified, which he called the *referential,* the *poetic* and the *metalingual,* functions which correspond to the outside world, the message itself and the language system that makes it possible. For Jakobson, these three functions of language are there in any communication, so that any discourse is capable of conveying meaning about the world, about itself and about the system of codes by which it operates simultaneously. Some discourses, he argues, seem more orientated towards one of these functions than others. Poetry, for example, foregrounds the poetic function of language by drawing attention to the way in which things are said to the point where reference seems like a lesser consideration; prose, on the other hand, seems to use language in a more transparent way and so foregrounds the referential function. But this is not the whole story. If the poetic function seems to dominate in poetry, this does not mean that the referential function is negated or absent, nor that the poetic function of prose is absent. A scientific analysis can focus on any aspect of the communication that it pleases – the poetic function of prose for example – so that the analyst has some input into which aspect of the communication to foreground. In other words, foregrounding is not something determined only by the nature of the language under analysis, it is also an active process on the part of the analysis, the critic or the reader. Put simply, this means that if you ask a question about the metalingual aspect of an utterance, you get a metalingual answer, but this doesn't mean that the referential aspect dissolves, or that the outside world ceases to exist.

Nothing very controversial so far. If the functions of language coexist happily, Jakobson's call for a *poetics* of all verbal art is just an attempt to institute a branch of literary criticism with a linguistic bent and a particular interest in the poetic function. Others, of course, remain free to speculate on how much Captain Wentworth still loves Anne. And yet, after 'Closing Statement', those who did so somehow branded themselves as naive fools. A.D. Nuttall, speaking of Jakobson's similarly uncontroversial argument in 'Realism in Art', notes the effect of this in the university seminar:

> The student who says in a seminar that Lawrence is splendidly true to life will be answered with smiles of conscious superiority as if he had committed some mild *betise*. The assumption behind the smiles is, quite simply, that modern literary theory has exploded the idea that literature is in any way authentically true to life.   (Nuttall, 1983, p. 54)

Here again we have that shaky feeling that the radical reputation of structuralist narratology might rest on nothing more than a claim that realism has a conventional element, and that behind the smug look of the poststructuralist student there lies the false assumption that Jakobson or Saussure had denied the relation of narrative realism to reality.

If we jump forward to 1979 and Paul de Man's *Allegories of Reading*, we find him looking back with unease at this ambiguity in the linguistic model: between bracketing off and denying the referential dimension of language:

> By an awareness of the arbitrariness of the sign (Saussure) and of literature as an autotelic statement 'focused on the way it is expressed' (Jakobson), the entire question of meaning can be bracketed, thus freeing the critical discourse from the debilitating burden of paraphrase. (1979, p. 5)

For de Man, the bracketing of content is good, but not good enough. It merely ignores referential content when he wants to obliterate it. He finds the more 'radical' critique of referential meaning in Rousseau:

> [Rousseau's] radical critique of referential meaning never implied that the referential function of language could in any way be avoided, bracketed, or reduced to being just one contingent linguistic property among others, as it is postulated, for example, in contemporary semiology. (1979, p. 204)

In other words, semiology implicitly denies reference by ignoring it and transforming form into the primary content of a discourse, but de Man is looking for a position which will more explicitly purge language of its referential content. When de Man represents semiology positively, he reveals a kind of revulsion at the idea of reference: '[Semiology] demonstrated that the perception of the literary dimension of language is largely obscured if one submits uncritically to the authority of reference' which asserts itself 'in a variety of disguises'. It even becomes a kind of germ requiring 'some preventative semiological hygiene' (1979, p. 5).

The argument against reference in *Allegories of Reading* can be summarised like this. If Jakobson sees the total meaning of a discourse as the sum of the six functions he identifies, the bracketing off of reference in the name of *poetics* produces a partial reading of that discourse. No matter how much scientific attention is poured onto the formal and self-referential aspects of that discourse, the referential aspect is still there, lurking but ignored, in happy co-existence with the other functions. De Man argues instead that reading should sustain the contradiction between different aspects of language. If semiology gives the impression that form *is* the *total* meaning of a discourse, it does so by ignoring its other aspects and allowing a partial reading to present itself as a total reading. This is *totalisation* – the great enemy of deconstruction – or *synecdoche,* whereby a part stands for the whole. This is a useful preliminary way of understanding the impact of deconstruction in narrative theory: a deconstructionist reads a narrative for contradictions and aims to sustain them, not to reduce the narrative to a stable, single structure or meaning.

One of the interesting aspects of de Man's attitude to reference in a narrative is that he cannot express it theoretically: it is 'a difficulty which puts

its precise theoretical exposition beyond my powers' (1979, p. 9). It is only
by reading texts that a critique of referential meaning emerges, so that the
linguistic theory is always embedded in the reading of a particular text
and remains unextractable from that context. A narrative example is his
analysis of the parable used by Rousseau as part of a discussion of the
relationship of metaphor to literal denomination in *Essay on the Origin of
Languages*. In this parable a primitive man, encountering other men, fears
them and names them accordingly not as *men* but as *giants*. When he later
discovers that these men are not different from himself (larger, stronger)
but the same as himself, he renames them with a term that he has in common with them such as *man*. Rousseau used this parable to illustrate the
priority of metaphor over denomination – that metaphor comes first. But
for de Man, whose revulsion at reference is mounting in intensity, the narrative yields a different insight. For Rousseau, the first act of naming is
metaphorical because it confuses subjective and objective properties: it
'displaces the referential meaning from an outward, visible property to an
inward feeling' (de Man 1979, p. 150), where *giant* substitutes for the feeling *I am afraid*. This is what a metaphor is. It posits similarity between
things that are different. But for de Man, this is an exact description of
denomination as well as metaphor. To name a particular tree *tree* is to
recognise a common essence between trees, so that any act of naming is
an act which posits sameness where there is difference. This makes the
word *man* in the parable doubly metaphorical – just as much an illusion
of sameness as the metaphor *giant*. His conclusion is that 'it is impossible
to say whether denomination is literal or figural' (1979, p. 148).

Simple as this argument may seem, it represents a profound shift for
narratological theory. For Jakobson, the linguistic model is a foundation
or a premise for the analysis of a narrative. For de Man, the narrative is
the premise which yields linguistic knowledge. The Jakobsonian notion of
the linguistic model as a premise can be found in many of the key works
of structural narratology. In 'Introduction to the Structural Analysis of
Narratives' Roland Barthes states the difference as a preference for the
deductive over the inductive scientific method:

> Linguistics itself, with only some three thousand languages to embrace,
> cannot manage (an inductive) programme and has wisely turned deduc-
> tive, a step which in fact marked its veritable constitution as a science and
> the beginning of its spectacular progress, it even succeeding in anticipat-
> ing facts prior to their discovery. So what of narrative analysis, faced as it
> is with millions of narratives? Of necessity, it is condemned to a deductive

procedure, obliged to devise first a hypothetical model of description (what Americans call a 'theory') and then gradually to work down from this model towards the different narrative species which at once conform to and depart from the model. (1977, p. 81)

'It seems reasonable', says Barthes a few sentences later, 'that the structural analysis of narrative be given linguistics itself as founding model.' Looking back, the deductive method was the downfall of structural narratology. It translated the rich diversity of narratives in the world into a bland sameness, as instances of grammatical rules, or as abstract structures illustrating the enabling conventions of narrative meaning. It was a sameness imposed on difference by the method of analysis, and for many this was the weakness of a scientific analysis of narrative.

But there was a philosophical modesty about this kind of science. It was not science that purported to know the true nature of its objects. It was Kuhnian or Popperian in the sense that the founding model was seen as a mode of invention by hypothesis rather than objective discovery. As Todorov puts it in *Introduction to Poetics*:

> The unity of a science is not constituted by the uniqueness of its object. There is not a 'science of bodies'... but a physics, a chemistry, a geometry... It is hardly necessary to repeat that the method creates the object, that the object of a science is not given in nature but represents the result of an elaboration. (1981, p. 8)

In *poetics*, then, the linguistic model creates the narrative object as a manifestation of linguistic rules without making any bold claims about the being, the objective nature, the ontology of narrative or indeed language in general.

This is the heart of the difference between structural narratology and deconstructive narratology, and it is not only a superficial difference in the way that linguistic terminology is deployed: by moving from general rules about language to the analysis of narratives, structuralism doesn't make bold claims about the objective nature of language; by moving from the analysis of narratives to general rules about language, deconstruction seems much more assertive and authoritative about the insights into language that literature can yield. The difference between Jakobson and de Man on the subject of the self-referentiality of language is an excellent example, and bears a little further exploration.

Jakobson's six functions of language correspond to what he calls the 'six constitutive factors of verbal communication'. When an *addresser* sends a *message* to an *addressee,* the message requires a *context,* a *code* and a *contact.* These six factors correspond to the six functions of language according to the following model:

Factors of Communication:

context

message

addresser   addressee

contact

code

Functions of Language:

referential

poetic

emotive   phatic   conative

metalingual

To return to the example of the parable, when de Man says that the word *giant* is 'based on a correspondence between inner feelings of fear and outward properties of size', he identifies two factors of communication: the *addresser's* feelings and the *context.* Correspondingly, the metaphor 'giant' embraces the emotive and the referential functions of language. This is the definition of metaphor which, for de Man, also provides the logic of denomination – an undecidable oscillation between emotive and referential functions of language. While Jakobson insists that the emotive and referential functions are not separable, de Man insists that they are not distinguishable; where Jakobson sees happy co-existence between the functions of language, de Man negates the distinction altogether.

Here we enter the counter-intuitive universe in which a narrative is seen to advance a proposition about its own inability to refer to the outside world. If there is no logical distinction between metaphorical and literal naming, there is a sense in which language can never point to the outside world. But nor can it be said that it merely points to an illusion inside the mind. The most simple act of reference – literal naming – suddenly becomes something which points to the name itself, blaming the name for the imposition of identity (all trees have a common essence) on difference (the irreducible differences between individual trees). Not only has all language become metaphor, but all metaphor has become autotelic. This is the ultimate general rule that de Man sees as the insight of the parable: 'If language is about language, then the paradigmatic linguistic model is that of an entity which confronts itself' (1979, p. 153). In other words, the breakdown of the distinction between the referential and the emotive functions of language leads directly into the poetic function, which is orientated towards the message itself, and the metalingual function, which conveys information about the language system in general.

If my preliminary account of the impact of deconstruction on narratology was that it refused the view of narrative as a stable structure, everything I have said since then points to an important qualification. Narrative is not only something that can't be pinned down by scientific (semiological) analysis. By being unpindownable, narrative destabilises the model of analysis and in this sense yields its own linguistic knowledge. For de Man, the model of analysis at stake is what he calls the inside/outside model in literary studies, a brief contemplation of which will be of enormous explanatory value in this discussion.

The main characteristic of the inside/outside model is that nobody knows which is which. The opposition of form and content implies that form is external, yet in another sense the form of a work is within it while its content is often something which is pointed to outside the work. For this reason the opposition of intrinsic and extrinsic criticism has never been clear. Intrinsic criticism in the hands of New Criticism was formalist while extrinsic brought external information such as historical, biographical or referential perspectives to bear. Many critics after the New Criticism began to express the relationship between the outside of literature and formalism the other way around. Here is A.D. Nuttall again: 'There are two languages of criticism, the first "opaque", external, formalist, operating outside the mechanisms of art and taking those mechanisms as its object, the second "transparent", internal, realist, operating within the world presented in the work' (1983, p. 80). This confusion is de Man's starting point: 'The recurrent debate opposing intrinsic to extrinsic criticism stands under the aegis of an inside/outside metaphor that is never being seriously questioned' (1979, p. 5). The problem with literary semiology, for de Man, is that even if it seems to understand reference, on Saussurean lines, as a purely internal effect of language, it still imports the inside/outside model by distinguishing between, for example, the referential and the autotelic.

In other words, literary structuralism has gone some way towards the reconciliation of form and content, or the inside and outside of language, but it has not gone far enough. This is the exact formula for Jacques

Derrida's engagement with linguistics: that even in the most monistic linguistic models, there is a residual dualist presupposition about the inside and outside. *Of Grammatology* therefore aims at dissolving the polarities of inside and outside in a similar way. Speaking of Saussure's justification to base his study of language on speech – the pure inside of language – as opposed to writing which is merely an external representation of speech, Derrida characterises the new relationship between the poles: 'the outside bears with the inside a relationship which is, as usual, anything but simple exteriority. The meaning of the outside was always present within the inside, imprisoned outside the outside, and vice versa' (1976, p. 100). I love the 'vice versa' at the end of that sentence, implying as it does that the possibility of chiasmic reversal between the poles had not been sufficiently established by the rest of the sentence.

This is what Derrida's engagements with linguistic theory are always like: they illustrate that language itself does not co-operate with any model which seeks to stabilise it, reduce it or close down its infinite complexity. As a result, linguistic terminology in Derrida's work tends to take on ironic force, no longer naming some feature of language, but naming some problem in a prior theory or tradition. *Différance* is a good example of a term which does its utmost not to designate anything except the unstoppable motion of language in the face of attempts to keep it still for a moment; or, to put it another way, if it designates anything it is the inadequacy of the Saussurean term 'difference'. Simple terms such as 'writing', 'metaphor' and 'signifier' are used by Derrida in ironic ways to upturn and collapse the oppositions to which they belong in linguistic theory at large, so that again they designate the presuppositions of former accounts of meaning more than they designate anything about the nature of language: language will always undermine the categories and distinctions by which linguists attempt to define and totalise it.

Perhaps the most famous misrepresentation of Derrida's engagement with language theory is the way that critics and philosophers have interpreted the slogan '*Il n'y a pas de-hors texte.*' If I am right in stating in the paragraph above that Derrida never attempts to say anything of his own about language but only to show that it disrupts, exceeds and resists its own analysis, the slogan does not mean there is nothing outside the text as most commentators have taken it. It is closer to 'There is no outside-text.' Derrida does not mean that reality does not exist except as an illusion foisted on us by language, but that it is not possible to distinguish categorically between what is within and what is outside. So, for example, the idea often associated with Derrida that all language is metaphorical is a problem in the definition of literal meaning, not an ontological claim. A rare example of a commentator who makes this clear is John Llewelyn:

> ...what is at stake is a philosophical theory of metaphor and the part metaphor plays in the philosophies of say Plato, Leibniz, Bergson or Derrida. Derrida is not denying that one may be speaking the literal truth when one says such things as 'This pencil is red', any more than he is denying that there are objects we refer to and persons who refer to them. It is a certain construal of sense and reference that he deconstructs. (1986, pp. 78–9)

Rodolphe Gasché is another who gets this emphasis right when describing de Man's deconstruction:

> ...deconstruction is, according to de Man, the negative insight' into the misleading assumptions and effects of metaphor and concept. Deconstruction amounts to the epistemological gesture of falsifying the pretentions to truth and completeness of all totalising principles... It is a knowledge about the mechanics of knowledge, a knowledge destructive of knowledge, but a knowledge nonetheless. (1981, p. 45)

Those who claim, in those stupid arguments in university bars, that deconstruction rests on a theory of language which denies reference to the outside world are mistaken on two grounds. First, they assume that the linguistic model comes first, like a premise which is then applied to instances – the realistic novel for example – of language. As I have said, theoretical knowledge, however negative, comes if anything from reading narratives against the grain of any linguistic model for analysis. Second, they assume that deconstruction is a kind of knowledge of language when it would be safer to see it as an argument against the knowability of language which shifts attention away from knowledge of language towards the language of knowledge.

What does this mean for narratology? Some have argued that it has been nothing less than the death of narratology as a science. Thus, when Barthes argued in 'Introduction to the Structural Analysis of Narratives' (1977) that it was the deductive character of the linguistic approach to narrative that made it scientific, he defined clearly what it was that was killed off by poststructuralist approaches. Analysis of narrative could no longer take the deductive path which sought to apply a linguistic model to any narrative. It turned inductive, which is to say that the particularity of each narrative revealed the weakness of the deductive approach. If the semiological approach to narrative was essentially deductive, the poststructuralist approach was to demonstrate that the structure of narrative was created rather than revealed by the deductive approach, so that the analysis projected the structure of its categories and distinctions onto the work and, as de Man and Derrida have demonstrated, projected a lot of philosophical assumptions about the inside and outside of language onto narrative in the process.

I have also argued here that linguistic terminology began to play a very different role in narratology after the transition from deductive science to inductive deconstruction of linguistic knowledge. For the structuralist, linguistic terminology was primarily descriptive. The structuralist would stand back from narrative and describe its codes and conventions, its internal structure, its figures and tropes from a distance. For the structuralist, linguistics was a metalanguage which could describe narrative, reveal its operations and mechanisms, from a stance of scientific objectivity. If the implication of this kind of analysis was that language constructed rather than reflected the world, created rather than revealed the structures that we think of as reality, the excitement of scientific discovery was distracting structuralism as a whole from a glaring flaw in this position of assumed objectivity: if language creates, rather than reveals, the world, surely metalanguage also creates, rather than reveals, the structures of language. Reference to language is, after all, no different from reference to the so-called 'outside world'. There can surely be no position outside language from which language can be viewed objectively. Derrida calls this a repetition and a redoubling of structuralism's basic insight.

The consequences of this redoubling for narratology are twofold. The first is that the assumed distance between a narrative and its reading is abolished: the narrative and its reading become identical – the narrative is the reading and the reading is the narrative. This sense of the impossibility of standing outside the text clearly lies behind Derrida's slogan, '*Il n'y a pas de-hors texte.*' It also underlies de Man's formula for an allegory of reading, which can either be seen as a narrative which folds back on itself and becomes self-referential or as a reading which narrates the allegory of the impossibility of reading where no final reading is possible. In both cases it is potentially misleading to see the relation of the primary narrative and the critical metalanguage as an inductive process, in the sense that the metalingual knowledge yielded by narrative is a property of both. Deconstruction therefore translates narratives into self-referential, metalingual tracts about the impossibility of an outside reading or, as in the case of Rousseau's parable, about the impossibility of denomination.

The first consequence of this is that some of our best-loved canonical narratives are rendered unrecognisable by the translation of a deconstructive reading. Proust's *A la recherche du temps perdu* is a good example, a narrative traditionally viewed as an exposition of memory which becomes, in the hands of Gillès Deleuze, a metalanguage better capable of exploring the semiotics of narrative than any critical language, or, in the hands of Paul de Man, a deconstruction of the distinction between metaphor and metonymy.

The second consequence is that a critical reading can no longer assume its own transparency to the narrative under analysis and must instead constantly declare its own active role in producing that narrative. This results in a reflexive critical language: a kind of criticism acutely aware of its own textuality or its own inability to stand outside language and narrative. Redoubling then is a kind of in-built self-referentiality in critical language: a self-awareness in which narratological critical performance subverts any illusion of its own transparency just as it subverts the illusion of transparency in the language under analysis. Where Barthes once characterised narrative theory as an abstract deductive process transparently revealing the actual structures of narrative, he came round eventually to a very different definition of the theoretical discourse:

> Theoretical does not of course mean abstract. From my point of view it means *reflexive*, something which turns back on itself: a discourse which turns back on itself is by virtue of this very fact theoretical. (Quoted in Young, 1981, p. 1)

Suddenly theory is no longer a prescriptive model for critical practice but part of the critical performance itself. In other words, it was not sufficient for structuralism to imply that the content of a narrative was its form, to dismantle the opposition between reference and self-reference, only to re-establish those oppositions in practice: it became necessary to recognise and signal the textuality of one's own critical language – to practise what one preached.

Writing only four years after his 'Introduction to the Structural Analysis of Narratives', presumably after having read Derrida, Barthes describes these two consequences in a key statement of the transition from structuralism to poststructuralism:

> The subject of the analysis (the critic, the scholar, the philologist) cannot in fact, without bad faith and smugness, believe he is external to the language he is describing. His exteriority is only quite provisional and apparent: he

too is in language, and he must assume his insertion, however 'rigorous' and 'objective' he may wish to be, into the triple knot of the subject, the signifier and the Other, an insertion which writing (the text) fully accomplishes, without having recourse to the hypocritical distance of a fallacious metalanguage. *The only practice that is founded by the theory of the text is the text itself.* The consequence is evident: all in all, it is the whole of criticism (as a discourse held 'on' a work) which is outdated. If an author comes to speak of a past text, he can only do so by himself producing a new text . . . There are no more critics, only writers.   (1973, p. 44; his emphasis)

Bearing in mind that there was no French equivalent of the word *poststructuralism* at that moment, this is a clear statement of what the Anglo-American tradition would call a poststructuralist tenet: that the boundary between literary and critical writing disappears as a consequence of the impossibility of metalingual distance. Barthes himself therefore becomes the transitional figure *par excellence,* not only because his thinking has shifted from a certain confidence in the deductive, linguistic approach towards a more deconstructive scepticism about the possibility of metalanguage, but also because he effectively declares the end of criticism in the conflation of critical and literary writing. When Barthes was hit by the apocryphal milk truck – some say laundry truck – in Paris in 1980, he was reported to be writing a novel, the significance of which lay in the idea that the future of narratology lay within narrative itself. If this seems like saying that the future of botany lies in flowers, it nevertheless points to a discernible trend towards what I would call the theoretical fiction, or the narratological narrative – the product of a new kind of literary academic, the writer/critic, who personifies the boundary between fiction and criticism, and will be the subject of the next chapter.

With this trend in mind, we do now appear to be staring at the corpse of narratology as we knew it. The redoubling of the conditions of reference to encompass the relation of a metalanguage to the language it describes seem to have brought the dream of a narratological science to an end. A more positive view would be that it is only by turning back on itself that structuralism can remain faithful to its own insights into language in general and literary language in particular. Robert Young manages to illustrate both views when he says that 'poststructuralism traces the trace of structuralism's difference from itself' (1981, p. 8) – a sentence of the kind that I had in mind at the opening of this chapter. From this formula it would appear that narratology has no future, or that it degenerates in the poststructuralist phase into self-contemplation –

or contemplation of the inadequacy of structuralist narratology. What is poststructuralist narratology like if it is not a metalanguage, not a programme for analysis, and if it takes former theories rather than narratives as the primary object of critique? Barthes's answer to this question – the convergence of fiction and criticism under the term *writer* – is not really adequate. Clearly the academic study of narrative has not simply come to an end. My answer would be that there were three responses to the poststructuralist critique of structuralist narratology. The first was to carry poststructuralist insights onwards to the analysis of narratives everywhere, both literary and non-literary, so that narratology evolved into a thoroughly self-conscious deconstructive textualism. The second was to reject deconstruction's critique as introverted twaddle and to carry on with business as usual. The third was simply to displace the philosophical questions inherent in deconstruction's engagement with language theory with political and historical ones deemed of greater importance. These contradictory responses can all be found in the New Historicist engagements with narrative theory in the 1980s and are discussed in Chapter 4.

If the role of linguistic terminology in narratology turns out to be a useful way of charting the transition from structuralism to poststructuralism, or of indicating the provisionality of metalinguistic claims, the language of criticism is no less ugly for it, as this sentence illustrates. The theoretical fiction – narratology as narrative – may be one kind of attempt at redemption, transforming criticism into art. Many theorists have taken this path, and many others cannot. Derrida opens his tribute to Paul de Man – *Mémoires* – with the declaration, 'I have never known how to tell a story.' He was not joking. But the difficulty, even impossibility, of narration explored in *Mémoires* is not a deficiency limited to Derrida's own story. It is an effect of deconstruction which questions the possibility of narrating personal or historical memory: 'Deconstructive discourses have sufficiently questioned, among other things, the classical assurances of history, the genealogical narrative, and periodisations of all sorts' (1986, p. 15). Whether in fiction or in criticism, the ugliness of the new, self-reflexive theoretical languages cannot be seen as mere superficiality if it subverts something as deep as the knowability of the past.

3   Theoretical Fiction

Some fictional narratives seem to be more theoretical than others. Sometimes writers seem to choose consciously between fiction and the dry abstractions of a theoretical work. Proust is a good example. At the start of his manuscript notebooks for *A la recherche du temps perdu* he poses the question, 'Should this be turned into a novel, a philosophical essay?' If fiction is sometimes a better vehicle for ideas than the essay, it is fiction with theoretical intent or theoretical fiction. There have always been philosophers and historians who have forsaken theoretical discourse for the advantages of fiction, for its subtle mechanisms of persuasion, for its ability to explore ideas or historical forces as they are lived by individuals. Sometimes it is exactly the imprecision of narrative fiction which appeals, as when Sartre turned to the novel to express ideas which escaped systematic knowledge. Literary theory has seen the same kind of defection.

Is it perhaps sexier to be a writer than a critic? Barthes seemed to think so, turning from rigorous scientist of literature towards the erotic pleasures of the text and finally to fictional writing. David Lodge cut his teeth on the distinction between metaphor and metonymy, then wrote novels about academic sex lives, spreading structuralist and poststructuralist ideas about fiction more widely than anyone else in the process. The same could be said of Umberto Eco, as critic-turned novelist of ideas. There is a kind of academic frustration at work here – frustration on the one hand at the dispassionate character of critical science and on the other at audience size. When Julia Kristeva wrote her first novel *The Samurai* in 1990 she posed the question inspired by Proust: 'Knowing how to deal with a topic that preoccupies us is an ever recurring problem, should we treat it theoretically or fictionally?' One answer reflects the frustrated suppression of passion in intellectual life:

> The imagination could be considered as the deep structure of concepts and their systems. It may be that the crucible of the symbolic is the drive-related basis of the signifier, in other words, sensations, perceptions, and emotions; and to translate them is to leave the realm of ideas for that of fiction: *hence, I have related the passion filled life of intellectuals.* (Kristeva, 1993, p. 78; her emphasis)

In other words, yes, it is sexier to be a writer than a critic, even if the passion concerned, understood as the drive-related basis of the signifier, doesn't sound that wild. Her second answer reflects a frustration in the suppression of intellectual life in a world of passion:

> Furthermore, I may be forgiven for believing that the French genius consists in a close relationship between common passions on the one hand and the dynamics of intellectual tensions on the other. One finds such closeness nowhere else, even if in certain times, particularly those of national depression – in which I believe we now live – there is, in France, an increasing distance between intellectuals and others. I have thus tried to reconstruct for nonspecialists the work and very existence of intellectuals. (1993, p. 78)

Can this be forgiven in a book titled *Nations without Nationalism?* I am reminded for the wrong reasons of a book titled *Narcissistic Narrative.* How many different forms of narcissism, individual and collective, are there in this justification of the decision to treat a subject fictionally?

The right reason to be reminded of Linda Hutcheon's title is surely that this defection from theory to fiction inevitably results in narrative self-contemplation. Bearing in mind Barthes's definition of a theoretical discourse as a self-reflexive discourse, the export of critical expertise into the novel is not only a way of disseminating theory more widely. It is a way of giving the novel a critical function, the ability to explore the logic and the philosophy of narrative without recourse to metalanguage: it renders fiction theoretical. In this sense, theoretical fiction resolves some of the problems that deconstruction, and my last chapter, raised about critical metalanguages. The theoretical fiction is a performative rather than a constative narratology, meaning that it does not try to state the truth about an object-narrative but rather enacts or performs what it wishes to say about narrative while itself being a narrative. For this reason I prefer the term 'theoretical fiction' to the term 'metafiction', by which this kind of narrative self-contemplation has been named in the past two decades. Metafiction implies a difference between normal fiction and its metalanguage, even when that metalanguage is fiction itself. Theoretical fiction implies a convergence of theory and fiction of the kind Barthes describes.

The borderline between fiction and criticism has been a point of convergence where fiction and criticism have assimilated each other's insights, producing a more inventive kind of criticism and a new species of the novel of ideas. If the defection from criticism to fiction represents some kind of vain aspiration on the part of the critic to be a fictional writer, there has been a reciprocal aspiration on the part of novelists to assimilate the perspectives of criticism into the narrative process. It might be possible to explain this second kind of aspiration in similarly biographical terms. Writers like Martin Amis, John Fowles and Salman Rushdie, as graduates of Oxbridge English departments, are also writer-critics in the sense that they import academic criticism into the novel. But a theoretical fiction cannot be defined in such biographical terms. A writer-critic may personify the boundary between fiction and criticism, but a theoretical fiction has to be seen as a discourse which dramatises that boundary or uses it as an energy source. Sometimes this might involve the dramatisation of academics in fiction, as in David Lodge's novels, A.S. Byatt's *Possession,* Kristeva's *The Samurai,* John Updike's *Memories of the Ford Administration,* Umberto Eco's *Name of the Rose* J.M. Coetzee's *Disgrace* and *Elizabeth Costello,* Ali Smith's *The Accidental* or Zadie Smith's *On Beauty.* Some kind of narratological or historiographical self-consciousness can be imported into the novel by the inclusion of a literary academic, but it can also be incorporated in more subtle ways by the theoretical fiction.

The academic critic is an extreme, perhaps heavy-handed, version of a well-established fictional device which narratology has called, among other things, the surrogate reader: somebody within a fiction who represents the reception of the narrative. We are just as accustomed to the surrogate author, a figure in a narrative who dramatises the process of fictional production. Nobody could argue that these are new games in literature. Chaucer's elaborate framings of the *Canterbury Tales,* Shakespeare's plays within plays, the epistolary forms in seventeenth- and eighteenth-century poetry or the intrusive narrators of Fielding and Richardson are all in a sense versions of this kind of theoretical self-consciousness. The sensible commentators have pointed out that the metafictional device is 'a function inherent in all novels', as Patricia Waugh puts it, or, as Gerald Prince would have it, that the metanarrative sign is a moment of reflexivity in narrative which, like Jakobson's referential function, can happily co-exist with straightforward referential aspects of the narrative. But if narrative self-consciousness is not new, why have so many commentators emphasised it as the definitive characteristic of the postmodern novel?

One answer to this question would be that nothing described as postmodern can also be described as new. Newness was the leading value of literary modernism, whereas postmodern literature obsessively revisits and rereads its own past. Another answer would be that narrative self-consciousness has always been a feature of the novel, but that it has become more so in contemporary literature. This could either be a reflection of a wider cultural self-consciousness which can be pointed to in film, architecture, fashion and the TV game show or it could be a more specific response to developments in the theory of language and literature which make it more difficult to write a novel that does not reflect on its own role in the construction of reality. The broader issue of a generalised self-consciousness will be explored later. The focus of this chapter is the idea of reciprocal influence between literary theory and fiction which led the novel into narratological territory or, as Patricia Waugh puts it, into an exploration of 'a theory of fiction through the writing of fiction' (1984, p. 2).

Criticism as fiction

It would be misleading to describe new directions in literary theory as the cause of fictional change. There is a chicken-and-egg problem with fictional and a more general linguistic self-consciousness. The relationship between Saussurean linguistics and literary modernism is a good example. Both are places where the self-referentiality of language was emphasised alongside its ability to refer to an external world. For Saussure, referential language is implicitly self-referential in the sense that it depends on the hidden system of differences, systemic and contextual, which give each sign its value. According to this argument, language hides the conditions which permit meaning production, and the task for the structuralist is therefore to make those conditions – differential relations, contextual factors and conventions – explicit. But what order of causation or cosmological coincidence was at work in animating the modernist novel around the same project at around the same time, seeking as it did to foreground the hidden conditions – structural principles, the creative process, the conventions and the artifice – of fiction?

The self-referential dimension of literary modernism consisted partly in rejecting conventions of realism, traditional narrative forms, principles of unity and transparent representational language for techniques of alienation, obtrusive intertextual reference, multiple viewpoints, principles of unity borrowed from myth and music, and a more demanding, opaque, poeticised language. In modernist fiction these tendencies are of two kinds: those which foreground fictional conventions, and those which foreground language itself. In both cases, transparent and invisible structures are transformed into defamiliarised and visible techniques, so that referential meaning is articulated alongside a self-reference to the conditions of its own possibility. A dramatised version of this conjunction is the artist in fiction, such as Joyce's Stephen in *A Portrait of the Artist as a Young Man* in which the narrator becomes increasingly alienated from the referential aspects of words, seeing them instead as a kind of material self-activity, at the same time as the novel experiments poetically with the representation of his thoughts. *Ulysses* similarly portrays Dublin in all its newly achieved extremes of naturalism within a verbal and literary universe which paradoxically reminds us at every turn of the artificiality of the depiction. And then there is *Finnegans Wake* which almost completely abandons representation for a radical self-referentiality where language itself is the only player on the stage. Could it be said that in Joyce's work there is either some spooky prescience, or even direct causation, of the insights of structuralist and poststructuralist literary theory?

Joyce is a fascinating example partly because several poststructuralist theorists in the 1970s and 1980s looked to his work as a kind of inspiration and an origin for their theoretical insights. In other words, Joyce was a writer of theoretical fiction not in the sense that he defected from theory to fiction, but in that he was perceived afterwards as a writer who was exploring the theory of fiction through the practice of writing fiction. If some novels are more theoretical than others, Joyce's writing has repeatedly been represented as the ultimate theoretical fiction, not because academic theory has been imported into his fiction, but because academic theory has in a sense extracted the theoretical implications of his fiction. Poststructuralists in particular have identified Joyce as a proto-poststructuralist in a way that seriously confuses the relationship between cause and effect, fiction and criticism, or a narrative and its reading. Attridge and Ferrer's volume *Post-structuralist Joyce*, from its title onwards, declares the ambiguity: is it Joyce or the readings that are poststructuralist? J. Hillis Miller addressed the Seventh International Joyce Symposium in 1979 under a title which declared a similar uncertainty about the direction of influence between the fiction and theory – 'From Joyce to Narrative Theory and from Narrative Theory to Joyce' (1982b). Jacques Derrida has repeatedly invoked Joyce as an influence on his own writing as if we would be better to look to Joyce's fiction than Saussure's linguistics for the theoretical basis of poststructuralist writing. Again it could have been some narcissistic self-imaging on Derrida's part that inclined him to associate himself with a glamorous (if bygone) literary avant-garde more than with a Swiss linguist. Reading his work as a whole, his implicit hostility to linguists and his barely masked love of modernist writers, only confirm this. But they clearly also create a profound confusion between the theory and practice of writing, between the notions that poststructuralist attitudes to language were discovered in Joyce or invented by poststructuralist readings – a confusion which threatened to remove the boundary separating fictional representation from philosophical or critical statement, beginning a fashion for their mutual contamination.

To see fiction as theoretical or criticism as creative is to recognise their mutual contamination. The ambiguity designates the problem of whether literary meanings are discovered or invented by a critic, revealed or created by the act of reading. With the kind of contempt for cause and effect that Derrida would call *supplementarity,* the suggestion is that poststructuralist theoretical perspective is not only something that came later in the revision and rereading of Joyce, but that it was there in the first place. At the Seventh International Joyce Symposium in 1979, J. Hillis Miller seemed unsure about whether the displacement of concepts of unity by those of heterogeneity came from Joyce to narrative theory or vice versa. Ultimately, Miller seems convinced that Joyce's work articulates a theory of heterogeneity in a way that other narratives (he names Dickens and George Eliot) do not: 'There is little that deconstructive theory of narrative knows about the undecidability of words or of story lines which Joyce did not already know' (1982b, p. 4). The implication is clear enough: some narratives are more theoretical than others. But the paradox is also clear: if some narratives are more theoretical than others, they must be theoretical in themselves, objectively or intentionally, and not merely construed, constructed, created or invented as theoretical by the reading. There are many accounts of deconstructive criticism that give the impression that the critic is unconstrained by the objective structure or the authorial intention of a text – free to make anything of it that he or she pleases. But Miller seems to be saying something different: that there is something about Joyce's writing that invites, licenses or prescribes deconstruction because it knows deconstructive narrative theory in advance. How then can deconstruction claim this and at the same time reject, as it must, the traditional authority of critical metalanguages based in objectivity or intention?

Derrida's reading of *Ulysses* in 'Ulysses Gramophone' is a fascinating attempt to shed the authority of critical metalanguage and still say something truish about the particular nature of Joyce's narrative. The trick is to make the reading itself a work of theoretical fiction. The essay is a strange disjointed narrative which relates several apparently irrelevant journeys of Derrida's own, funny things that happened on the way to the conference and daft digressions. The fragmentary narrative is punctuated with theoretical declarations of the impossibility of a critical metalanguage and comic apologies to the intimidatingly expert conference audience. Having begun his career as a Joyce critic with a ridiculous essay about two words in *Finnegans Wake,* his reading of *Ulysses* compounds the joke by focusing on one word – *yes* – and saying nothing serious about it. This might not sound like narratology as we know it, but it is clearly a performative and not a constative narratology. It doesn't attempt to stand at a distance from *Ulysses* and tell the objective truth. Its mode is imitative: it is a parody of the Homerian symbolic journey which attempts to reproduce the theoretical implications of *Ulysses* without stating them.

Derrida sometimes gives the impression that *Ulysses* is a monument erected to deconstruction before it ever happened. Like Miller, he sees Joyce's work as a prescriptive constraint on the freedom of the critic: as a 'rigorous programme of prerecorded necessity'. He claims that:

> Nothing can be invented on the subject of Joyce. Everything we can say about *Ulysses,* for example, has already been anticipated ... All the gestures made in the attempt to take the initiative of a movement are found to be already announced in an overpotentialized text that will remind you, at a given moment, that you are captive in a network of language, writing, knowledge and even narration.   (Derrida, 1992, p. 281)

The implication here is that some narratives are more theoretical than others, and that *Ulysses* is a particularly appropriate text for deconstruction because it *programophones* its own deconstruction, predicting and prenarrating the assumptions of deconstructive narrative theory. While this makes some sense of the many declarations, his own and those of others, that Derrida's work is written under the influence of Joyce (Miller concludes that Derrida could not have written *Glas* except under the influence of *Finnegans Wake*), it has to be taken with a pinch of salt. The whole idea of *Ulysses* as a *monument* to deconstruction is just an ironic confusion of the temporality of cause and effect, which is also a way of confusing the object-text seen as theory and the critical text which is going to such lengths to foreground its own creativity.

It also seems to fly in the face of an explicit warning from Attridge and Ferrer in the introduction to *Post-structuralist Joyce*:

> The point is not that Joyce is the most perfect illustration for such a theory – for one of the convictions that the authors of the essays included in this book have in common is that there is no metalanguage: the text reads the theory at the same time as it is read by it.   (1984, p. 10)

This formulation of the theory–fiction relationship accords closely with the arguments of the volume – Heath's argument about the reader's freedom to invent contexts to interpret *Finnegans Wake* only to have those contexts destroyed by the text's ability to generate different contexts, Derrida's metaphor for the theory–fiction relationship as interacting computer softwares, Aubert's injunction that reading has to move both with and against the flow of words at the beginning of *Finnegans Wake*, and Rabaté's distinction between structural and serial thought which produces an oscillation between the critical poles of discovery and invention. These are all two-directional, interactive models of the relationship between the object and the critical text. They correct the impression that Derrida's essay on *Ulysses* can give, that Joyce's work represented some kind of discovered origin for Miller's or Derrida's poststructuralism.

These two-directional accounts of the relationship between Joyce and poststructuralism mean that the deconstructive reading of Joyce will usually oscillate between the poles of metalingual reference to their object and the subjective pole which sees reading as creative invention. In this sense, the deconstructive reading of Joyce is positioned astride the boundary of fiction and criticism, being both a secondary critical act and an act of creative production. An academic metalanguage is always there, in co-existence with an overtly metaphorical language which highlights the inability of the reading to refer transparently to its object. The oscillation is evident in 'Ulysses Gramophone' which tries at all times to 'avoid the platitude of a supposed academic metalanguage' (1992, p. 60) and at the same time avoid the anarchy of an entirely introverted critical writing. It is a co-presence of different voices in the reading, one of which holds academic competence in disdain for its implication that 'a metadiscourse is possible, neutral and univocal with regard to a field of objectivity, whether or not it possesses the structure of a text' (1992, p. 282); the other kind of

voice is that which claims that this impossibility of a metadiscourse is precisely a field of objectivity: 'For reasons connected with the structure of
the corpus, the project and the signature, there can be no assurance of
any principle of truth or legitimacy' (1992, p. 283). An academic transparency to the structure of the Joyce corpus is not possible, and yet 'one
can always at least dream of writing on Joyce and not in Joyce' (1992,
p. 281).

The point here is that Derrida's essay is itself a fiction which imitates
Joyce's fiction, and that in the act of imitation the problem of critical reference to a textual object reproduces the problem of fictional reference to
Dublin: it is a fiction with a theoretical performance. Derrida's oscillation
is itself an imitation of Joyce's own oscillation between the poles of naturalism and symbolism in *Ulysses*, meaning that the problem in critical
reference is itself predicted and prenarrated by *Ulysses* in what is traditionally called the *myth fact paradox*. This paradox is the movement that
allows the wealth of authenticating detail in *Ulysses* to achieve an extreme
of naturalism while functioning simultaneously in an intertextual system which assigns symbolic or metanarrative value to that authenticating
detail. Aspects of *Ulysses* that work in the service of a referential illusion –
the lack of plot, authorial absence, the disunity of the narrative voice,
the general multiplicity of voices, the blurred distinction between inside
and outside worlds, the mimetic experiments which create the illusion
of a lack of fictional technique, the sense of direct access to the minds
of characters, to the syntax of their thoughts, the vivid and unmediated
presence of Dublin, the factual detail of its presentation, redundant visual
detail, the sometimes comically objective scientific voice and the demotic
particularity of Dublin society – are inextricably embedded in layers of
illusion-breaking technique.

The trouble with this new, performative mode for criticism and theory
is that it leaves the subject–object relation between a text and its reading
mysteriously untheorised. The act of imitation implies a kind of collusion between Joyce and poststructuralism that could not exist for *Jane
Eyre,* implying that metanarrative aspects of *Ulysses* prescribe a critical
response which adopts the same duplicity with regard to the conditions
of its own referentiality. To argue that poststructuralist critical language
operates under the obligation to repeat, to imitate or to parody the myth-
fact paradox would be to argue for the remonumentalisation of the text
as an object – as a monument to aporia that prescribes the metaphysical
assumptions of further response to that monument.

Derrida's 'Ulysses Gramophone' does not exactly argue that *Ulysses* contains a critical prescription and is careful to avoid the remonumentalisation of the text as a philosophical tract about language and referentiality. Yet it is the imitation of the myth-fact paradox which characterises Joyce's influence on Derrida. In the spirit of Derrida's often repeated claim that a literary text assumes a metaphysics, it is a metaphysical attitude to reference which creates the collusion between reading and text that I am identifying. If the word *parody* implies a critical distance from the object-text, the word *collusion* designates more accurately the dynamic between monumentalising the object-text in terms of its metaphysics of reference and the demonumentalising of the text on which that metaphysics seems to insist. The tendencies of this dynamic, though apparently opposite, affirm both that *Ulysses* is a theoretical fiction and that its theoretical content is a deconstructive metaphysics.

So there is a theoretical content in *Ulysses* which is not entirely generated by Derrida's reading and which is enacted rather than explicitly stated by both: a performative and not a constative knowledge of narrative theory. If Derrida's object-text were a realistic narrative, assuming rather than questioning the possibility of reference, it might still be said to have theoretical content. But it would not be a deconstructive theoretical content, or if it were construed as such it would be an unconscious theoretical content, discovered only by a reading that went against the grain of the text: a reading of a realist text could not create the same sense of collusion and co-operation between the object-text and the reading. This collusion cannot really be anything other than an appeal to intention. It may not be singular intention, and the comic partiality of Derrida's reading of *Ulysses* signals his refusal to totalise at every stage. Neither is it necessarily a conscious authorial intention which underwrites the reading. But appeals to 'the structure of the corpus', in conjunction with ideas of prediction, prenarration and the programophone, are nevertheless appeals to the conscious structure of the text. They seem to define the idea of the 'influence' of Joyce on Derrida as Derrida's uptake of Joyce's consciously implied metaphysics.

Derrida's strategy in 'Ulysses Gramophone' then is to invest his reading with the authority of this vague theoretical collusion without invoking the authority of signifying intention or objective reference. The legacy of this collusion for Joyce studies is equally powerful because it recruits Joyce for theoretical fiction, constructing him as a proto-poststructuralist. It creates a narcissistic plane of mutual reflection between poststructuralism and Joyce across the boundary of literature and criticism. This might be one valid contextualisation of Joyce among others but it shows no such modesty, presenting itself as an internal necessity in the Joyce corpus. It is a high-cultural collusion which places Joyce and poststructuralism in a relation of mutual support, emphasising the shared theoretical assumptions of both. Taken together, the subtle reintroduction of authorising criteria in poststructuralist readings of Joyce and the high-cultural character of the collusion it creates make it difficult to accept Derrida's judgement of the subversive power of the deconstructive reading: that it is capable 'of destroying the very root of this (academic) competence, of this legitimacy, of its domestic interiority, capable of deconstructing the university institution, its internal or interdepartmental divisions, as well as its contract with the extra-university world' (1992, p. 283). Poststructuralist readings of Joyce, like theoretical fictions in general, establish a new theoretical competence to guide the performances of criticism, placing Joyce's texts the more firmly in the sphere of this academic competence by constructing them as philosophical and theoretical performances themselves. Is this Kristevan narcissism again? By getting inside it, by getting as close to it as a critic can, by claiming it as his own, Derrida seemed to wish that he had written *Ulysses*, but, as he told us, he didn't know how to tell a story.

Fiction as criticism

It would be difficult to count the number of metafictional novels that have appeared since the 1960s: novels written by people who do know how to tell a story but whose narratives turn back on themselves in differing levels of self-consciousness, self-awareness and ironic self-distance. It is not only Barthes's definition of theory as a discourse that turns back on itself which renders these narratives narratological. One of the major thrusts of structuralist narratology was to demonstrate that the realistic novel constructs, rather than reflects, the real world, or, to put it another way, that the outside world is always mediated by language and narrative, however much it is naturalised by the transparency of realistic language. If narratological criticism insisted this about realistic fiction from the outside, metafiction does so, and always did so, from within. It is in this sense that fiction can have a critical or a theoretical function in relation to itself and its own conventions. What I have just been describing in poststructuralist readings of Joyce is a meeting of metafiction and metacriticism. Both are characterised by self-consciousness about the way that they construe their objects; both foreground the same metaphysics of reference; both simultaneously assert and deny the authority of their referential mode; both, in my terminology, are theoretical fictions.

The conflation, or the mutual contamination, of criticism and fiction may elevate the critic to the status of writer, but what does the novelist gain from the new contract? The defection of critics to the novel is easy to understand, but why would the novelist want to defect to the obscurity of criticism? Why would they even consider allowing the perspectives of academic criticism a place in their stories? Why would an author, for example, subscribe to the idea of the death of the author? Or disinvest the novel of its power to refer to the real world? In the poststructuralist world, the novelist who assimilates critical perspective is subscribing to self-critique or signing his own death warrant.

When David Lodge turned his mind to this question in 1987, he argued that, far from there being a general convergence between fictional writing and poststuctruralist theory, there was a growing gap between, on the one hand, the humanist view of fiction which emphasised the mimetic and author-controlled aspects of fiction and, on the other, the poststructuralist views which denied the importance of these aspects. For Lodge, the actual experience of writing fiction was becoming increasingly divorced from the opaque and counter-intuitive claims of academic theory because an author tends to subscribe to the humanist view of what fiction is. The metafictional device, in his view, is not an anti-realist device with poststructuralist tendencies, but the opposite:

> ...consider the work of James Joyce. Almost every incident and character in his novels and stories can be traced back to some fact of his own life and experience, and he boasted that if the city of Dublin were to be destroyed it could be reconstructed from his books, yet at the same time he made large explicit and implicit claims for the timeless and universal significance of those narratives. Novelists are and always have been split between, on the one hand, the desire to claim an imaginative and representative truth for their stories, and on the other the wish to guarantee and defend that truth-claim by reference to empirical facts: a contradiction they seek to disguise by elaborate mystifications and metafictional ploys such as framing narratives, parody and other kinds of intertextuality and self-reflexivity or what the Russian formalists called 'baring the device'. These ploys are not as is sometimes thought, absent from the classic realist novel – one finds examples in for instance *The Heart of Midlothian, Northanger Abbey* and *Vanity Fair*; but they do seem to be particularly marked in contemporary fiction

as if in response to or defence against the epistemological scepticism of contemporary critical theory.   (1990, p. 18)

If there is some ambiguity here between the view of metafictional devices as a response to and a defence against poststructuralist theory, it is soon cleared up:

> The foregrounding of the act of authorship within the boundaries of the text which is such a common feature of contemporary fiction, is a defensive response, either conscious or intuitive, to the questioning of the idea of the author and of the mimetic function of fiction by modern critical theory. (1990, p. 19).

This is a difficult logic to follow. How can a metafictional ploy or 'baring the device' disguise the contradiction between the factuality and the fictionality of a novel? How can Lodge reconcile the two halves of this sentence: 'Indeed it would be false to oppose metafiction to realism; rather, metafiction makes explicit the implicit problematic of realism' (1990, p. 19)? If realism aspires towards mimetic transparency, any ploy which foregrounds the fictionality of realism tugs in the opposite direction, towards the opacity of language and the visibility of the devices by which a fiction constructs, rather than mimetically reflects, the world of facts and experience. And what does Lodge mean when he says that it is a defensive response? Is it defensive in the sense that the novel that declares its fictionality is less open to the charge that it is fictional? If so, is it defensive in the manner of a statement that anticipates an objection on the part of the audience, or tries to preclude the objection that it is false? Fiction which presents itself as real is, like a true lie, no less contradictory because it knows it and shows it.

Lodge's position is based on a falsely polar way of understanding the difference between poststructuralist and humanist views of fiction. It is not that the humanist view of fiction believes in reference to an outside world where poststructuralists deny it. The poststructuralist is committed to both positions, to their co-presence in a single text and to the irreducibility of the text to either one or the other. The poststructuralist, quite simply, loves the contradiction, and novels which celebrate the contradiction, like *Ulysses*, are better understood as poststructuralist novels than as novels defending themselves against contemporary theory. Another way of saying this would be that the postmodern novel is the novel in rebellion against two major laws of philosophical logic. The first is the law of non-contradiction which says that an argument is flawed if it contradicts itself. The second is the law of cause and effect which organises not only philosophical argument but the events of a novel, the relation of the novel to criticism, the relation between modernism and postmodernism, or personal and historical experience in general, as a linear sequence. The novel is superior to philosophy exactly because it is not constrained by such laws. It has acquired an epistemological importance in contemporary culture because it has always had the power to question the certainties of traditional philosophical argument, to be dialectical, to be complex.

Linda Hutcheon takes these points up in *A Poetics of Postmodernism* where she argues that the themes of self-reflexivity and the relation of fiction to history define the postmodern novel. Self-reflexivity, in her mind, gives the novel a new philosophical weight:

> This self-reflexivity does not weaken, but on the contrary, strengthens and points to the direct level of historical engagement and reference of the text. Like many postmodern novels, this provisionality and uncertainty (and the wilful and overt construction of meaning too) do not 'cast doubt upon their seriousness', but rather define the new postmodern seriousness that acknowledges the limits and powers of reporting or writing the past, recent or remote.   (1988, p. 117)

I would like to know what Hutcheon would make of the episode of *Columbo* where the murderer is a writer of murder stories, or *Fame* where American showbiz brats play the roles of American showbiz brats in search of the fame they have already found, or *Beavis and Butthead* where MTV morons sit on sofas watching each other with their televisions back to back. Her point is clearly not that self-reflexivity is in itself a kind of philosophical weight, but that the postmodern novel has become the serious, high-cultural version of a widespread phenomenon:

> Postmodern novels raise a number of specific issues regarding the interaction of historiography and fiction ... issues surrounding the nature of identity and subjectivity; the question of reference and representation; the intertextual nature of the past; and the ideological implications of writing about history.   (1988, p. 117)

This is what Hutcheon calls *historiographic metafiction,* a new kind of experimental writing which is uniquely capable of fulfilling the poetics of postmodernism precisely because it is epistemological: it raises issues about knowledge of the past and the bearing that narrative has on that knowledge. It has become more or less accepted in the world of literary and cultural studies that the postmodern novel is a philosophical novel, much better qualified than traditional discursive philosophy to address the question of the knowability of the past because it is stuck in the orbit of fiction and narrative.

The *historiographic metafiction* is a theoretical fiction in the sense that it writes out in fictional form what poststructuralist theorists say about historical narratives. As criticism has been circular in the twentieth century, first rejecting the historicist paradigm of the nineteenth century for a rigid formalism, then rejecting that formalism for a new historicism, so too has the novel moved from an essentially historical realist mode, through a period of formal self-consciousness and experimentation, into a new kind of ironic history. I can't remember who said that a little bit of formalism takes you away from history and a lot of formalism brings you back to it, but it is clearly true for the parallel histories of fiction and criticism. It is as if the war between historicism and formalism has come to an end, and it has become possible to admit that history has a narrative form and that narrative form has a history. Perhaps this is the best way of understanding what motivates a novelist to incorporate academic critical perspective into the novel. It is a way of acquiring the weight of academic philosophy, theory or criticism without conceding to the boredom of those discourses – or without loss of sex appeal. The novelist who wants to sell film rights might be better to stick with the contemporary topic and the documentary style, but for those in search of the intellectual weight that gets a novel onto a university reading list or wins them a literary prize, historiographic metafiction is the right path.

The common denominator among historiographic metafictions is that they explore the paradox of history as at the same time real and discursive. Some have seen this paradox as the outcome of the structuralist model of history. When structuralist narratology turned its attention to historical narratives, as for example in Hayden White's *Metahistory,* it reproduced the logic of an ongoing critique of fictional realism, which can be summarised as a challenge to the objectivity of realist narratives. One of the key narratological functions of historiographic metafiction is to foreground the subjectivity of historical novels. White has argued that structuralist narratology defines the objectivity of a narrative in linguistic terms. Following the work of Emile Benveniste and Gérard Genette, White argues that the objectivity of a discourse is determined by grammatical features which foreground or hide the narrative voice. A subjective narration will draw attention to the narrative voice with pronouns like 'I', with indicators of the time and place of writing, such as 'here', 'now' or 'tomorrow', and through tenses such as the present and the present perfect. An objective narration, on the other hand, will exclude indications of the person who narrates, presenting events as if they are telling themselves, as if nobody is speaking. In other words, the linguist can distinguish precisely between a historical discourse that openly adopts a subjective viewpoint on the world and one that 'feigns to make the world speak itself and speak itself as a story'. White calls the first of these *narration* and the second, which narrativises events while maintaining the pretence that there is no narrator, *narrativity*.

A novel like John Fowles's *The French Lieutenant's Woman* produces its theoretical effects by transposing narrativity into narration. It is a novel in which the objective voice of conventional Victorian fiction is constantly subverted by inappropriate interventions from an authorial narrator. Such interventions were in fact containable by Victorian convention, which allows for an oscillation between the modes of showing and telling in the narrative voice, or the intrusion of an authorial voice into the fiction to address the reader directly. But where the Victorian intervention operates as a kind of narrative candour to enhance realism, Fowles turns this into an illusion-breaking self-reflexivity, reminding the reader that the history being presented is a species of creative writing. The narrator regularly interrupts his own recognisably Victorian tone with a narrative comment from the late twentieth century, or with an explicit declaration of the artificiality of the events being narrated: 'The story I am telling is all imagination. These characters I create never existed outside my own mind.' Clearly this kind of intervention can be seen as a gain in subjective realism, as the candour of a narrator prepared to announce his presence in a text which otherwise hides him. The point here is that the poles of narration and narrativity combine to form a paradox, baring the device of impersonal omniscience on which the objectivity of historical narration depends by revealing it as subjective invention.

In 'The Value of Narrativity in the Representation of Reality' White argues that one of the functions of narrativity, where historical events tell their own story, is to disguise the moral argument of a historical chronicle. To narrativise history is, for White, a process of imposing structural principles on the chaos of historical experience. An example is narrative closure, the sense of an ending in a story which renders events meaningful, especially in moral terms: 'The demand for closure in the historical story is a demand, I suggest, for moral meaning, a demand that sequences of real events be assessed as to their significance in a moral drama' (1981, p. 20). Speaking here of non-fictional historical narrative, White identifies a function of closure that historiographic metafictionalists have exploited for its critical insight: that endings are ways of projecting values onto events, rendering the remainder of the narrative sequence intelligible in retrospect. A frequent feature of historiographic metafiction is to carry the modernist experiment of open-endedness into the domain of historical representation, highlighting its moral function. Salman Rushdie, in *Midnight's Children,* a novel preoccupied with the philosophy of history, with the constraints of plot and with the subjectivity of historical narrative, places its endings and beginnings in the middle of the narrative to avoid any obtrusive moral conclusion. Kurt Vonnegut's backwards war film in *Slaughterhouse Five* and (a work that it inspired) Martin Amis's *Time's Arrow* both invert the relationship between good and evil by narrating events the wrong way round. *The French Lieutenant's Woman* offers the reader a choice of endings in a way that paradoxically highlights both the God-like power of the authorial narrator and the freedom of the readership. The function of these games is basically critical, to draw attention to the normally subtle moralising in which an ending partakes, to highlight the ideological package that linear narrative and closure deliver to us, and therefore to explore the ideological function of narrativity in the presentation of the past.

It is probably clear that the mode of this kind of theoretical fiction can no longer be one of uncomplicated mimetic referentiality. By highlighting the role of narrativity in shaping history as a story, the mode is fundamentally *intertextual,* forcing us to contemplate not what the past was actually like but how it has been represented by other texts. These are not really novels that contemplate *themselves* so much as novels which contemplate the logic and the ideology of narrative in the act of construing the world. Like a word or a person, no narrative is ever an island. The narrative which develops historiographic self-consciousness should be seen less as an introverted novel than as one which looks outward to other narratives and the way they impose values under the pretence of neutral depiction of the world. Novels like *The French Lieutenants's Woman* and *Midnight's Children* make this intertextual orientation abundantly clear, the former by invoking and imitating novels and scientific texts of the period, the latter through parodies of the Anglo-Indian novel and continual references to the new Indian media as the mediators of contemporary history. These are novels that advance the proposition that historical sources are always textual, or that historical representations are always constrained by the conventions of representation in which they operate. They depict a world of texts in which historical fact, historical representations and historiographic ideology are inseparable.

This is where the concept of self-consciousness starts to look misleading. As John Updike puts it, self-consciousness is 'a mode of interestedness which ultimately turns outward'. If I inspect my own inner life I encounter only the system of differences or the traces of contemporary history through which I conceive of myself as an individual. So too for the novel. Elizabeth Dipple says this of Umberto Eco's network of intertextual reference in *The Name of the Rose*: 'The major point of the novel is that no book is an independent entity, and private existential self-referentiality is an impossibility. The degree to which the mind is formulated by written data and our perusal of them is immeasurable' (1988, p. 128). Self-contemplation, or reflexivity, is fundamentally critical because it refers us to other texts, to narrativity in general, not from some Olympian position of metalingual distance but from within the discourse on which it reflects.

If Derrida's reading of Joyce aspires to a performative rather than a constative narratology, historiographic metafiction often does the opposite, incorporating into the fiction some explicit, constative statement which would traditionally belong to the discourses of criticism or theory. Dipple, for example, finds the following passage in Eco's *The Name of the Rose* to illustrate the text's position on intertextuality:

> Often books speak of other books. Often a harmless book is like a seed which will blossom into a dangerous book, or it is the other way around: it is the sweet fruit of a bitter stem. In reading Albert, couldn't I have learned what Thomas might have said? Or in reading Thomas, know what Averroes said?
>
> 'True' I said amazed. Until then I has thought each book spoke of things, human or divine, that lie outside books. Now I realised that not infrequently books speak of books: it is as if they spoke among themselves.   (quoted in Dipple, 1988, p. 128)

Here is a passage which would not be out of place (save for the elegance of its expression) in a critical guide to intertextuality, stating the relation of the novel in which it is embedded to its historical sources, explicitly declaring its own theory of intertextuality. Dipple comments that this is non-novelistic thinking and links it explicitly to poststructuralism: 'The poststructuralist argument that language is always the subject of language has created a plethora of fictive ironies' (1988, p. 130). I would agree with a qualification, that the novel should not be seen as poststructuralist because it articulates a poststructuralist view on intertextuality, but rather because it enacts that view, performs that view, in its intertextual relation to other novels, other historical novels, other detective stories and the texts of academic theory. In short, it is not what a novel says but what a novel does that links it to poststructuralist theory, so that narratological knowledge of other texts derives from its intertextual performance and not from the statements of a metalanguage.

The idea of criticism as an intertextual relation and not a metalanguage is what unites theoretical fictions on the border between fiction and criticism. Intertextuality posits a model of referentiality which cannot distinguish between reference to the world and reference to another text, since textuality is woven into all. This is the starting point for what has been called, in the United States, the New Historicism, which is part of the discussion in the next chapter. It is also a heavy emphasis in many theories of postmodern culture at large, which is the subject of Chapter 5. For the moment the conclusion is simply that the wall between academic literary studies and fiction has been demolished from both sides, and that postmodern discourse has been dancing for three decades on the new space between.

Part II

Narrative Time and Space

4 Narrative, Politics and History

We must conceive of power without the king. So Foucault tells us throughout his work, as if to dissociate historicism from the idea of a single sovereign force and from the model of linear succession from which kingly power derives. We must conceive of power instead as a multiplicity of forces in permanent battle, and the movement of history in terms of discontinuity and rupture, not linear succession. How embarrassing then that Foucault should be the new king, and how contradictory the battle cries: formalism is dead, long live the New Historicism. There were two paradoxes inherent in these battle cries. The first was that the New Historicism was committed to the dissolution of kingship while enjoying its privileges, its supremacy and its institutional power. The second was that the New Historicism was new, constructing the analytical methods of the recent past as old hat, implying a kind of technological progress or teleological evolution that the new historiographies flatly denied.

The irony was compounded by the fact that this kind of pragmatic contradiction had prevailed in the reign of deconstruction. A pragmatic (or performative) contradiction can be defined as a discourse which claims one thing and does another. Deconstruction had always been accused of subverting the idea of any truth-claim while continuing to expect its own claims to be taken as true. This was also the premise of much New Historicist thought: that the New Historicists aimed to place in question the traditional idea of historical truth while claiming that the new things they said about the past were true. What this points to is that the New Historicism was more like an extension of deconstructive insights into new realms than the displacement of one set of critical assumptions by another within the same kingdom. (A full discussion of these themes can be found in John Brannigan's book *New Historicism and*

Cultural Materialism in this series.) The aim of this chapter is to show that deconstruction did not die in the 1980s, and that the new historical narratologies that have developed over the last two decades can be characterised as a kind of deconstructive historicism, in which the precepts and strategies of deconstruction find their way to new narratives.

The idea that New Historicism displaced deconstruction as the governing critical paradigm is very misleading, and yet there were institutional reasons, especially in the United States, for believing that this was the case. 'Deeco, deeco, deeco' moaned a prominent American publisher in 1990 when I told him that I was working on deconstruction, 'What's happening now? What's next?' Fishing for approval, I found that the right answer was not to point at any radical avant-garde in criticism, but to point to the right sort of politically progressive has-been whose work could be resurrected and recontextualised for the new age. Like new age philosophy, the re-release of *Star Wars* and the reappearance of flared trousers, criticism was on its way back to the future in the grips of what is called, in the world of advertising, accelerated recontextualisation, or a kind of nostalgia industry for the increasingly recent past. As such, criticism was returning to something in the past, something prior to deconstruction, but making it new: criticism was returning to history, and more specifically to Marxism, to questions of the ideologically constituted subject, and giving them a deconstructive inflection.

One more pragmatic contradiction is relevant here. It is the contradiction between being a professional academic and espousing a radical politics. It is relevant because the view of the New Historicism as a radical successor to an apolitical deconstruction was constructed by a more-radical-than-thou polemic which reached a peak of absurdity in the early 1980s. The opponents of deconstruction started writing books which can be summarised like this: the ideas of literary theory are all very interesting, but how do they help people who work in factories? Frank Lentricchia argued this in *Criticism and Social Change*. Terry Eagleton did the same in *Literary Theory: an Introduction*. It seemed that deconstruction, for all its radical posturing and philosophical sophistication, could be brought to its knees by an argument on this level. And there were places, such as Imre Salusinski's book of interviews with literary theorists, *Criticism in Society*, where the argument was conducted on this level. This is Harold Bloom on the new academic lust for social enlightenment and the pragmatic contradiction of the tenured radical:

> If they wish to alleviate the sufferings of the exploited classes, let them live up to their pretensions, let them abandon the academy and go out

there and work politically and economically and in a humanitarian spirit. They are the hypocrites, the so-called Marxist critics, and all of this rabblement that follows them now in the academies. They are the charlatans, they are the self-deceivers and deceivers of others...I am a proletarian; they are not. I am the only person I know at Yale who was born and raised in a working-class family. I'm the son of a New York garment worker... These critics are versions of the Parisian intellectual and social disease I can least abide... which is the high bourgeoisie being unable to stand its status as the high bourgeoisie, while continuing to enjoy it in every respect.   (Salusinski, 1987, pp. 66–7)

And this is Frank Lentricchia's angry reply:

Those who speak cynically of left intellectuals should examine the implications of suggesting that the university is not a good place to pursue social change. What the fuck are they doing? If they believe that, they should resign their jobs.   (Salusinski, 1987, p. 190)

I think there are lots of people in the academy who have had this argument, or pre-empted it with declarations of deprived backgrounds. I personally have listened to many academic biographies which begin in New York garment factories and which are designed to underwrite New Historicist political motives. But in the end, academic criticism cannot operate at this socio-biographical level. The move towards a socio-narratology needed the deconstructive inflection to lend some intellectual credibility to a debate which belongs in the Socialist Workers Party, and to imply progress from the old Marxist historiographies. There is, and should be, a limit to the academic value of a socio-narratology whose principal function is to signal that the critic is in solidarity with the oppressed.

Hundreds of readers may have abandoned me between the last sentence and this one because thousands of academic careers are currently predicated on this kind of solidarity. But this is not a call for some return to academic neutrality. I agree with Eagleton that neutrality is delusory and dishonest:

The idea that there are 'non-political' forms of criticism is simply a myth which furthers certain political uses of literature all the more effectively. The difference between a 'political' and 'non-political' criticism is just the difference between the prime minister and the monarch: the latter furthers certain political ends while pretending not to, while the former makes no bones about it. It is always better to be honest in these matters.   (1983, p. 209)

Where I disagree with Eagleton is in the rest of his book, which repeatedly returns to the unsupportable view that structuralism and post-structuralism, by retreating from history, have furthered some kingly pretence of neutrality while advancing a conservative politics. The thesis of this chapter is that this polemical moment in the 1980s, which construed the opposition of non-political formalism and political historicism as that of deconstruction and New Historicism, was wildly wrongheaded. It was wrong at the time, and it looks even more wrong from the twenty-first century. It was tempting for polemicists like Lentricchia and Eagleton to tell the story this way because it deployed all the resources of narrative explanation in the service of self-promotion without heed to the tangible ideological effects of deconstruction. What it belies is the role played by deconstruction in exposing (1) the fallacy, even tyranny, of a neutral science of narrative, (2) the ideological presuppositions of certain narrative structures, and (3) the ideological effects of history when structured as a line through a disparate past. When these deconstructive legacies are recognised, the return to history becomes, for socio-narratology, something much more than a flag of political allegiance, something more like an ideological unmasking which operates at the level of engaged textual analysis. There are three foundation stones for new socio-narratologies which can be identified within deconstruction and serve as a useful introduction to the New Historicism, which will be discussed here as the deconstruction of narrative time, the deconstruction of narrative exclusion and the textualisation of history.

Narrative and time

One of the main lines of attack on the formalism of structuralist analyses of narrative was their so-called 'synchronic orientation'. The Saussurean model of the sign had dictated that meaning be analysed as a spatial structure in relation to a snapshot of the language system as a whole at any one time. It was a common perception that this banished time and history entirely from structuralist narratology, and yet it doesn't take much exploration in the structuralist handbooks to determine that the internal temporality of a narrative – the order and frequency of its events – was one of the major concerns of the structuralists. Nor was it ahistorical in itself to take such a snapshot of the language system since, in theory at least, that might involve reconstructing the system of conventions, oppositions and codes as a kind of linguistic-historical context for any given utterance. In practice, however, there were few structuralist linguists who would go to the trouble of reconstructing the system of antonyms and synonyms that would give a sign its meaning at the time of its utterance or point out historical differences between the system at the time of the text's production and the time of its analysis. In practice there was a kind of disregard for the possible historical dimension of synchronic analysis and a tendency to view the internal, temporal sequence of narrative as a spatial or structural organisation of narrative elements. In theory structuralist narratology was neither ahistorical nor disinterested in the temporal organisation of narrative, but in practice anything temporal was quickly translated into spatial relationships or differences.

The Derridean concept of *différance* seemed to qualify the structural model of difference by allowing time back into the analysis: *différance* carried with it a temporal as well as a spatial meaning. At the level of a sentence, the model of difference would direct the analysis towards the syntagmatic relations between the components of the sentence, or the relationship between any sign and the sentence as a whole, as if these were stable structural relations. The model of *différance,* on the other hand, implied that the relationships between the elements of a sentence were always in motion, or that the meaning of any sign was somehow always qualifying those which preceded it in the sequence or waiting to be qualified by those which followed. This is what Derrida referred to as the *trace* structure of the sign: any sign is embedded in a context and its meaning bears the trace of the signs which surround it, which have preceded it and which follow it. In short, the meaning of a sign is not complete in itself, or is not present within itself, but somehow spread out across all the others. Nor is there any limit to the dissemination of meaning across other signs. Derrida talks of meaning as having no respite in the 'indefinite referral from signifier to signifier' (1978, p. 25) because the model of *différance* posits that neither the beginning nor the end of a sentence or a book can stop this movement.

The importance of the trace structure of the sign is that if it does reintroduce time into the analysis of meaning it also seems to strike at the concept of time itself:

> The concepts of present, past and future, everything in the concepts of time and history which implies evidence of them – the metaphysical concept of time in general – cannot adequately describe the structure of the trace. And deconstructing the simplicity of presence does not amount to accounting for the horizons of potential presence, indeed of a dialectic of protension

and retension that one would install in the heart of the present instead of
surrounding it with it.   (Derrida, 1976, p. 67)

The co-implication of meaning, time and history is strikingly clear here
as a kind of metaphysics based on presence. When Derrida refers to the
metaphysical concepts of meaning, time or history he is drawing attention
to this foundational illusion of presence which is destroyed by the trace –
by the fact that the present, or presence itself, is a crossed structure of
'protensions' and 'retensions', bearing within it the spectres of its own
past and future. If time and history are being readmitted here, it is in
an unrecognisable form that destroys the linear sequence of past, present
and future with the logic of the trace, which understands the components
of any sequence as constitutive of each other.

In the context of a polemic between a political criticism committed
to historicism and a depoliticised formalism, this was a very confusing
logical position. It seemed to be disturbing the simplicities of formalism
with the complexities of time that had been so reductively excluded from
structuralism, and yet it also seemed to be disrupting the simplicities of
time with a formal argument about the relations between the signifiers
in any chain. Even if some Marxists, like Lentricchia, heralded Derrida's
historical consciousness as liberation from formalism, turning the attack
on de Man instead, others were still scratching their heads about what all
this meant for people who worked in factories or who still had to get up
with the alarm clock in the morning.

In *Positions*, which was enormously influential in the United States,
Derrida summarises the implications of this non-metaphysical theory of
time for history. The position, however, became no clearer. Resistance to
the metaphysical concept of history, according to Derrida, entails resistance to both 'history in general and the general concept of history'.
Discussing the first of these, Derrida waves a big red flag, suggesting that
resistance to 'history in general' might involve subscribing to something
like Althusser's critique of Hegel's concept of history, which 'aims to show
that there is not one single history, but rather histories different in their
type, rhythm, mode of inscription – intervallic, differentiated histories'
(1981, p. 58). If this rebellion against a single, general history was politically motivated, the rebellion against the 'general concept of history' was
less obviously so and consisted in guarding against the presumption of
any common denominator which might link different histories together.
In *Positions* Derrida makes it quite clear that the common denominator that links histories together into a general, metaphysical concept of

history more than any other is linearity, the implication that one thing leads to another, which supports 'an entire system of implications (teleology, eschatology, elevating and interiorising accumulation of meaning, a certain type of traditionality, a certain concept of continuity, of truth etc.)'. Whereas the first argument seems to encourage the writing of more histories – the histories of those excluded by history in general for example – the second seems to undermine completely what we think of as, and how we might write, history. We might then ask why we should not follow the political impulse to democratise the writing of history by breaking the dominance of general history without worrying about the more formalist issue of the linear form of history and all of the implications it supports. What, after all, is so wrong with the linear concept of history in general? Why has deconstruction been so concerned with deconstructing the linear concept of time, of meaning, of narrative and of narrative history? I think the best answer to this question is that narrative linearity is in itself a form which represses difference, a proposition which is best explained in relation to the second foundation stone of the new historicisms – the critique of the structure of exclusion.

Narrative and exclusion

For Derrida, the sign was a structure of exclusion. The whole idea of the sign as a carrier of meaning was based on the principle that its meaning could be fenced off from other meanings. Saussure may have argued that it is the differences between signs that enables them to signify, but he did not go as far as to say that the meaning of a sign is actually constituted by those differences. Even in the radical terms of structural linguistics there is a sense that the meaning of a sign is pure. The sign is not internally divided. It is surrounded by difference but not contaminated by difference. Derrida's account of the sign can be summarised as an opposition to this idea of the pure self-identical sign, to show that the sign is always internally divided, different from itself. The sign then represses difference in at least three ways. The first is that, like the word *history*, the sign always posits some common denominator, some sameness between the things that it denominates, so that the word *dog* posits a common essence between dogs that effaces the rich variety of dogs in the world or represses the differences between dogs. The second is that the sign represses the differences between dogs and cats, because every time that *dog* presents itself as an apparently autonomous word, it hides or excludes the other words from which it differs, pretending that its meaning is constituted by itself and not by difference. The third kind of repression of difference is the one that will be most significant to this discussion of the ideology of narrative – that the sign represses the temporal differences between itself and the other signs in the sequence in which it is embedded.

My aim here is to show that these notions about the sign as a structure of exclusion act as a kind of foundation for most of the political criticism of the 1990s, which characteristically argues at the level of discourse that what is not there in a discourse is constitutive of what is. For the moment I want to digress for the sake of further illustration of the third kind of repression of difference. For linguists, the word is the 'minimum free form', which means that it is the smallest linguistic unit that can be taken out of its context, used in another and still mean the same thing. This makes the word different from the phoneme, since the phoneme doesn't have meaning on its own: it must be combined with other phonemes into a word for meaning to occur. In other words the meaning of a phoneme is context-bound whereas the meaning of a word is free. This is the traditional view that Derrida's *différance* challenges. One of the many jokes contained in the word *différance* is that one little phonemic change, a phonemic change which cannot even be heard, can alter the meaning of the word *difference* from a structural to a temporal relation. This tiny change highlights a principle that has large consequences for narrative thought in general. Not only are words internally divided by an alterable sequence of letters which have an individual potential to disrupt meaning, but the meaning of a word is also context-bound in the sense that it bears the trace of other words in the sequence to which it belongs. Like the phoneme, it is only as part of a combinative sequence that the word accrues meaning, so that it is marked by the temporal process of the discourse of which it is part. And it is marked by the trace of words which are not part of the discourse at hand, like the structuralist *difference*, which are ghostly intertextual presences inhabiting the word. What all these factors conspire to show is that a word is not simply a free form or the bearer of meaning as presence, since that presence is always contaminated by absences, traces of context, both immediate and distant. As Jonathan Culler puts it, meaning is context-bound, but context is boundless.

A concept as apparently innocent as the 'minimum free form' turns out to be a multidimensional repression of difference, a structure of exclusion which seeks to establish hard and fast boundaries around its meaning as if that meaning were not marked by protensions and retensions of other signs in the discourse, of former discourses and those still to come. What happens when this principle of the trace is scaled up to the level of a sentence, a narrative episode or an entire discourse? One answer is that the attempt to isolate any larger discursive unit and repress the trace of differences within it gives the concepts of autonomy, purity and presence a discernibly political importance, where the assumed linearity of a discourse can be seen as an agent of particular ideological bent. Two examples of the structure of exclusion at this level and the role of narrative linearity in the repression of difference are the critique of origins and the critique of positivist history, for both of which I will offer a brief summary.

One of the obvious consequences of this kind of argument that the word cannot be extracted from the *process* of language, or that it is always marked by the past and future, is that there can be no such thing as a moment. A moment, like a word, only comes into being as a structure of exclusion or an undivided presence. A moment can only be present when it is not yet in the past and no longer in the future. But any definition of what a moment is, any attempt to cleanse the moment of the trace of past and future and see it as pure presence will be forced to impose arbitrary boundaries which mark off the present from past and future. As with any structure of exclusion, the moment then becomes an entity in its own right but only by virtue of the fact that it has arbitrarily excluded the relations that constitute it. One is hard pressed to explain what one means by a moment without reference to the past and the future because it is structured by their exclusion. According to Derrida, the elusive nature of the moment is like the elusive nature of undivided presence in general. Its autonomy or purity is mythical. It is a desire rather than an actuality. One reason that undivided presence can be understood as a desire is that it helps to bring the explanation of something to rest on something stable, something no longer in motion, no longer referring backwards or waiting to be altered.

The desire for presence helps to explain what Derrida means when he talks about *metaphysical* history. Metaphysics, for Derrida, is the metaphysics of presence, any science of presence, so that metaphysical history is any history which sees the passage of time as a sequence of present moments, any one of which can be isolated from the sequence and seen in terms of this mythical purity and presence. It also helps to explain why Derrida devotes so much of his writing to the deconstruction of origins. An origin is the first moment in an historical sequence. It is, in a sense, an easier moment to mythologise as presence because nothing comes before it and, at the time it occurs, it has not yet been marked by subsequent moments. This means that when you want to explain something, its origin is a useful bedrock for the explanation, very often narrating the history of that something from the point of originary purity and self-presence, very often narrating its history as a fall from that original state of presence. At one level the sign itself is a fall from presence, since it can be circulated, repeated and used without the thing to which it refers being present. Interpreting the sign then becomes a process of working backwards to the originary and mythical moment when the sign and the thing were unified, when the meaning of the sign was present. Writing is also a fall from presence since, like the sign, it is exterior to what it means, capable of signifying in the absence of the writer, demanding a kind of nostalgia for its origin, the moment when the mind that produced it was present, when it was full with signifying intention, or when it was speech. Speech is also the origin of writing in the sense that it comes first, in childhood or in the history of humankind, and this temporal priority is often seen as a kind of logical or metaphysical priority. To explain writing, it then becomes necessary to trace it back to its origin in speech, where language can be seen in its purest form.

These examples of origins as underpinning moments of purity and presence are all taken from the question of language. They are narrative explanations of language, which present metaphysical presuppositions as historical processes, investing origins with some special explanatory power. They are myths functioning as memories. This formula can be used to describe the politics of other explanations which see history as a fall from some mythical purity. Culture, for example, is often seen as a fall from nature, implying that nature has some metaphysical priority against which the history of culture can be seen as a process of deterioration. This is a particularly absurd claim, demanding as it does that the historian trace culture backwards in time to a moment of pure nature, before its adulteration by human history. What date would that be? No wonder that God has so often functioned to bring a halt to this kind of archaeology, from the book of *Genesis* to *A Brief History of Time*.

A more common version of this narrative supposition is to make the poles of nature and culture relative, so that past history is seen as more natural than the present. Dry stone dykes are more natural than reinforced concrete walls, pens are more natural than personal computers, fires more natural than radiators, bicycles more natural than cars. Often nostalgia for a more natural past is based on a myth which confuses nature with a former state of culture. One of the characteristic strategies of New Historicist criticism is to demythologise the past either by extracting it from this kind of narrative perspective or by exposing the operations of power through juxtaposition with the contemporary world. To use Derridean language, narrative history is often constructed around an opposition between an origin and a supplement, or that which comes later, so that the story is one of loss of innocence or original purity. To show that the terms of this narrative opposition are in a relation of mutual contamination, narratology has to destroy two of its founding suppositions: the supposition of a pure, undivided origin and the supposition that the ensuing fall into difference was a process of linear consecution whose events could be excluded from the origin itself. Derrida's term *supplementarity* can be thought of as a narratological concept in so far as it names the counter-logic to this narrative logic, disrupting the linearity and the exclusion on which it depends. This counter-logic is as follows: the supplement does not follow from the origin except in terms of the metaphysical concept of time; the supplement is not added on later but is 'a possibility [which) produces that to which it is said to be added on'. In other words the possibility of what comes later is the origin of the origin, so that the origin always contains within it the mark of what is to come. Or, to use another Derridean phrase, the fall from presence has *always already* occurred, and the idea of some undivided originary presence which precedes difference is a delusion foisted on us by narrative.

Supplementarity names one of the ways in which a structure of exclusion can be opened up to difference, where the purity of an origin is seen as already structured by the loss of purity which follows from it. This might be called an intra-narrative structure of exclusion, since the mythic origin excludes the future events which form the remainder of the same narrative. I want to turn now to another kind of structure of exclusion which could be called inter-narrative exclusion, which also illustrates the complicity of narrative linearity and certain ideological functions of narrative, and which also links common New Historicist strategies with a deconstructive logic. Deconstruction was always obsessed with absences, with the constitutive role of the Other in the identity of anything. What I have been describing over the last few paragraphs is a logic based on the idea that a sign, an origin or a narrative episode can bear the traces of its syntagmatic relations – bears the traces of past and future parts of the discourse to which it belongs. What I want to turn to now is the idea that a narrative history is a structure of exclusion in the sense that it bears the traces of other stories, stories that are not told, stories that are excluded, stories of the excluded.

It is a common criticism of Jane Austen's fiction, for example, that it describes only a very small part of the world and only a very small part of society within that small world. On the first count, critics have pointed out that Jane Austen's fiction excludes any reference to major world events of the period in which her narratives are set, such as the Napoleonic wars, and on the second, that there are no servants, no cooks, no housekeepers, no carriage drivers, no gardeners, village idiots or toe-rags to be found in her novels. This is a reading that to some extent depends upon excluding certain uncooperative details (like *Mansfield Park*) in the corpus but expresses a broad truism about the narrow lie that is a Jane Austen novel. The rigid geographical boundaries around Highbury in *Emma,* for example, prevent us from following Frank Churchill even as far as London, while the class boundaries prevent anyone from below the top end of the mercantile class from playing a role. What are we to make of these exclusions? Some critics, like one of my undergraduate lecturers, defend them on the grounds that these are artistic choices and not limitations. Others, like Raymond Williams, will painstakingly reconstruct aspects of the historical context which have been left out, just so that we know that early nineteenth-century England was not all balls and picnics. But how could a narrative include everything? And why don't critics argue that there are no rounded middle-class characters in *Trainspotting*? Clearly it is a political argument, not objecting to exclusion itself but to the exclusion of certain people or certain aspects of society, to the exclusion of the powerless from representation. It is an argument which posits a kind of complicity between narrative exclusion and a broader and more systematic kind of exclusion from economic and political power. One critical strategy which can tentatively be called New Historicist then is the telling of a different story, the story of the excluded, which delves into historical context to counteract the exclusions of an object-narrative as a demonstration that the apparently autonomous world of that narrative depends vitally on what it leaves out. In other words, the New Historicism takes the basic argument of semiology – that the meaning of a sign can only be explained with reference to the systemic relations which it hides and scales it up into a principle for a whole discourse.

This strategy was the subject of a disagreement between Derrida and Foucault which reveals a subtle difference in emphasis between deconstruction and New Historicism. In *Madness and Civilization,* Foucault had argued that the age of reason could only construct itself, or be constructed in retrospect as the age of reason, by excluding madness. Again there is a sense here of the complicity between society's need to incarcerate mad people and the need of a narrative history to exclude the mad from representation of the era. Madness, after all, is just as much a part of history as reason. Derrida's review of Foucault's argument, 'Cogito and the History of Madness', does not accept that the New Historian merely has to write the history of the excluded:

> ... if the decision through which reason constitutes itself by excluding and objectifying the free subjectivity of madness is the origin of history, if it is historicity itself, the condition of meaning and of language, the condition of the tradition of meaning, the condition of the work in general, if the structure of exclusion is the fundamental structure of historicity, then the 'classical' moment of this exclusion described by Foucault has neither absolute privilege nor archetypal exemplarity.   (1978, p. 42)

For Derrida, Foucault's New Historical writing is a sample of the structure of exclusion from which it seeks to distinguish itself both in the appeal to a historical moment which is the origin of exclusion and in the way that the history of madness merely reproduces the metaphysics of a linear history for the excluded: it gives the privilege of representation to the deprived and therefore upturns the power relation without changing the way that history is written. Paul de Man argues the same case against Foucault, that he operates within the pattern of a genetic historicism while claiming to displace it. In fact this nuance was a central debating point in the early 1980s: did the politics of historical narrative reside in the genetic and linear form of the story (in exclusion itself) or in the material power of those doing the excluding or being excluded? Another example would be Samuel Weber's critique of Fredric Jameson's defence of Marxist historicism in *The Political Unconscious*:

> ... Jameson's defence of Marxism is caught in a double-bind: it criticises its competitors for being ideological in the sense of practising 'strategies of containment', that is of drawing lines and practising exclusions that ultimately reflect the particularities – the partiality and partisanship – of special interests seeking to present themselves as a whole. But at the same time its own claim to offer an alternative to such ideological containment is itself based on a strategy of containment, only one which seeks to identify with a whole more comprehensive than its rivals.   (1983, p. 22)

Here again is the pragmatic or performative contradiction that if one opposes a particular strategy one cannot continue to use it oneself. To do so is like taking money from the rich and giving it to the poor without addressing the principle of inequality. This dichotomy can be expressed in historiographic terms: that it is not enough to oppose the positivistic assumptions of history by writing a positivist history of the oppressed – it is the traditional practices of historical writing themselves which operate as ideological containment.

Foucault's reply to Derrida, translated as 'My Body, This Paper, This Fire', does little more than call Derrida a cheeky bastard and a pot calling the kettle black. The argument for all its apparent complexity descends again to the level of Bloom versus Lentricchia: that Foucault and Derrida both deploy the resources they denounce, but that Foucault is closer to changing the world than Derrida because the latter has his textualist head further up his own backside. Foucault's head, according to Edward Said in 'The Problem of Textuality: Two Exemplary Positions', is at least moving in and out: 'Derrida's criticism therefore moves us into the text, Foucault's in and out of it.' One of the interesting things about this formula, which was very influential in the uptake of Foucault's work in the United States, is that it seems to make a structure of exclusion out of textuality itself, in so far as it posits an outside of the text and implies that Derrida is simply ignoring it. So where do New Historicists stand on this issue? Does textuality have limits? Does it stand in opposition to the real world?

Textuality and history

I have been arguing that Derrida and Foucault are theoretically quite close together on the role of exclusion, the part played by narrative linearity in the construction of exclusion and the commitment to conceive of power as dispersed in difference. Foucault states that 'we must not imagine a world of discourse divided between accepted and excluded discourse' and that 'we must conceive of power without the king'. Derrida writes that 'structure has always been neutralised or reduced, and this by a process of giving it a centre', that it became 'necessary to begin thinking that there was no centre', and that '[the centre] is never absolutely present outside a system of differences' (1981, pp. 278–9). Both Foucault and Derrida therefore reject the idea that history is knowable through any single narrative account which would inevitably reduce an irreducible difference to a single centre. Derrida may bury his head in philosophical and literary texts and speak of signifiers, origins, supplements, traces and *différance* where Foucault talks of prisons, hospitals, kings, political power and other obviously societal institutions. This may make them opposites in the terms of a factional debate between form and history, but in terms of the broad transition from literary narratology to socio-narratology Derrida and Foucault should be seen as the twin pillars on which the diversification of narratology rests, or as a way of linking poststructuralist linguistic tenets with politics and ideology.

For critics like Stephen Greenblatt, the New Historicism became a historicism of power and politics in two principal senses. The first was a recognition of the textuality of history which derived directly from this poststructuralist emphasis on exclusion, origins and closure. In his introduction to *Shakespearean Negotiations,* for example, Greenblatt argues that history has to renew itself by moving away from 'realist' assumptions about the meaning of a historical text towards a recognition that history and literature are discourses which construct rather than reflect, invent rather than discover, the past. This first claim, that history is textual, is much more than an argument that historical knowledge is based in texts rather than empirical facts. It is a recognition that the history carries within it the values and assumptions imposed on it by narrative exclusion and plot, so that historical knowledge often unwittingly subscribes to those values while assuming some transparent access to the past. The second is a redoubling of this insight to reflect on the interpreter's own values, or the textuality of modern interpretations of historical texts. Greenblatt argues something very close to Eagleton on apolitical criticism when he claims that power and politics are at work not only in historical representations, but in the interpretations of those discourses which can never be neutral or disinterested. In other words, the New Historicism exactly reproduces the double movement that I have been attributing to deconstruction over the last two chapters, where the displacement of 'realism' with textuality applied equally to the reading and the thing read.

If deconstruction developed a self-consciousness about the role of its own language in the rewriting of its object-texts, the New Historicism placed a similar emphasis on its own textuality at the level of constative statement and critical performance. So for example it is characteristic for a New Historicist reading to declare its subjectivity as a kind of rewriting of history, as an active reinvention of the past which wears its political allegiances on its sleeve. Greenblatt's early impact on literary studies derived from this sense that the Renaissance could be completely rewritten and reinvented, destroying any notion of its timeless and durable character. Suddenly autobiographical details about the critic's proletarian origins or skin colour took on the intellectual importance of a self-aware textuality – a poststructuralist recognition of the irreducible subjectivity of interpretation – which openly declared the values on the basis of which the Renaissance was to be reconstructed. At the level of performativity, Greenblatt and his followers often foregrounded the anecdotal and narrative character of their own autobiographical and contextual elaborations, the open textuality of which adopted a kind of productive intertextual juxtaposition with the text being read. If the fictional subjectivity of these narratives was ever thought to be in conflict with the facts of history, so much the worse for the facts.

Greenblatt's introduction to *Shakespearean Negotiations* has been taken by several commentators as a kind of manifesto for the new historicisms and the *cultural poetics* that they imply. Like deconstruction, the new historicisms never thought of themselves as a unity, nor of their critical procedures as governed by any applicable methods or rules. Like deconstruction, the New Historicism is based in performance, in particularity and locality, which resists formulation. But performativity, as the commentators of deconstruction have shown, has no real power to resist formulation, and there are always those who, like me, make a living from reducing and abstracting critical performances to a set of communicable or teachable principles. Veeser did this for the new historicisms when he isolated five common assumptions:

> New Historicism really does assume: (1) that every expressive act is embedded in a network of material practices; (2) that every act of unmasking, critique and opposition uses the tools that it condemns and risks falling prey to the practice it exposes; (3) that literary and non-literary 'texts' circulate inseparably; (4) that no discourse, imaginative or archival, gives access to unchanging truths or expresses unalterable human nature; and (5) that a critical method and a language adequate to describe culture under capitalism participate in the economy they describe.   (1989, p. 2)

It hardly seems necessary to point out the trace of deconstruction in this list. It is more useful to contemplate the slight shifts in emphasis, particularly in points (1) and (5): the assumptions that the object of criticism is capitalist culture and that culture is comprised of material practices. At first sight, the emphasis on the material practices of culture seems inconsistent with a textualism that asserts the constructedness of those practices. The term 'materialism' is often used to describe a philosophy which subscribes to the priority of real material things over the idealities of mind, language, text and perception. For the materialist, things exist whether or not they are represented, perceived, articulated and written. This was always, I believe, a point of misunderstanding between the traditions of Marxism and poststructuralism, the clarification of which points not only to the possibility of a poststructuralist Marxism but also to the philosophical basis for socio-narratology.

The misunderstanding was that Derrida's work was a form of Idealism which claimed that the world of things was all in the mind, as perception constructed by language. W.J.T. Mitchell, for example, argues that Derrida's theory of meaning 'remains a form of idealism strictly speaking, for semantic value is produced entirely within the confines of language, without reference to the world of things' (1982, p. 73). Mitchell was not alone, and I am thinking not only of works like Coward and Ellis's (1977) volume *Language and Materialism* but of a host of British cultural materialists and teachers of literary theory who have represented Derrida in this way. Any semi-alert reading of Derrida will produce a different conclusion: that language *is* a material practice not only in the sense that it is to be understood in isolation from the mind as the material marks of writing but also in the sense that textual and linguistic constructs are (to use a word that Derrida avoids) *reified* or transformed into material things and practices in the world. As always with Derrida, the point is to liberate meaning from the duality of mind and things, the strategy for which is to untie the bond between language and consciousness and represent language instead in its material forms: as writing, as recording, technology, externality and so on. The clarification then is that textualism, for Derrida as for Foucault, does not belong in an opposition with materialism. The consequence for a socio-narratology is that narratives are not inventions of the mind but political and ideological practices as much a part of the material texture of reality as bombs and factories, wars and revolutions.

Nothing is more offensive in the postmodern sensibility than a statement like Paul de Man's that 'the bases for historical knowledge are not empirical facts but written texts, even if these texts masquerade in the guise of wars or revolutions' or Baudrillard's notorious claims that the Gulf War was a hyperreal media event. But such statements are only offensive when they are misunderstood as claims that wars and revolutions are mere texts, mere representations, appearances and not things in themselves, from within the position that stories and writing are external to politics. The role of narrative in characterisations of postmodern culture in general is the subject of the next chapter. I want to finish this one with an illustration of the complicity between politics and narrative based on specifically deconstructive notions of the ideological function of narrative.

Nations and narrations

Thankfully, since the polemics of the 1970s and 1980s, there has been a sense of convergence of formalist and historicist thought that no longer poses a choice between political commitment and apolitical aestheticism in criticism. A good example is postcolonial criticism, especially in its dealings with narrative, where it is common to find narratological methods being drawn from a wide range of sources with the specific purpose of illustrating the role that can be played by narrative in the 'discourses' of nation and empire. Those interested in a detailed illustration of postcolonial criticism as it draws on narratological resources can find it in the discussion of the history of the reading of *Heart of Darkness* in Chapter 6. The remainder of this chapter will be an exposition of Homi K. Bhabha's ingenious essay 'DissemiNation: Time, Narrative and the Margins of the Modern Nation' (1989) which attempts to link the deconstruction of narrative time – notions of origins, margins, discontinuity and supplementarity – with the material experiences of national identity, an essay that has acquired a seminal status in socio-narratology.

Bhabha begins from the notion that the nation is a notion – a powerful political idea or, in Benedict Anderson's phrase, an *imagined community* to which individuals affiliate themselves. Perhaps it would be more accurate to say that he locates the nation somewhere between a thing and an idea: that the nation may be notional but that it is an idea which forms a part of the material experience of society, underpinning national institutions or experiences as real as migration and wars. In this sense there is an echo of Derrida's refusal of the dichotomy between the material and the ideal which allows him to pass freely between statements about narrative and politics. The most obvious point to make about a nation is that, if it is a thing in any sense, it is one of the most complex things one could think of, so that any attempt to represent it in its totality will be forced to employ a strategy of totalisation: that is, using some parts or characteristics to represent the whole complex entity. The nation is the structure of exclusion *par excellence* in that any attempt to totalise it will have to exclude, or marginalise, those parts of the nation that are not deemed representative of its total essence.

Hence there is a Foucauldian sense in Bhabha's essay that the nation is a discursive formation, a thing that only comes into being through discourse, but where no single discourse can convey the multiplicity of forces which make up that formation. The reduction of this unthinkable complexity to a single story of a singular thing is not adequate, and yet, for

Bhabha, this kind of reduction is exactly what takes place in the established relationship between the nation and realist narrative: a transparent medium creates the impression of a continuous community. Bhabha also points out that, when the realist narrative tells the story of a nation, it smuggles into the explanation the supposition of an origin, since the story has to begin somewhere, and an endpoint which sees the modern nation as the outcome of this singular history. If these seem like harmless suppositions, it is worth bearing in mind the use that they have been put to in Nazi Germany or the battle over territory in Bosnia, where positivist histories were marshalled to the causes of ethnic cleansing and genocide. But these are extreme cases. It could be objected that the evil use of metaphysical history does not logically support the idea that metaphysical history is evil in itself, any more than the use of a pillow as a murder weapon reflects badly on pillows in general. Bhabha does not make this point about the histories that Hitler commissioned or the Serbian appeals to national origins, but he does explain what makes narrative history different from pillows: the ability to homogenise time.

Bhabha talks about the 'homogeneous time of social narratives' as if they were evil because linear time conveys the impression that the continuity from national origins to the modern nation is natural and real rather than constructed by exclusions. So, for example, the narration of a national community from indigenous origins through the age of mass immigration will tend to view immigrants at best as late additions to the nation which do not alter its historical character and at worst as a contamination of the purity of that character. Hence homogenous time underpins ideas of the homogeneity of the nation seen as natural rather than exclusionary. Speaking of the inadequacy of single explanations which refer to single origins, Bhabha writes:

> If, in our travelling theory, we are alive to the *metaphoricity* of the peoples of imagined communities – migrant or metropolitan – then we shall find that the space of the modern nation-people is never simply horizontal. Their metaphoric movement requires a kind of 'doubleness' in writing; a temporality of representation that moves between cultural formations and social processes without a 'centred' causal logic.   (1989, p. 293; his emphasis)

I have never quite understood why Bhabha says 'metaphoric' and not 'metonymic' here, since the relation of a modern national community to some single part is surely one of contiguity (synecdoche), not similarity. But pedantry aside, the important emphasis is that a sense of nation is the product of a kind of centred linear writing – a kind of metaphor.

This is an emphasis that informs many New Historicist revisions of old historiographic assumptions, and here, as elsewhere, dissent becomes a writing strategy which opens narrative out from its singular linear character. From the early new historicisms to recent postcolonial writings there is a sense that material things and metaphorical discourses are inseparable, often becoming part of an individual's material experience through a psychoanalytic identification with an imaginary and symbolic structure such as the Western nation.

Bhabha's essay contains two counter-emphases to the homogenous time of social narratives which can be interpreted as anti-historical. The first is the displacement of homogenous time with double-time which reflects the disjunction between historical explanation of a nation and its living present:

> We then have a contested cultural territory where the people must be thought in a double-time; the people are the historical 'objects' of a nationalist pedagogy, giving the discourse an authority that is based on the pre-given or constituted historical origin or event; the people are also the 'subjects' of a process of signification that must erase any prior or originary presence of the nation-people to demonstrate the prodigious, living principle of the people as that continual process by which the national life is redeemed and signified as a repeating and reproductive process. The scraps, patches, and rags of daily life must be repeatedly turned into the signs of a national culture, while the very act of narrative performance interpellates a growing circle of national subjects.   (1989, p. 297)

This tension between the pedagogical and the performative has the potential to dismantle the conspiracy between the past and the present, so that signs of national culture in the present are not doomed to repeat the exclusions constructed by traditional historicism. The second counter-emphasis follows from this: that it is possible to produce the signs of a modified national culture from a position that would have been marginal to the national character in the terms of traditional history: 'From the margins of modernity, at the insurmountable extremes of storytelling, we encounter the question of cultural difference as the perplexity of living, and writing, the nation' (1989, p. 311). In other words, Bhabha understands the 'living' and 'writing' of national consciousness as part of the same process: a process which must surrender to the complexity of the modern nation with a new, disjunctive narrative temporality rather than repeat the homogenising strategies of historicist narration.

I think the only real problem with Bhabha's essay is the volume of intellectual noise he uses to express a weak political argument. I think he succeeds in showing that the deconstruction of time has a political application and in illustrating the false dichotomy of the ideal and the material in academic approaches to culture. But in terms of political consequence, the argument amounts to little more than a conviction that there is more to being British than beefeaters and the lineage of kings. *Bhabhababble* is a kind of language that declares its inspiration from deconstruction, Marxism and psychoanalysis at every turn, but when the politics of this double writing are unravelled, there is a sense of disproportion between the intellectual apparatus and the result, like the use of heavy artillery to dispense with a gnat. It should also be added that this essay does not represent the kind of approach to criticism that Eagleton or Lentricchia would have had in mind in the early 1980s as the political antidote to formalism. But it is characteristic of a certain direction in criticism – a path back to history but concerned to displace historicism with the temporal aporias of narrative time, a certain mix between historical writing and a psychoanalysis of exclusion in the construction of identity, a self-conscious textuality in which material processes are transposed into stories and metaphors – which narratology has followed. The focus on national identity was always a preoccupation of deconstructionists like Derrida, Hélène Cixous, Julia Kristeva and Gayatri Spivak, making it a political topic marked from the beginning by the deconstructive inflection. It was a kind of textualist thought that presided over the beginnings of postcolonial narrative theory more than it did over British cultural materialism, for example, which aimed to sustain the importance of history to class consciousness in the study of narrative, has probably succeeded better in establishing a dissident criticism, but has contributed little to narratological knowledge.

I said earlier in this chapter that the value of socio-narratology should not be assessed on the basis of the critic's positionality alone: that is, as declared solidarity with the oppressed. I would conclude that, if narrative is as central to the experience of history, knowledge of history, the construction of personal or collective identity as the various new historicisms have claimed, the value of a socio-narratological approach is measured by its contribution to the knowledge of narrative mechanisms and strategies that perform these decidedly political functions rather than by their revolutionary potential. The revolution will not be like the new historicisms. The revolution may never happen and, if it does, will be more like a consumerist atavism than a progressive Marxism.

5 Culture and Schizophrenia

By what right have literary critics appointed themselves as critics of culture at large? Or, to limit the question slightly, what special expertise does narratology bring to the analysis of culture? It is perhaps easy enough to understand why narratology should export its insights to non-literary narrative forms such as narrative history, but can it presume to go further, to attempt a narratological explanation of culture at large? I think there are two arguments which lend some weight to the idea of a cultural narratology. The first is the idea that narrative is ubiquitous in the contemporary world, in fact so commonplace that it would be difficult to think about ideological issues and cultural forms without encountering it. The second is that culture not only contains narratives but is contained by narrative in the sense that the idea of culture, either in general or in particular, is a narrative.

The project of this chapter is to show that narratology has made a significant contribution to the study of culture beyond the boundaries of literature, and is all the more able to do so since its transformation from a scientific semiology into a deconstructive quest for paradox and aporia. Far from being a holistic theory, this chapter wallows in contradiction on the understanding that the special expertise of the new narratologies is in the dialogic and the contradictory logic of culture, linking what I have been describing as the deconstruction of narrative time to culture at large through the concept of what Deleuze and Guattari call cultural *schizophrenia*.

Accelerated recontextualisation

The Janus face of narrative has already been widely discussed in this book. What Paul de Man describes as the simultaneous assertion and denial of the authority of reference is visible in deconstructions, in theoretical fictions and in new historicisms *ad nauseam*. It is also visible on television, where different kinds of narrative adopt different attitudes to the authority of storytelling. On the one hand, there is the authority of reportage, of news stories, of documentary realism, while on the other there is an atmosphere of spoofery, of ironic imitation and of declared fictionality. In itself this is not unsettling: we might expect the real and the fictional, or the serious and the comic, to go hand in hand without having to declare a state of cultural schizophrenia. But my aim here is not to synthesise these opposite tendencies into an easy co-presence, a dialogue or a dialectic, but to highlight what is incommensurable in their attitudes to reference in a way that might yield knowledge of contradictory processes in culture. In particular it is through the disjunction between the different narrative temporalities of these attitudes that interesting cultural insights emerge.

With the help of Fredric Jameson, let me begin by describing a link between the narrative and the tempo of contemporary history:

> ... our entire contemporary social system has begun to live in a perpetual present and in a perpetual change that obliterates traditions of the kind which all earlier social formations have had in one way or another to preserve. Think only of the media exhaustion of news: of how Nixon and, even more so, Kennedy are figures from a now distant past. One is tempted to say that the very function of the news media is to relegate such recent historical experiences as rapidly as possible into the past.   (1992, p. 179)

I'm not sure that I agree with Jameson when he concludes from this that the function of news media is 'to help us forget' or create a 'perpetual present'. The speed with which events are consigned to the past could more convincingly be analysed as a flight from the present, as an impatience to narrate current events, to hurry everything into the past even while it is still happening. This makes it a way of remembering, of archiving, that actually displaces the experiential present tense with a historical self-consciousness. Historical self-consciousness does not then mean the same thing as historiographic self-consciousness: it is the sense that one is a narrative, or that one is part of the narrative of history, so that the present is experienced as if it were always already narrated in retrospect. That this narrative consciousness is memory and not amnesia is particularly demonstrable in the age of media capitalism in the way that news selects stories worthy of representation and discards others, the collective awareness of which conflates the lived experience of a society with the narrative form in which that experience might be represented in the media. There was a moment, for example, in the 1980s, when the BBC reformed its early evening news to include a summary which hastily historicised the day's events: 'Tuesday, June the 4th, 1987: the day on which ... '. In other words, it was only 6.20 p.m. GMT, and the complexity of global events was already being reduced to the form of a historical archive, canonising some as historical significance and excluding the rest well before dusk. The situation is compounded when events themselves are designed for media representation before they occur, like sound bites and terrorist attacks which are conceived in advance as narrations of past events. And this is not only a mode of experience for those lucky enough to have to worry about news management. The tourist in Notre Dame shows the same self-conscious contempt for linear time by experiencing its impressive windows through a camera lens, as if the recordability of the view for the future constitutes its importance in the present, as if always already archived. How many of us live our adventures as future narrations of the past, even if they are recorded only in our private archives, our photo albums, or the narrative form of our memories? Derrida has recently called this syndrome *archive fever*, and Warren Beatty summarised it nicely in *In Bed with Madonna* with his ironic question to Madonna: 'What is the point of doing anything off-camera?'

The theoretical issues connected to archive fever and narrative consciousness multiply uncontrollably when the impatience to record, narrate and monumentalise events actually takes over from the experience of them, constituting them in the present tense. It suggests a kind of reverse mimesis, where people's lives imitate stories rather than the other way around. I will be returning to this idea later. For the moment I want to propose that the authority of storytelling which consigns the present to the past as quickly as possible is subverted by other kinds of contemporary narrative which are impatient to resurrect the past and reinstall it in the present. The subversion of narrative authority is particularly clear in the culture of television and cinema advertising. It often seems that a narrative advertisement must pre-empt its own critique by unmasking itself. It might do this in the manner of the double-glazing advertisement in which the actor reading the Autocue falters in disbelief at the lack of marketing trickery in his script. At the moment of faltering – 'Hang on. What kind of a double-glazing company is this?' – the narrative ironises the hard sell and uses the process of resistance itself as persuasion, while at the same time turning the camera on the studio set, its spotlights, the crew, the Autocue, baring its devices, revealing its artificiality self-consciously.

Or the Mercury telephone advertisements which use Harry Enfield's special skills for imitating postwar television voices, picture quality and heavy-handed narrative styles of persuasion to create an ironic nostalgia which foregrounds and satirises the act of persuasion that it advances – a historiographic metafictional advertisement. There have been, in recent decades, well-known repetitions of well-known film scenes, like Peugeot's use of *Thelma and Louise,* Stella Artois imitating *Jean de Florette* or the less specific parodic references of Volkswagen's American flying saucer documentary and Gold Blend's absurd romantic soap operas. There is an atmosphere of spoofery, of ironic self-distance, sometimes of ideological candour which reproduces the experimental techniques of postmodern fictional narratives as if this kind of knowingness were the only remaining mode of narrative persuasion. The narrative of a television advertisement often has to distance itself from the product, or from conventional marketing rhetoric, to sell it, creating a complicity between the narrative and its suspicious, resistant viewers through the device of baring the device. If the process of interpellation as Althusser described it was the process of positioning a reader within the narrative through identification, this new kind of interpellation seems to hail the reader into a position of narratological distrust.

Narration and intertextuality seem inseparable in the contemporary context. It is particularly this idea of ironic recontextualisation that seems to have become dominant, leading many commentators on postmodern culture to view it as a defining characteristic. In the era of MTV and video, rock and pop stars have all but abandoned sincere rebellion to narrate themselves as recontextualised imitations of former stars, whether in Madonna's back references to mid-century sex symbols, David Bowie's chain of fictional, rock star personae, the parodic excesses of glam rock and new romanticism, the derivative imagery of Beatlemania in 1990s Brit-pop or the imitations of imitations of Lady Gaga and La Roux. The culture of recontextualisation touches every domain of style and design. It is often described as existing in a condition of acceleration: that is, of recontextualising not only long gone historical forms, as in the pastiches of classical architecture, but also the forms of an immediate prehistory. There is a feeling in the clothing industry, for example, that recontextualisation follows a linear progress through past styles, recycling the 1960s before moving onto the 1970s. In this case, the two main consequences of accelerated recontextualisation are (1) that recycling the past will eventually catch up with the present, and (2) that the process of recycling will become a recontextualisation of recontextualisations. Both of these consequences seem to point to a spiralling self-referentiality in the history of style which recalls the deconstruction of narrative time, where signs are nothing in themselves but the traces of other signs in the past and future. Many characterisations of the postmodern condition derive from this accelerated recycling of cultural forms: the idea that po-mo culture is above all an advanced stage of consumerism; the idea that it is a culture of imagery which dissolves history into a theatre of intertextual references and signs; that it differs from modernity in being unable to propose originality as a radical break from the past.

Two processes are at work here. The first is a kind of impatience to relegate contemporary events to the past, and the second is an impatience to resurrect them and reinstall them in the present. It is probably accurate to say that the first kind of impatience applies to realistic media like news and home video while the second applies to the kind of narratives which most readily arouse suspicion and resistance, like the television advertisement. The first process suggests that we do not really believe something to be real until it is archived as narration, or that we seek objective confirmation of what has occurred from recording media like news reports and videos. If this first process seems to confirm the cultural authority of narrative, the second is a way of undermining its authority through ironic recontextualisation. It could be concluded from this that postmodern narratives at large are organised around the same poles as fictional narratives, one being realistic, transparent and aiming to disguise the codes and conventions that mark its textuality while the other is overtly artificial, declaring its textuality by exposing its codes and conventions. And just as in the postmodern novel there is a convergence of these poles within the same work, it might be speculated that postmodern culture in general has witnessed the same kind of convergence of realistic and ironic modes within other domains of representation. In fact it takes very little exploration of the contemporary media to support this speculation. Whether it be the characteristic mixing of real footage and filmic narration in an Oliver Stone film, the self-awareness of television sitcoms like *Seinfeld* or *Moonlighting,* the fashionable combinations of journalistic reportage and fictional invention in newspapers, the experimental use of multiple narrators and points of view in documentary, or the imitation of hand-held camera wobbles to create the pseudo-documentary realism of *ER* or *NYPD Blue,* there is widespread evidence in the media of what David Harvey calls an 'increasing interpenetration of opposite tendencies in capitalism as a whole'.

Time-space compression

Whether understood, with Jameson, as a perpetual present or, with me, as a flight from the present, the increasing speed of the cycle which consigns events to the past and then recontextualises them, of narration and rewriting, is a type of time compression. But if this can be seen as a deconstruction of linear time within a cultural process, it ought not to be seen as the dissemination of poststructuralist philosophy in culture at large. The quickening cycle of narration and renarration reflects the time compression of commercial life in general where the pressure to renew the style of a commodity is part of the process of renewing markets. Capitalist culture issues us temporary contracts with everything, enforcing a sense of modernity with the ever-increasing speed of its obsolescence. Washing powder is a good example. How long does a washing powder such as biological Ariel remain at the vanguard of washing technology before it is supplanted by some pseudo-scientific innovation? In the relatively recent past the technological progress of Ariel was unfolding in a linear pattern towards the goal of absolute whiteness. Its progress was narrated by white-coated scientists in laboratories full of washing machines experimenting on hitherto unconquered kinds of stain. Modernity would momentarily present itself as a state of whiteness becoming consigned to the past as dirt, in preparation for some revolutionary advance which restarts the cycle from a position of even whiter whiteness. In obeisance, the domestic cycle was forced to accelerate in an increasingly technical campaign against grime, where shirts are peeled off children as they come in the door and washed in the blink of an eye, restoring a state of hygiene several times a day. But for all its metaphoricity, absolute whiteness could not be sustained as the telos of an accelerating domestic cycle. For one thing, many people's clothes were not white to begin with. The introduction of New Ariel Colour fragmented the grand narrative of whiteness, introducing a new value in washing culture, preserving the newness of colour and relegating the idea of ageing, of fading, to history. The technological project shifted from an emphasis on progress towards a more negative concern with arresting the ageing process. The logical next step was to retract the values of progress, and the implied inferiority of former washing powders, by recontextualising Original Ariel, the origin and not the telos, casting aspersions on the values of science in the name of nature and authenticity. There is a kind of schizophrenia involved here between the idea of history as progress and of history as a fall from nature, a kind of time compression which presents the history of Ariel spatially,

as co-presence or as product choice on the shelf at Tesco. It is as if marketing has changed its narratological assumptions, no longer interpellating
customers into a grand narrative of progress but accommodating different identities and values by reflecting them in the diversity of products
and their affiliations.

The suspension of narrative in time is collapsed into a moment of
consumer choice. This formula provides an illuminating link between
consumer society and schizophrenia which has been pursued by several commentators of postmodernity, particularly Jameson, Deleuze and
Guattari, and Harvey. There are few postmodern thinkers who believe in
the idea of an inner life or a private domain of subjectivity. Like the private home and its domestic cycle, there is a feeling that the mental life of
an individual finds its explanation in the outside world. This is reflected
in the widespread use of psychoanalytic terminology in cultural theory
and should be understood less in the spirit of an analogy between the
mind and the world than as a dismantling of the boundary between them.
The term *schizophrenia* is one such terminological link between states
of mind and cultural processes. Jacques Lacan, the poststructuralist psy-
choanalyst, defines schizophrenia as a kind of linguistic disorder, but as
poststructuralists tend to view language as the primary organising principles for reality, a linguistic disorder becomes a different way of construing
reality and experience. Traditionally we think of schizophrenia as a disunity in the personality, where different states of mind cannot be unified
in the pronoun 'I'. As Deleuze and Guattari notice, there is a tendency for
the schizophrenic to refer to himself in the third person, drawing attention to the link between narrative self-consciousness and schizophrenia.
Lacan understands this disunity as a breakdown in the temporal chain of
signification: that is, an inability to sustain the linearity of things – the
suspension of language in time, the order of narrative linearity, a sense
of sequence. To be normal, as opposed to schizophrenic, it is necessary
to have a linear concept of time, not only because it is the basis of guilt
and moral action – as fictions like *Time's Arrow, Slaughterhouse Five* and
Memories of the Ford Administration remind us – but because the narrative of personal identity and the experience of selfhood are at stake.
The interpretation of a sentence depends upon 'a certain temporal unification of past and future with the present before me', and the same can be
said of the narrative of personal identity, the linearity of which serves to
'unify the past, present and future of our own biographical experience or
psychic life'. For Jameson, without the ordered sequencing of meanings
in a sentence, 'we have schizophrenia in the form of a rubble of distinct

and unrelated signifiers'. If time compression is experienced in the supermarket as the suspension of narrative in time collapsing in a moment of consumer choice, the schizophrenic exists in a similar collision of different meanings, personae and psychic states which are no longer strung out in time. Deleuze and Guattari use this principle of the loss of temporal sequence to suggest that the schizophrenic experience is somehow more faithful to the condition of postmodern culture than the normal controlled admission of meanings as an unfolding sentence or narrative. Or, to put it another way, the schizophrenic lives out a poststructuralist perspective on meaning which deconstructs the normal intelligibility of things. The schizophrenic is seen as an interpreter whose disorder is to multiply and destabilise meanings, as an inability to observe the proper boundaries between meanings, to experience the world spatially as a theatre of signs and discourses which cannot exclude each other and which constitute a babble of voices: to experience selfhood not as an ordered narrative but as multiple identification amongst the babble of discourses. The schizophrenic is not so much nature's poststructuralist sociologist as the product of a schizoid culture which seems to aspire to the collapse of linear meaning into the compressed time of a perpetual present.

There may then be a sense in which we are all moving towards a schizophrenic mode of cultural experience, as our minds change in response to space-time compression, which sounds like a form of torture from *Star Trek* because it is intimately linked to the themes of travel speed and an extra-terrestrial perspective on the unity of planet earth. Postmodern social theory has taken the spatial compression of the globe into a global village, the theme of *globalisation,* as a key area of cultural change, suggesting as it does that it is not only history which has been compressed but geography. Traditionally travel may broaden the mind, but it also compresses the globe in the sense that, at jet speed, the temporal gap between places is reduced to a co-presence, encouraging us to think of the planet as a simultaneous unity, an effect obviously enforced by the simultaneity of other, electronic forms of communication. But most cultural theorists since Heidegger have recognised that if globalisation is conceived as a process of unification, it is at the same time a process of diversification, of an increasing awareness of diversity or an increasing individuation of cultures on the global stage. In the same way that Europeans have become more aware of the diversity of the European sausage in the face of attempts to standardise it, there has been a worldwide counter-politics by which local cultures assert difference in an increasingly public way as resistance to the standardising tendencies of globalising processes. As we might expect, cultural difference becomes increasingly commodified when the globe is compressed by trading and travelling technologies.

The schizophrenia of contemporary culture is partly about the super-market shelving – literal and metaphorical – of history, but geographical compression is just as obvious at Tesco. For the consuming classes, the supermarket offers a kind of compressed tourism which erodes the traditional relationship between identity and place. It is an experience dedicated to cultural diversity which offers the shopper an interna-tional spectrum of possible identifications, where the signs of other cultures compose the shopper's identity through affiliation with various ethnicities, as if shopping itself were a process of identity construction. Stuart Hall describes this new commodified and cosmopolitan sense of identity as a compressed tourism when he says:

> But side by side with [the old identities] are the new exotics, and the most sophisticated thing is to be in the new exotica. To be at the leading edge of modern capitalism is to eat fifteen different cuisines in any one week, not to eat one. It is no longer important to have Yorkshire pudding every Sunday. Who needs that? Because if you are jetting in from Tokyo, via Harare, you come in loaded, not with 'how everything is the same' but how wonderful it is that everything is different. In one trip around the world, in one week-end, you can see every wonder of the ancient world. You take it in as you go by, all in one, living with difference, wondering at pluralism, this con-centrated, corporate, over-corporate, over-integrated, over-concentrated, and condensed form of economic power which lives culturally through difference and which is constantly teasing itself with the pleasures of the transgressive Other.   (1991b, p. 31)

According to this view, globalisation is divided between processes tak-ing place at home and abroad, both of which amount to an increased experience of other cultures. If there seems to be a logical drift between the two in Hall's passage, it is probably due to their convergence in the global theatre of signs. How, for example, is one to differentiate between the American phenomenon of Disneyworld, where it is possible to visit a simulacrum of most of the world's nations conveyed as national sings, and the very contemporary mode of tourism which travels the world pho-tographing the signs of national culture (I think of Barthes's analysis of the Eiffel Tower) as mediated for the tourist industry. One may dispense with the tiresome business of travel, but they are equally semiotic modes of experience, and it is hard to think of a more striking example of the transformation of narrative depth into surface images than the shorthand cultural signs of the tourist industry.

These ideas of commodities as signifiers and of space-time compression are the substance of a running debate in cultural theory. The reader interested in deeper exploration is best advised to start with David Harvey's *The Condition of Postmodernity* (1989) and follow it with *Mapping the Futures* (1993, edited by Bird et al.), both of which attest to the increasing interpenetration of cultural and literary theory. It might seem, from the account of the debate above, that the compression of space-time is an account of the obliteration of narrative, or the dissolution of narrative into space, or the transformation of identity narratives into identity by commodity affiliation. It may be true that there are tendencies in postmodern culture to reduce stories to images, or that narrative has been the subject of prolonged assault not only from the new temporalities of culture, but academically, in the novel, in literary studies and in departments of history. But narrative remains at the forefront of the debate about postmodernity in a number of ways. One obvious point is that narrative cannot simply be done away with by a band of sociologists more interested in cultural geography. Clearly one version of the dichotomy between space and time in cultural theory is the oscillation between geography and history which could never be settled as the conquest of one pole by the other. Another obvious point is that a historical epoch – that vast and irreducible totality – could never be understood adequately except as a site of contestation or a discursive war. Few commentators, and perhaps Baudrillard is one of the few, are dumb enough to advance the view of postmodern culture as some abrupt change in everything, sweeping aside tradition and conventional wisdom. Harvey and Hall both recognise a contest in the contemporary world between an old and a new order of things, so that the postmodern world is always a dialogue between old and new processes of identification. Both Harvey and Hall emphasise that what they call the Fordist project of modernity is still alive in culture, so that, for example, a traditional sense of identity as a narrative based in the origins of place co-exists with any fancy postmodern sense of identity as unfixed commodity affiliation. Likewise there are commentators who give the impression that postmodern identities are forged entirely in the act of shopping, as if nobody worked any more. It may be that there is an act of affiliation involved in buying a jar of pesto sauce, a connotation of Italianicity, as Barthes would have it, but such a connotation is unlikely to inflect the identities of the work-forces, agricultural and industrial, involved in the production of pesto?

Before I start sounding any more like Terry Eagleton, I would point out that, as with pesto, so with narrative the issue still has to be addressed in terms of the difference between the production and consumption of narratives. Some postmodern commentators, and I fear Baudrillard is one of them, give the impression that the pole of production has all but disappeared, overwhelmed by the cultural importance of consumption, as if work had given way to pleasure on a global scale. In short, the allegation that narrative has somehow been obliterated by the process of space-time compression is melodramatic, ignoring the fact that some narratives are more victimised than others in the postmodern debate. Specifically, grand narratives are the object of critique whereas, for little narratives, it is business as never before.

Narratives grand and little

'Small is beautiful' could serve as a slogan for the phase of capitalism associated with the postmodern. It seems to indicate something fundamental about recent approaches, both corporate and academic, to globalisation. At one level it represents a recently fashionable spirit of advice among American economic gurus who favoured the downsizing of corporations over the established values of economies of scale, expansion and diversification. At another level it represents a much analysed shift in marketing, which can be summarised as the shift from catch-all advertising to niche marketing. A similar emphasis can be found in much postmodern theory which valorises the local over the global, an emphasis that derives from Francois Lyotard's discussions of the fragmentation of grand narratives into little narratives. If there is an initial confusion here between whether the emphasis on locality represents a counter-politics to the standardisation of the world by transnational corporations, whether those corporations actually thought it up first, and indeed whether transnational corporations stole the idea from leftist theory in the way that they have stolen from leftist semiotics, radical philosophy and sociology, it is a confusion which runs deep. Think of Margaret Thatcher's fear of the large unit of an integrated Europe in the 1980s. The dichotomies of large and small seemed to be under ideological stress in this period, when the idea of devolving into ever-decreasing units of identity seemed to defend the political right wing, their traditional nationalist stance, the emphasis on individuality, the idea of sovereignty. Society was seen as a socialist or even Soviet concept, a concept without a referent, in Thatcher's much-quoted view. Yet the European community, especially as it was conceived in the 1980s, was nothing more than an enormous free-trade zone, a capitalist monolith underwritten by the values of the free flow of capital.

The ideological incoherence of the big-small dichotomy is not surprising. Who would suggest that a dichotomy so abstracted, so intelligible or so easily put into practice could make political sense of the vast unknowability that most of us have taken for temporary culture. Before I answer that question, it might be worth considering the interaction of grand and little narratives in other contexts. One of the major impacts of the new historicisms in literary studies was the busting of the canon: the demythologisation of literary value, the breaking of male Anglo-Saxon hegemony in literary studies, the destruction of the boundary between high and popular culture. These were campaigns waged by leftist intellectuals against the traditional values of high culture. The enemy in intellectual terms was totalisation: the idea that the history of literature in its entirety could be represented by such a tiny fragment of literature. The literary canon was a grand narrative in the sense that it represented the history of literature as a whole, as a linear story constructed by sweeping exclusions. With narrative events the size of historical epochs, the canon could only operate this way, representing national literary history as a sequence of eras, with names like the Renaissance, Romanticism and Modernism, which could be represented in shorthand by a handful of hypercanonised texts. Many of the political problems with the canon were associated with its national character. Within a nation, the canon was understood as a kind of trickle-down economics, where the value and values of great works, as arbitrated by great people with the discrimination to know the good from the bad, functioned as top-down instruction. A kind of narcissism presided over the canon, translating the values of a critical elite into the value of great literature, alleging the universalism of those values. They were values to be adopted by the excluded for edification. If Hitler commissioned positivist histories which argued for the linear evolution of the Aryans from the dinosaurs, he was repeating a historiographic strategy which had always applied to the description of European culture. The construction of a culturally cohesive national society often has to colonise its extra-national origins as well as its national competitors, treating Jesus, Homer and Joyce as part of the story of English literature, as universal rather than national subjects.

Canon-busting can be understood then as part of a general assault on grand narratives that advance such universalistic pretensions. The national canons, to the postmodern critic, seemed to fall between the poles of the global and the local, requiring a counter-politics which might attempt simultaneously to globalise and to localise literary historical perspectives. If departments of comparative literature or the new field of postcolonial criticism have contributed to the globalisation of literary canons, it has not been in the name of some enormous new cosmopolitan canon based on universal values. Literary studies shows a marked tendency towards fragmentation, or towards little narratives, local narratives, small identity narratives, which break the hegemony of universal values, demoting grand narratives and their universalistic pretensions to the status of local histories of local elites. Like nations themselves, national canons have undergone a revolution which has entailed the twin processes of, on the one hand, an increased recognition of diversity and polyethnicity within national traditions and, on the other, a devolution of canons to narrate the literary histories of hitherto unnarrated identities: women's canons, gay canons, black canons and so on.

The canon illustrates a new kind of cultural schizophrenia and a new kind of doubleness in narrative which also pervades the sociology of globalisation. A canon is a narrative of narratives, a kind of master narrative which tells the story of stories. If we imagine for a moment the construction of a global canon which represented a global literary history, such a canon would in effect be the story of all stories. This would make it a metanarrative which took other stories as the object of its narrative and sought to reveal their true meaning in the light of their place in the total narrative. But it would be a kind of narrative which was incapable of conveying the complexity and difference that it purported to represent, and therefore cannot have the authority and mastery which it implies for itself. Effectively the grand narrative is no more than another narrative, no different from the stories it analyses, and just as open to narratological analysis or deconstruction as the narratives it narrates. Once again we encounter two characteristic postmodern attitudes to narrative. The first is a collapse of the distinction between narrative and metanarrative, since the universal pretensions of the metanarrative are reduced to being just one narrative among others. The second is an elevation of the particular, fragmentary little narrative as a counter-politics of the local. Clearly narrative has not disappeared. It has polarised around Lyotard's distinction between the grand and the little, where the former is big and bad and the latter small and beautiful, where the former is a metanarrative delusion and the latter is a form of assault.

Suppose I were a white male cosmopolitan with universalist delusions and no regional accent (which I am). Clearly in the war against totalisation, between the deconstruction of grand narratives and the elevation of little narratives, my possible identifications are limited. I could either carry on with my power-crazed, imperialist project to see the world as a single place (the option that I decline), or find myself without a counter-identity or a little narrative to produce. I become, in Lyotard's terminology, a discourse without phrases, or in my own terms I seem to be up a tree without a trunk. I become a cipher in the sense that I cannot produce little narratives without reproducing my imperialist pretensions, so that the only course open to me seems to be to redeem myself through solidarity with the oppressed. I become a kind of consumer of identities, like a tourist or a shopper with a taste for ethnic cuisines, apologising for my power through affiliation. In the great diversity of language games, mine is a cosmopolitical point of view, which means that my lack of a resistance identity positions me as a consumer and not a producer of little narratives. I seem to be identifying with somebody else, like the reader and not the writer of little narratives.

Luckily for me, and for Lyotard, the poles of the grand and the little narratives, or the cosmopolitical and resistance communities, are not so reductive:

> The resistance of communities banded around their names and their narratives is counted on to stand in the way of capital's hegemony. This is a mistake. First of all, this resistance fosters this hegemony as much as it counters it. Then, it puts off the Idea of a cosmopolitical history and generates the fear of falling back onto legitimation through tradition, indeed onto legitimation through myth, even if that legitimation also gives shape to the resistances of peoples to their extermination. Proud struggles for independence end in young, reactionary States.   (Lyotard, 1988, p. 181)

This is a simple point, often made about political revolutions, that if the resistance to some hegemony uses the same resources as the oppressor, the revolution will simply substitute one form of domination for another. Its interest lies in the way that it advances the Kantian idea of a cosmopolitical (translated elsewhere simply as *cosmopolitan*) history as the positive pole in opposition to the narratives of myth and tradition, where an imagined resistance community legitimates itself through narration. The cosmopolitical narrative stands in opposition to the savage narrative for Lyotard because it sustains an awareness of its co-existence with other incommensurable stories rather than present itself in the moment of its telling as the final word:

> A non-cosmopolitical (or 'savage') narrative proceeds by phrases like On that date, in that place, it happened that x etc. The question raised by cosmopolitical narrative would be the following: since this x, this date, and this place are proper names and since proper names belong by definition to worlds of names and to specific 'savage' narratives, how can these narratives give rise to a single world of names and to a universal narrative? – The question may seem absurd: aren't these communities human ones? – No, they are 'Cashinahua' and they call themselves the community of 'true men', if not in exception to others, then at least in distinction from them. The bond woven around 'Cashinahua' names by these narratives procures an identity that is solely 'Cashinahua'. Were this identity already human in the cosmopolitical sense, it would not entail the exception of other communities, or even the difference between them, and the universal history of humanity would consist in the simple extension of particular narratives to the entire set of human communities.   (1988, p. 155)

In other words, Lyotard is arguing that, in a world in which there is no recourse to grand narratives or metanarratives, a political problem arises when any little narrative presents itself as universal. I cannot possibly do justice to Lyotard's argument in *The Differend* and elsewhere, but I would like to draw attention to two important emphases in this account of the cosmopolitical. First, there is the suggestion that a cosmopolitan subject occupies a kind of moral and political high ground exactly by being a kind of consumer of other narratives and other identities, by producing narratives which sustain an awareness of other narratives which cannot be subsumed or mastered. Second, there is the idea that we have already met that the traditional form of narrative itself is the agent of a savage politics. It is not just that narrative traditionally excludes all parallel narratives for the sake of its linear order, but that it subsumes what Lyotard calls *differends* – incommensurable disputes between little narratives where there are no external criteria for litigation or judgement – in the coherence of a single identity narrative. In other words, narrative and narratology share the political responsibility to highlight the co-existence and the incommensurability of different stories, not so much in the semiotic spirit of acknowledging the constitutive role of difference in the abstract but to base political action on a view of humanity as a matrix of unresolvable narrative disputes.

Many philosophers, sociologists and critics have laughed at Lyotard's pompous and confusing attempts to link narrative and political responsibility in this way, especially when that responsibility seems to amount to a resignation to the complexity of things. My interest in him here is in relation to the increasing interpenetration of opposite tendencies in capitalism as a whole, the phrase that I borrowed from Harvey to describe the mutual contamination of realistic and ironic modes, or simulation and reality. What is clear from Lyotard's sense that resistance lies in the little narrative, in locality and particularity is that these terms have a relationship with the opposite tendencies of globalisation and standardisation as intimate as the relationship between production and consumption. The dichotomy of the universal and the particular, the cosmopolitan and the parochial, seems only to deepen in Lyotard's work because the local is where the global happens. If the cosmopolitical narrative is a little narrative, as it must be, it is a little narrative acting out its particularity on a singular, global stage. The proliferation of difference and the standardisation of the world seem to go hand in hand, and the politics of the dichotomy produce confused laughter. The American bumper sticker 'think global, act local' speaks as clearly to the transnational executive as it does to its implied environmentalist reader.

This view of globalisation *as* proliferation of difference differs markedly from the dominant sociological account. It also provides a narratological basis for the difference between modernity and post-modernity. Sociology has until recently understood the process of globalisation as standardisation. Many cultural critics have argued that this is above all a process of Americanisation, where the political and economic dominance of the United States is felt across the globe, spreading its cultural hegemony through an army of cultural forms from Donald Duck to Ronald McDonald. The model of Americanisation was a particularly modernist idea in the sense that it was seen in terms of a grand narrative progressing towards global homogeneity perceived as modernisation and perfectibility. But in the age of space-time compression, globalisation is no longer understood as a linear narrative of progress towards homogenisation, so that post-modernity is often characterised in Lyotardian terms as the conquest of difference over the narrative of standardisation:

> If one of the characteristics associated with postmodernism is the loss of
> a sense of common historical past and the flattening and spatialization
> out of long established symbolic hierarchies, then the process of globaliza-
> tion, the emergence of the sense that the world is a single place, may have

directly contributed to this perspective through bringing about a greater interchange and clashing of different images of global order and historical narratives. The perception of history as an unending linear process of the unification of the world with Europe at the centre in the nineteenth century and the United States at the centre in the twentieth century, has become harder to sustain with the beginnings of a shift in the global balance of power away from the West.   (Featherstone, 1993, p. 171)

Featherstone seems to acknowledge here that the fragmentary character of postmodernity may be no more than a transition from one form of domination to another. Some have seen the process as no more than the diversification of capital, where the process of standardisation masquerades as diversity by commodifying all cultural difference. Others have seen it as no less than the end of history. For me, it is the conquest of cultural schizophrenia over narrative identity. Far from being the death of narrative identity or the death of totality, it is the playing out of savage narratives on the global stage, where fragments have acquired a new awareness, a new self-consciousness of their role in an increasingly visible totality.

It doesn't seem contradictory to me to argue that globalisation and fragmentation are part of the same process. They are poles apart and they are poles together. Recent media studies often gives the impression of a complete loss of shared events in the displacement of broadcasting with narrowcasting. The rise of CNN testifies on behalf of the theory that broadcasting has been enforced, not displaced, by narrowcasting, and that documentary realism has been authorised and not subverted by the atmosphere of parody and pastiche. When Jakobson argued for linguistics as the global science of narrative in 1960, it was a minority cry for the standardisation of narratological method in a context of diverse approaches. It was the voice of a little narrative seeking a hegemony which never occurred. Now there is a babble of voices all saying the same thing, all insisting on specificity and particularity in a context of ever-increasing orthodoxy and homogeneity. There is something lumpen in the new diversity of resistances, some principle of imperial convergence at work, in narratology and at large, which has succeeded in making an orthodoxy out of a rebellion.

Part III

Narrative Subjects

6 True Lies: Unreliable Identities in *Dr Jekyll and Mr Hyde*

If I tell you that I am lying, I create a perpetual logical rebound. If it is true, then it is false, so how can it be true? And if it is false and I am not lying, then I am telling the truth, in which case I am lying. The undecidability in this predicament comes to rest only if the statement about myself and the moment of saying it can be separated in time, so that I am no longer a liar while I am saying so: 'sometimes I lie' or 'I used to be a liar' make perfect logical sense because they separate the reliability of the narrator from the unreliability of the narrated, even when they are the same person. The pragmatic contradiction is resolved by splitting the 'I' between the past and the present.

One of the uses of narrative in psychoanalysis is to produce this schism. Psychoanalysis *is* self-narration or, in J.M. Bernstein's phrase, 'theory-mediated autobiography'. In the Freudian tradition it operates on the assumption that mental disturbance is a state of self-ignorance to be over-come in the moment of narration by self-knowledge. This idea can be linked to the theme of lying because, for Freud, self-ignorance is not just a state of needing to be told the causes of a disturbance, it is a kind of self-deceit or repression. The past was a lie, and the present is the cure in the form of truthful, reliable self-narration. A beautiful paradox is born, because the received view of psychoanalysis as the cure of schisms is forced to ignore the schizophrenia involved in self-narration and the split that it entails between the subject and object of narrative. It could be argued that psychoanalysis itself is forced to ignore the schism of self-narration because it permits the domination of the narrated by the narrator, allowing self-narration not only to operate as self-knowledge but also to consign one's own mental disturbance to the past. But isn't this like using one form of madness to cure another?

Contemporary approaches to narrative generally insist on the idea that narrative constructs a version of events rather than describing them in their true state, that it is performative rather than constative, or inventive not descriptive. I have been describing an increasing self-consciousness in narrative in the form of an awareness of the constructedness or fictionality of what that narrative purports to describe. If self-narration can function as a form of therapy by recognising the truth about a past lie, it can do so only at the expense of this kind of narrative self-consciousness because it has to present itself as reliable narration in order to distance itself from the unreliability of what is narrated. In other words, in order to stabilise one's identity as narrative, one has to erase or naturalise a new kind of madness which is performed in the process of narrating oneself as if one were another person, exposing the schism of the past by disguising the schism between the present and the past. The premise of this chapter is the formula for this trade-off between self-consciousness as narrative and narrative self-consciousness: the reliability of self-narration depends on temporal distance between the narrator and the narrated but has to sacrifice the candour of narrative self-consciousness if the narrative is to be believed. It might not be an exaggeration to say that all narrative exists in this condition of fictional truth, as true lies.

Inner distance

In Chapter 1, my discussion of *Emma* illustrated the narrative principle that the control of distance by narrative point of view was a device employed for the control of moral judgement. But *Emma* is a third-person narration, meaning that this kind of moral distance can be achieved naturally in narrative commentary as a result of the structural distance between the narrator and the narrated. But what happens when a first-person narrator wants to make moral self-judgements? The simplest and most common strategy is to use temporal distance as moral distance, as at the beginning of Dr Jekyll's confession in Stevenson's *Dr Jekyll and Mr Hyde* (*JH*):

> I was born in the year 18—to a large fortune, endowed besides with excellent parts, inclined by nature to industry, fond of the respect of the wise and the good among my fellow men, and thus, as might have been supposed, with every guarantee of an honourable and distinguished future. And indeed the very worst of my faults was a certain impatient gaiety of disposition, such as has made the happiness of many, but such as I found

it hard to reconcile with my imperious desire to carry my head high, and wear a more than commonly grave countenance before the public.　(*JH*, 1886, p. 81)

Moral self-judgement here can take the same form as the narrator's opening remarks on Emma's faults because temporal distance substitutes for distance in the third-person point of view. But whereas Austen's narrator can adopt this kind of moral distance throughout the story, Dr Jekyll's narrative is faced with the problem that the time of the narrated is rapidly catching up with the time of the narration, so that the temporal distance which allows this kind of moral self-distance is diminishing fast as the narrative proceeds. In the previous chapter I commented that the schizophrenic is often seen as somebody who cannot unify himself under the pronoun 'I' and consequently often refers to himself in the third person, as 'he'. One of the immediately interesting things about Dr Jekyll's narrative is that two different types of schizophrenia are hurtling into collision. On the one hand, there is the obvious metaphor of doubleness in Jekyll's drug-induced metamorphoses into Mr Hyde, a metaphor which is literalised in the sense that it transposes the idea of twin personalities within a single body into two separate bodies. On the other hand, there is the less obvious doubleness of the narrator and the narrated, representing the kind of schizophrenia which will occur when narrated time catches up with the time of narration and temporal distance collapses into the present. If Mr Hyde can be seen as a literalisation of schizophrenic self-reference in the third person, this passage looks like a state of double schizophrenia, or quadrophrenia:

> Henry Jekyll stood at times aghast before the acts of Edward Hyde; but the situation was apart from ordinary laws, and insidiously relaxed the grasp of conscience. It was Hyde, after all, and Hyde alone, that was guilty. Jekyll was no worse; he woke again to his good qualities seemingly unimpaired; he would even make haste, where it was possible, to undo the evil done by Hyde. And thus his conscience slumbered.　(*JH*, 1979, p. 87)

Several aspects of the narrative seem to be in collaboration here. Jekyll is referring to himself in the third person not only as Hyde, which is permissible in terms of the fiction of another body, but also as Jekyll, as if the relationship between Jekyll and Hyde and the relationship between Jekyll and Jekyll as narrator and narrated are operating in parallel. And the schisms are linked not only because they transpose self-narration into the third person, but also because they allow moral judgements

which describe both Jekyll's moral superiority to Hyde at the time and
the superiority of Jekyll the narrator over Jekyll the narrated: if the narrated Jekyll is morally aghast at Hyde, he is in turn reprimanded for a
slumbering conscience by the narrating Jekyll.

This doubled doubleness is perhaps glimpsed by Jekyll at the start of
his confession:

> With every day, and from both sides of my intelligence, the moral and the
> intellectual, I thus drew steadily nearer to the truth by whose partial dis-
> covery I have been doomed to such a dreadful shipwreck: that man is not
> truly one but truly two. I say two, because the state of my own knowledge
> does not pass beyond that point. Others will follow, others will outstrip me
> on the same lines; and I hazard the guess that man will be ultimately known
> for a mere polity of multifarious, incongruous and independent denizens.
> I, for my part, from the nature of my life, advanced infallibly in one direc-
> tion and in one direction only. It was on the moral side, and in my own
> person, that I learned to recognise the thorough and primitive duality of
> man.   (*JH*, 1979, p. 82)

Jekyll seems to know that there is more to this doubleness than the moral
duality of Jekyll and Hyde. There are also two sides of his intelligence,
named as the moral and the intellectual. The statement that 'man is not
truly one but truly two' becomes ambiguous: normally understood as the
formula for his moral duality, Jekyll seems to begin the passage by saying
that there are two dualities towards which he is advancing, before limiting
it to the single direction of the moral. The paradox here is that he seems to
consciously consign any intellectual duality to the unconscious, leaving it
to others, me perhaps, to expand the picture of man's multifarious polity
of denizens. It reads like an invitation to plot the duality of the narrator
and the narrated alongside that of Jekyll and Hyde. It seems to place the
pronoun 'I' under a stress much greater than mere doubleness, referring
at the beginning of the passage to an awareness of a double doubleness
that has evaporated by the end.

This is one of the moments in the confession when Jekyll's, and possibly Stevenson's, unconscious seems to surface. The logical problems for
the reader begin to deepen because what is coming to the surface at such
moments is an unconscious self-consciousness about the problems of self-
narration. I said a moment ago that the moral and the narrative dualities
of the story were operating in parallel, but there is clearly a sense in which
they also come into collision: the duality of Jekyll and Hyde is the internal, realist substance of the narration but the duality of Jekyll and Jekyll

diverts attention from that substance towards the logic of self-narration itself. The realist illusion of the confession, with all of its professions of candour and truth, is in an allegorical relation with the hidden mechanisms and assumptions of the narration, so that the narrative illusion is referring allegorically to the destruction of its own illusion.

As Paul de Man and others illustrate, one of the features of contemporary narrative criticism is to disassociate the term 'allegory' from authorial intention. I do not know whether Stevenson carefully plotted this collision of dualities for the purpose of making his narrative as janus-faced as Jekyll and Hyde, as a kind of critical self-consciousness. Perhaps the idea, from the previous paragraph, of an unconscious self-consciousness should act as a warning that the idea of self-consciousness cannot really be sustained. It describes too many different levels of the logic of narration: the idea that identity is narrative in form, the idea of reference to the self as if to another, the possibility of authorially intended narrative self-consciousness and now the possibility that it is the narrative itself which has this consciousness and not any of the people, internal and external, involved with it. But I want to keep it exactly because it encompasses the characters, the narrator, the author, the reader and the narrative itself, to describe a situation in narrative which should not be thought of as a carefully plotted authorial intention but one which is produced by the unavoidable collision of these levels.

Narrative shipwreck

For Jekyll, the narrative process is one of drawing 'steadily nearer to that truth by whose partial discovery I have been doomed to such a dreadful shipwreck' (*JH*, 1979, p. 82). But Jekyll is doomed to moral shipwreck because the two parts of his formerly integrated personality have separated into two bodies. This bodily separation operates as a metaphor for self-narration in two distinct ways. The first is that Hyde has a name, even a signature, of his own; and the second is that Hyde and Jekyll can no longer coincide in time. But this bodily separation is much more complicated than it first appears, and I want to argue now that the further we delve into these complications, the more we encounter the co-implication of identity and narrative, to the point where Jekyll and Hyde cannot really be understood as an allegory or an analogy for the problems of self-narration but as nothing other than the problems of narration, or that Jekyll's shipwreck is more narratological than moral.

At first sight, the bodily split of Jekyll and Hyde is a division of labour between good and evil: 'Even as good shone upon the countenance of one, evil was written broadly and plainly on the face of the other' (*JH*, 1979, p. 84). But it becomes clear, not long into the full statement, that it is an unequal bargain:

> Hence, although I now had two characters as well as two appearances, one was wholly evil, and the other was still the old Henry Jekyll, that incongruous compound of whose reformation and improvement I had already learned to despair. The movement was thus wholly toward the worse. (*JH*, 1979, p. 85)

Whereas Hyde is pure evil, Jekyll still qualifies as a human being according to his own conviction that such beings are 'commingled out of good and evil'. This is just as well. If Jekyll were pure good, not only would the moral theme of the story degenerate into an abstracted battle along the lines of *Paradise Lost,* but he would be an inhumanly angelic goody two-shoes with no sense of how much fun it is to be bad. But if the old Henry Jekyll had a wicked streak, personified but not purged by Hyde, are we to assume that the new Jekyll, the narrator, is exactly this kind of goody two-shoes, the inhuman voice of pure goodness, reformed and therefore qualified to pass judgement on his own past? The division of labour between good and evil is so far from being simple that the divisions will have to be numbered: (1) the split between new Jekyll and old Jekyll; (2) the internal divisions in old Jekyll; and (3) the split between Jekyll and Hyde.

The ending of Jekyll's narration and the entire narrative does not get its force from the resolution of action. The third-person narration of 'The Last Night' has already described events beyond the end of Jekyll's narrative, and Dr Lanyon's narrative has made it clear that Jekyll and Hyde are one. We know, therefore, that Jekyll will die, and will die in the body of Hyde. The real excitement of the ending is not waiting for him to croak: the open question, up to the last line of the confession, is 'at what point does he become Hyde?'. Bearing in mind that Jekyll is, at this stage, taking his powders not to transform but to ward transformation off, there is a sense in which Hyde is now catching up with Jekyll, closing on him from within, ready to displace him for the last time. What I find most interesting about this predicament is that the gap between Jekyll and Hyde is reducing at the same speed as the gap between narrated time and the moment of the narration: that the schizophrenia of Jekyll and Hyde and the schizophrenia of Jekyll and Jekyll are converging at the moment of death. The point about Jekyll and Hyde is that they cannot both exist in the same moment, and clearly the same is true of the narrator and the narrated, since there would be nothing left to narrate except narration itself.

This is what I am calling the narratological shipwreck: the collision of the past and the present after which narration is no longer possible. And if the narrative depends for its very existence on the separation of the narrated past and the narrating present, it also depends for its very existence on the separation of Jekyll and Hyde. Part of Jekyll's urgency in the closing paragraphs is to bring the narrative to an end because his transformation into Hyde will entail its destruction:

> Nor must I delay too long to bring my writing to an end; for if my narrative has hitherto escaped destruction, it has been by a combination of great prudence and great good luck. Should the throes of change take me in the act of writing it, Hyde will tear it in pieces; but if some time shall have elapsed after I have laid it by, his wonderful selfishness and circumscription to the moment will probably save it once again from the action of his ape-like spite.   (*JH*, 1979, pp. 96–7)

It is as if Hyde is not only the personification of Jekyll's wickedness but the personification of narrated time: the past catching up with the present and destroying the narrative in the moment of truth and death. The idea that Hyde is the personification of the narrative past is supported by the closing sentence in which Jekyll perceives his death as the end of writing: 'Here, then, as I lay down the pen, and proceed to seal up my confession, I bring the life of that unhappy Henry Jekyll to an end' (*JH*, 1979, p. 97). This is a fascinating sentence which I want to dwell on for a moment. It illustrates perfectly the crisis which takes place when narrative time catches up. It produces an illogical temporality in trying to narrate the end of narration, describing putting down the pen which is still writing the description. The end of the narrative is emphatic, ending as it does on the word 'end', and yet the simultaneity of Jekyll's end and the narrative's end is spoiled by the fact that the sentence draws our attention to Jekyll's continuation beyond the end of the sentence in the act of sealing the confession. The very existence of the narrative attests to the fact that some time has elapsed after he has laid it by, since this is the condition that has just been described by which the narrative escapes destruction at the hands of Hyde. And yet it is exactly this span of time, the implied narrative beyond the end of the final sentence, that is the great mystery of the story: the unknowable, unsolvable, unnarrated space in which Jekyll's transformation and death actually occur. The unknowable and unnarratable perhaps draw attention to the idea that identity is only identity when narration is in process, so that there is a sense in which Jekyll has no existence beyond the end of the writing: his fictionality ensures that he has no existence after writing has stopped.

The closing sentence sends one further shiver down my spine. In the final phrase, 'I bring the life of that unhappy Henry Jekyll to an end', one finds the last expression of that schizophrenia of self-narration: he refers to himself in the first and third person in a single breath. The shiver comes from an inkling into a much more radical reading of the text. Is it possible that Edward Hyde is doing the narrating? We know that the death of Jekyll is to be brought about by his final transformation into Hyde. Wouldn't it make perfect sense for the 'I' here to be the 'I' of Hyde the murderer of Jekyll? We know that he is discovered as Hyde on the floor of the room in which the narration is written. We assume that the transformation takes place somewhere in the unnarrated time beyond the narrative's end, but how would we know that it has not taken place already? Hyde has already forged Jekyll's handwriting several times in the course of the narrative. Hyde does not only hide in Jekyll as a refuge from the gallows, but he also hides behind writing, behind Jekyll's identity as writing. It is chilling to be reminded that our only access to the whole visual universe of the narrative is through the medium of writing, a medium that the narrative shows several times to be an unreliable guide to the identity of the writer.

But why should we jump to such a ridiculous conclusion? Isn't it just a wrongheaded inference? There are two kinds of objection. The first is that it makes no moral sense at all within the terms of the story. Why would Hyde, the personification of evil, vindicate Jekyll in the confession and take all the blame himself? Why, indeed, would he continue to narrate at all given his spiteful and selfish attitude to Jekyll? The problem with this objection is that it runs into the problem of the reliability of the narrative at every turn. The only information we have about Hyde comes from the confession of Jekyll, but if all of that information is unreliable, we no longer have any kind of handle on the moral personalities of Jekyll or Hyde. The second kind of objection is that it is simply an inappropriate question to pose because the answer is undecidable. The writing is all we have, and there is no underpinning reality with reference to which we might resolve the ambiguity. In other words, it may be a logical possibility that Hyde is narrating, but it would have to remain as an open possibility, an undecidability, without any point of reference for a solution. Nevertheless only the possibility is required to set the logical rebound in motion:

the possibility of unreliability renders all the information we might use in counter-argument unreliable.

We might view this possibility as a characteristic problem in the logic of self-narration; but I'm not sure that it can be dismissed on the basis of either of the objections above. The objection that it is morally illogical and the objection that it is critically inappropriate are both undermined by the extent to which the narrative suggests that it is conceivable that Hyde is narrating. Before Jekyll's narrative comes to an end, for example, we discover that it was Hyde who composed the following moral appeal in his letter to Dr Lanyon:

> There was never a day when, if you had said to me, 'Jekyll, my life, my hon-
> our, my reason, depend upon you,' I would not have sacrificed my fortune
> or my left hand to help you. Lanyon, my life, my honour, my reason, are all
> at your mercy; if you fail me tonight, I am lost. You might suppose, after this
> preface, that I am going to ask you for something dishonourable to grant.
> Judge for yourself.   (*JH*, 1979, p. 74)

Even if it is motivated by fear of the gallows, the fact that Hyde can write this appeal at all is subversive. It shows that he is just as capable of imitating Jekyll's moral personality as he is of imitating his handwriting. It installs suspicion in the reader for every moment of moral candour and self-judgement to follow, so that the possibility that the confession is a lie increases in proportion with its honesty. The effect is compounded by the fact that we discover this deceit at a moment in the narrative when the narrative pronouns are beginning to yield to the stress, reminding us of the difficulty of telling Jekyll and Hyde apart in writing. After several pages of narration in which Hyde is the referent of the narrative 'I', relegating Jekyll to the third person, the narrative identity crisis culminates in a moment of metanarrative self-realisation: 'He, I say – I cannot say, I' (*JH*, p. 94). Snapping out of one narrative voice into another, the logical absurdity of a sentence which says 'I' three times while proclaiming that pronoun impossible lies somewhere in the ambiguity of Jekyll's focalisation of the narrative through Hyde – between Hyde as narrator and Hyde as narrated.

A fictional confession is bound to produce paradoxes, generated in the tension between fiction and truth. But some narratives more than others will foreground the difficulties of telling truth from lies by dramatising the tension within the narrative as a reliability problem. Self-narration, in fiction and in life, may always generate this kind of suspicion; but when we are dealing with a story which subjects the narrator to a proliferating binary fission, the parts of which converge on its ending, a strange reversal takes place. It is as if the narrative proceeds towards a truth which is only partially glimpsed in the doubleness of Jekyll and Hyde: the shipwreck of subjectivity in narrative form when the distancing devices of the time gap and the third person self-address can no longer avert collision.

Writing and seeing

The problem that I have been pointing to here could be quickly eliminated by a film adaptation of the narrative. Filmic narration tends to imply the complete reliability and authority of the camera on questions of identity, on the basis that seeing is believing. The genre of the courtroom drama, for example, generally adjudicates between the unreliability of different versions of events by using the camera to reveal the truth of past events as a reliable contrast to their narration in words. Those flashbacks at the end of *Columbo* or Agatha Christie films function less as corroboration of the detective's version of events than as an indication of their complete authority as truth. And on the question of identity, film can only deceive through the use of implausible rubber masks and improbable doubles, and even this will not compromise the reliability of the medium itself. There is something about seeing, even fictional seeing, which overrules the authority of verbal narrative.

The tension between seeing and writing is a growth industry in contemporary narratology. In classical rhetoric, seeing and writing were generally understood as complementary media, not only because image and text could be juxtaposed productively, but because it was part of the power of a text to depict, to conjure visions. The rhetorical term *eckphrasis* referred to the power of words to create a picture or to operate like a painting, and Horace's formula – *ut pictura poesis* – represented the established view that writing aspired to the condition of an imitation or copy of the world it described. This is one of the assumptions about writing that didn't survive long into systematic narratology. The New Critics may have made use of the categories of showing and telling as if they were complementary modes of verbal narrative, but since structuralism the tendency has been to subsume any visual experience evoked by words in grammatical and structural perspectives. Recently there has been renewed interest in the interaction of words and images, not only as multimedia juxtapositions, but in the eckphrastic power of the written word to construct pictures. The subject is often broached in terms of a kind of power struggle between words and images, or through the broad idea that words are somehow on the retreat in an age which is dominated by images. I think the broad idea of this power struggle is nonsensical, but I am interested in a new division of labour between texts and images which has deepened since the invention of the photograph and which creates fascinating internal tensions within writing. The idea that language is not adequate to express everything in the human mind may be older than the hills, but it characterises a distinctly modern crisis in the relative ability of words to document visual experience. In the context of postmodern theories of identity as increasingly superficial and visual projections of meaning, it is a crisis which lies at the heart of the question of the importance of narration to identity. One facet of the tension between word and image in cultural studies at large is a kind of power shift away from the linguistic aspects of identity towards the visible signs of identity like clothing, the body and the face.

One of the interesting things about *Dr Jekyll* is that outward appearance clearly functions as a metaphor for the soul's moral character, and yet the narrative has immense difficulty in conveying the details of those outward manifestations of identity. Hyde, the third-person narrator tells us, 'had never been photographed', and 'those few who could describe him differed widely' (*JH*, 1979, p. 50). Everybody seems to agree that Hyde's face and body are deformed, but none of his observers can encapsulate it in a verbal description. The first attempt, from Mr Enfield, is a sorry failure:

> He is not easy to describe. There is something wrong with his appearance; something displeasing, something downright detestable. I never saw a man I so disliked, and yet I scarce know why. He must be deformed somewhere; he gives a strong feeling of deformity, although I couldn't specify the point. He's an extraordinary-looking man, and yet I really can name nothing out of the way. No, sir; I can make no hand of it; I can't describe him. And it's not want of memory; for I declare I can see him this moment. (*JH*, 1979, p. 34)

The inexpressibility of Hyde's appearance is at one level just part of the terror and suspense: horror is usually generated by suggestion and not description, even in film. What is frustrating here is that whereas the image of Hyde is luminous in Enfield's memory, the reader's experience is of no more than the provisionality and inadequacy of language to name it.

Utterson's first description is similarly couched in unutterable somethings and sort ofs:

> Mr Hyde was pale and dwarfish; he gave an impression of deformity without any namable malformation, he had a displeasing smile, he had borne himself to the lawyer with a sort of murderous mixture of timidity and boldness, and he spoke with a husky, whispering and somewhat broken voice, – all of these were points against him; but not all of these together could explain the hitherto unknown disgust, loathing and fear with which Mr Utterson regarded him. 'There must be something else' said the perplexed gentleman. 'There is something more, if I could find a name for it.' (*JH*, 1979, p. 40)

The narrative repeatedly fails to depict the mask of evil, or declares that it is beyond the power of writing to convey its complexity. And we are reminded several times of the opacity of writing in this regard in a more oblique way, when the metaphor of writing is used to describe Hyde's face, first by Utterson who reads 'Satan's signature' on it, then at the crucial moment of self-description when Jekyll first looks on Hyde in the glass and beholds evil 'written broadly and plainly on the face' and on the body 'an imprint of deformity and decay'. The moment at which we hope to overcome the opacity of writing in the transluscence of vision is ruined by the metaphor of writing, as if writing can only reflect itself at the moment of revelation.

The writer looks into the mirror and beholds writing. This is a metaphor which seems to undermine the aspirations of writing to depict, or to reflect, something other than itself. This is confirmed at the moment when Poole and Utterson break into Jekyll's chamber at the moment of his death and discover the doctor's narrative lying on the desk beside the mirror in which Jekyll has witnessed his own transformation. But what are we to make of this complex metaphor?

> Next, in the course of their review of the chamber, the searchers came to the cheval-glass, into whose depth they looked with an involuntary horror. But it was so turned as to show them nothing but the rosy glow playing on the roof, the fire sparkling in a hundred repetitions along the glazed front of the presses, and their own pale and fearful countenances stooping to look in.
>
> 'This glass has seen some strange things, sir,' whispered Poole.
>
> 'And surely none stranger than itself,' echoed the lawyer in the same tone. 'For what did Jekyll' – he caught himself up at the word with a start,

and then conquering the weakness: 'what could Jekyll want with it?' he said.   (*JH*, 1979, p. 71)

This is a multiply suggestive mirror. It is on one level a clue to the unsolved mystery, since the answer to the lawyer's rhetorical question points to the nature of Jekyll's experiments with his appearance. But Poole describes it as a witness. This is a powerful metaphor because, as a witness, it has seen so much more than Poole realises or than the reader will ever see in full: the face of Hyde as well as the unnarrated events between the end of Jekyll's confession and this moment. As such, the mirror acts as a metaphor for the vision to which the reader has no access through writing. But Utterson's response to Poole complicates the metaphor immeasurably. The mirror, which at a literal level allows a person to see himself, has witnessed nothing more strange than itself. Even when a mirror is personified as a witness, it would only be capable of witnessing itself by looking into another mirror. One way of reading this is to see it as an inversion of the roles of mirror and face, in which a mirror looks into the face of a person and sees itself. In other words, the mirror that sees itself in a face is a metaphor for the face that sees itself in a mirror, creating a giddy confusion about which is which. Either way, the image evokes another kind of unstoppable rebound: an infinite regress of mutually reflecting mirrors.

The relationship between the mirror and Jekyll's self-narration can be seen as both eckphrastic hope and eckphrastic fear. As a metaphor for self-reflection, the hope is that Jekyll's narrative will achieve the luminosity of vision with which the mirror has witnessed events in this very private chamber, or better still, that the narrative will provide the depth of understanding that the mirror cannot when Utterson and Poole look into it. The fear is that self-narration, like the mirror, will be incapable of conveying that private vision, or that Utterson will look into Jekyll's narrative in anticipation of depth and see only the pale face of his own fear. The metanarrative function of the mirror is at this moment poised between the hope that all will be revealed and the fear that writing is incapable of full revelation, just as it is undecided between the modes of seeing and writing as the most reliable guide to the depth of events. The key device here which encourages this metanarrative interpretation is the positioning of Utterson alongside the reader. He is our guide, our detective, our source of judgement and our access to further discovery. His role as a surrogate reader is made all the more explicit at this point in the narrative when, having led us from external sightings into this inner chamber, he undergoes a transition of his own from character in the narrative to reader of the two narratives in which this mystery was to be explained' (*JH*, 1979, p. 73). The narrative as a whole is organised as a journey into interiority. It stages Jekyll's self-narration as revelation of the truth behind appearances, as a process of unveiling, of stripping away layers of disguise only to discover the externality of writing or the truth that writing is the ultimate disguise.

Perhaps this helps to explain why *Dr Jekyll* has been so resonant of psychoanalytic meanings for the modern reader. It is not only that it is a narrative metaphor for the divided self, nor even that the division is repeated in the schism between the self as the subject and object of self-narration; it also stages a conflict between image and text as modes of subjectivity and identification – as mirror versus self-narration. While the logic of revelation and confession seems to elevate narrating above seeing as the reliable guide to identity, as depth over surface, there is a powerful counter-logic which reminds us that there is blindness in our insight, because we cannot see the identity of the narrator in the present any more than we can see Hyde's face through the materiality of the written word. If the mirror image has dominion over the present tense, it is incapable of grasping identity over time; and if self-narration has mastery over past events, the present tense represents a crisis in its power. This is not so much a general rule about about the power of image or text to represent identity. It is more like a way of locating the mystery of this text in the tension between the significance of the face and the significance of narrative time, in the logical rebound both within and between the two modes of subjectivity.

Self-conscious self-consciousness

I began this chapter by arguing that for self-consciousness to take a narrative form, it had to forsake self-consciousness of the moment of narration. This places self-consciousness in the same logical position as lying in the sense that when one is self-consciously self-conscious, the veracity of self-narration is questioned and any therapeutic value may be lost: when one becomes aware that one is performing or transforming oneself in the act of narration, it is at the expense of the constative force of narrative as the recuperation of past events. When I tell my own story, I must deny that I am inventing myself in the process in order to believe that I am discovering myself.

The same thing can be said of the relationship between narrative and narratology, or a particular narrative and its reading. I may be reinventing the story according to my own interests, but in order to do so I have to pretend that I am discovering something which was objectively there in the first place. It is as if the inventive and performative aspects of reading must be momentarily overlooked to keep the anarchy of self-consciousness at bay. This is the only way in which I can make sense of the idea associated with critics like Paul de Man and J. Hillis Miller, that deconstruction is something a text does to itself without any intervention from the critic. For de Man, 'deconstruction is not something we have added to the text but it constituted the text in the first place' (1979, p. 14); for Miller, 'Deconstruction is not a dismantling of the text but a demonstration that it has already dismantled itself' (1976, p. 141). The problem here is that the reading is claiming transparency for its own language while denying the possibility of transparency, seeing the process of deconstructing the referential illusion as if it were something which takes place autonomously on the book shelf after everybody has gone to bed. I want to pose this as a question about the reading I have just offered of *Dr Jekyll* – did I deconstruct it or did it deconstruct itself? – particularly because it is a reading which imitates critics like Miller and de Man. In fact it imitates a whole generation of critics who see literary texts as allegories of their favourite bits of literary theory and who imply constantly that this is what the texts are actually about.

The reading presented here set out to show that there is something inherently schizophrenic in the logic of self-narration. It aimed, therefore, to link Dr Jekyll's narrative with the ideas of the previous chapter, in which a whole culture was seen to be self-consciously narrating itself, and with the theme of space-time compression that that entailed. It was clearly convenient that *Dr Jekyll* is about schizophrenia, convenient that it involves self-address in the third person and that the third person is converging on the narrative 'I' as the end approaches in the forms of both Jekyll and Hyde. Was it also convenient that I found the theme of the opacity of writing in more than one place, in the ambiguity of Jekyll's handwriting, the personification of the mirror and a couple of metaphors linking vision to writing? These arguments gave the impression that the text itself yielded poststructuralist perspectives on the multifarious nature of subjectivity, the externality of writing and the self-referentiality of narrative. In other words, I was rewriting a well-known text, normally taken to be about the moral duality of human nature and the naughty-but-nice psychology that moral constraints produce, as if it were about literary and cultural theory.

I didn't choose Dr *Jekyll* for its co-operation with my argument. It was chosen for me by the series editor who wanted the discussions published in this series to have common literary reference points. If anything, I made it co-operate. I read through it underlining in pencil only those bits which referred to the act of writing itself or which illustrated difficulties in the logic of self-narration. I borrowed heavily from the argument of a lecture I give regularly on self-narration in a similar text, Hogg's *Confessions of a Justified Sinner,* in which an apparently reformed narrator tells us what a liar he used to be. In short I have forced the text to say what I want it to say, rewritten it as a theoretical fiction on the basis of selective evidence, surreptitiously translated it while conveying fidelity to it, ventriloquised through it without moving my lips.

Narratology has been doing this now for about 30 years. There have been two phases: the first was a collective intent to read texts as allegories of the problems of linguistic knowledge or reading, and the second has been to politicise the allegory, to find in texts a political and ideological unconscious. In the first phase the horizon of everything including politics was language, and in the second phase the horizon of everything including language was politics. Obviously these are broad enough to be horizons. If I were to start a movement in narratology on the basis that the horizon of everything is football, or to try to read *Dr Jekyll* as an allegory of Manchester United's 1997–98 season, I would be struggling. Flippant as it may seem, this tells us something important: that some topics are more narratologically universal than others. Evidence will be found in any narrative to support an allegorical reading based on language or ideology, and this means that the relation between such a reading and the object-text is more reciprocal than I have been implying: that the poles of discovery and invention, or objectivity and subjectivity, or constative and performative statement, are bound together in interaction. Stop me if I am stating the obvious, but a narrative and its reading are in a kind of dialogue with each other. They are a kind of mutually dependant pair, *nec tecum nec sine te,* a kind of suture which keeps them separate and prevents them from parting. A narrative does not speak for itself. It needs to be articulated by a reading, and a reading will always be a kind of rewriting, but the reading cannot interpret the text in complete freedom, cannot say anything it likes. There is always a kind of oscillation between objectivity and subjectivity in reading: the reading invents the narrative no more than it is invented by it.

A useful metaphor to describe this relation of mutual dependence is that of two mirrors facing each other. It is useful because it conveys the sense of a reading as determining and being determined by its object. Following Derrida's reading of Ponge in 'Psyche: Inventions of the Other' (1989) and Gasché's reading of Derrida in *The Tain of the Mirror*, the metaphor can be seen as one which equates the tain of the mirror, the silvering which prevents transparency and authorises the invention of the other, with writing. According to this model, my reading of *Dr Jekyll* is one kind of writing rebounding against another, but in order to authorise the reading as in any way transparent or faithful to the object-text, I am forced to disguise or naturalise the moment of reading in the same way that Jekyll is forced to naturalise the moment of narration for the sake of objectivity. I don't want to get lost in this new logical rebound. I simply want to observe that criticism, for all its recent self-consciousness about its active production of the object, has never really escaped the dualism of subject–object relations and has resorted to a strategy which is much more pernicious: it has displaced the prescriptive model of theory, the linguistic model in narratology, with something completely untheorised in terms of subject–object relations. Earlier in this book I discussed the idea that the most significant transition in narratology had been to demolish the boundary between narrative and narratology. On the whole I would see this as a very positive transition in so far as it is directed against the assurances of narratology as a deductive science. But I think the idea of the untheorised theoretical metaphor – like my mirror – which ambiguously divides responsibility for theoretical insight between the reading and text itself is an unwanted side effect.

My reading suggests, disingenuously I think, that Stevenson's mirror is a theoretical metaphor, an unwitting allegory for everything I think about the logic of self-narration, the reliability of writing and the relationship between fiction and criticism. It implies that I had discovered in the metaphor an encapsulation of deconstruction, and therefore that deconstruction was not something I had brought to the text but something that constituted it in the first place. I pretended to discover a truth which I had at least partially invented. I lied, my lie caught up with me, and now, as I write, I am lying dead.

7 The Dark Clouds of Enlightenment: Socio-Narratology and *Heart of Darkness*

Conrad's *Heart of Darkness* is the most analysed narrative in history. It has been used to demonstrate everything in the narratological universe, and I will use it here to survey some of the transitions through which narratology has passed in recent years. I want to make a simple point that despite the diversification, fracturing and deconstruction of literary studies, narratology is a common resource, a finite set of terms and concepts which can be deployed by critics with very different interests. Narratology is not a critical school and not a branch of formalism. In some ways narratology has followed the same course as globalisation. It has devolved into smaller units at the same time as it has converged into an increasingly shared vocabulary with increasingly similar objectives. This phenomenon marks a profound change from the condition of narrative criticism as recently as 15 years ago, when critics tended to draw terminology and critical concepts from disparate sources, and where those sources often had incommensurate aims and assumptions. Perhaps the most apparent change is the shift from a widespread fear of and resistance to theory in narrative criticism towards an almost wholesale acceptance of its perspectives and methods, towards the canonisation of certain theorists who have become the shared reference points for disparate narratologies.

The process of narratological standardisation also shows the signs of the time compression that I described in reference to the simultaneous marketing of original and biological washing powders. That is to say, many of the founding concepts of narratology which were viewed with some suspicion in their own historical moments have found their markets in more recent history alongside new developments. It is not only that the foundational insights of the analysis of fictional point of view are still in use or that the distinctions of structural narratology have a continuing validity, but predominantly that modern narratological concepts have found their inspiration in political, historicist and dialectical thinking which was perhaps marginalised in its own moment by the dominance of formalist criticism. For this reason the contribution to narratology of critics such as Williams, Bakhtin, Voloshinov, Althusser and Macherey can be felt at large in literary studies now for the first time. And whereas in the mid-1980s these were names used as weapons against critics like Propp, Greimas, Genette, Todorov, Barthes, Derrida, de Man, Miller and others, at the turn of the millennium there is no longer the same sense of conflict between schools. Some people will doubt this, but only if they misunderstand me. I am not suggesting that contemporary narrative criticism is a serene consensus, but rather that the alignment of certain theorists with certain critical interests is no longer as easy to plot. A good example is the change in the way narratologists have used psychoanalysis in the last decade. When I first specialised in literary theory in the mid-1980s, the Lacanian critic was a lonely interdisciplinary figure being carried along on the bandwagon of Derrideans with whom she could at least hold a conversation. Since then, the Lacanian critique of Freud has informed almost every issue in literary and cultural studies (see forthcoming volume by Andrew Roberts in this series) and has become the basis of recent perspectives in film studies, the new orthodoxy in feminism and the often undeclared inspiration for much postcolonial theory. Lacanian psychoanalysis, perhaps alongside reader-response criticism, has gone some way towards meeting the growing demand from different areas of criticism to account for readers with different identities and modes of identification. I would also argue that psychoanalysis has met a need for political criticism in general to say anything interesting and specific about a narrative, furnishing Marxism with the concept of a political unconscious and freeing critics like Althusser, Macherey and Jameson from the traditional quest for class allegory and socialist realism.

Could it be that the academic publishing industry has had some hand in this change? It is not only those works, which I have already mentioned, that gather narratological concepts together into handbooks which would bring about this kind of convergence. The death of the academic monograph and the growth of the critical anthology or the case study in critical performances could well also be a factor. I am thinking here particularly of those editions of literary texts, like *Heart of Darkness*, that offer several different critical perspectives on the text on which publishers are coming to depend. It would be a good party game for sad literary academics to try to tell which reading is which, so difficult have they become to tell apart.

I have strong sympathy for Elaine Jordan in her introduction to the *Joseph Conrad* volume of the *New Casebooks Series*:

> These papers belong more to postcolonial criticism than to feminism, but there is no necessary antagonism. Feminism like Marxism has led towards political and cultural thinking more widely concerned with differences, indeed this is the important development in modern feminism: not 'post-feminism', but insistence on feminism within other debates and struggles, and the insistence of other debates and struggles within feminism.   (1996, p. 8)

The difficulty for this kind of volume is that there are few easily labelled card-carrying critics remaining, as Jordan notes a few lines later: 'Few essays in this volume promote an exclusive methodology. Usually they articulate several approaches: narratology with psychoanalysis, Marxism with both, feminism with deconstruction' (1996, p. 8). Even when the readings are commissioned as exclusive methodologies, they seem to trespass all over each other's material. I don't like this supermarket attitude to critical method, and I see the labelling difficulties they are beginning to face in a positive light, not only because they suggest that narratological resources can be borrowed across the boundaries, but also because they release issues like gender, race and class from the ghettos to which they have been traditionally confined. The problem of distinguishing one critical approach from another is not really one of the sameness of all readings as much as it is the absence of any perceptible common denominator between readings encompassed by a single -*ism*.

The crossovers and contaminations between different critical methods are particularly relevant to the recent reception of *Heart of Darkness* because it is a text that lent itself to the controversy that raged between formalist and historicist criticism earlier in the twentieth century. Here was a text that was both a highly formal, self-conscious narrative which seemed to take the problems of narration and of seeing through words as a primary concern, and yet the manifest content of which was a critique of European imperialism through the example of the Congo Free State. It seems absurd that this should present any kind of dichotomy, yet early analyses rarely dealt with formal and historical aspects together. There was a tendency to focus a reading on one aspect only, not because the other didn't exist but because it was seen as a subordinate concern: that narrative form was merely the vehicle for historical themes or that the imperial context was a kind of alibi for loftier and more universal insights into human nature. The dominance of formalism in the early part of the century ensured that the specificities of history were viewed as extrinsic issues or allegorical vehicles, so that the colonial context of Marlow's journey was subordinated to its self-referential, narrative aspect or its reading as a symbolic journey into an inner landscape. Ideas of an inner journey or a symbolic journey were recruited to the formalist cause by virtue of their universalising tendencies, their transcendence of historical particulars and geographical detail.

One of the things at stake in the hierarchy of the universal and the particular was the character of high modernism as a whole. Until recently the modernist novel was defined chiefly as a shift from external to internal reality. The representation of subjectivity presented a new challenge and a new crisis: was language adequate to convey interiority? Traditionally the language of modernist fiction was understood as a response to this crisis: the poeticisation of prose, the fragmentation of narrative structure, new forms of focalisation, and a new self-consciousness of language and narrative structure were seen as attempts to cope with the new demands of the inner landscape. The modernist novel was seen as an introverted aesthetic experiment, turning its back on history to explore the relationship between narrative conventions and the possibilities for inner self-exploration. The analysis of point of view, obsessed with the use of narrative technique as access to minds, fashioned modernism in this mould, this conjunction of aesthetic experimentation and interiority.

The rereading of modernism has entailed different kinds of historical revision. One strategy has been to try to break the circular relationship between this view of modernism as a whole and the hypercanonicity of texts like *Heart of Darkness* which best exemplify it by reading other texts instead. This is not the strategy I want to focus on here, nor is it the predominant strain in the revision of modernism which has been the rereading of hypercanonical texts in a way that yields a different definition of the age by reopening them to historicist analysis. Jameson, for example, has argued that the crisis of language and representation in modernist fiction should be understood as a product of historical change rather than as a retreat into aestheticism. The age of Empire, he claims, has turned history into an ungraspable totality. It is no longer possible to encapsulate historical experience within the provincial English village because so much of it is taking place elsewhere. The relationship between the bourgeoisie and the proletariat is no longer complete within a locality because, in an increasingly global society, that relationship is only experienced in fragments. The crisis of modernist fiction is therefore historical through and through, so that the fragmentation of narrative and the interest in interiority are symptoms of the unrepresentability of history as a whole, and the traditional definition of modernism or reading of *Heart of Darkness* becomes a kind of geopolitical denial. 'Self-consciousness', says John Updike, 'is a mode of interestedness which ultimately turns outwards', and this is a good way of understanding the new 'symptomatic' emphases of contemporary narratology: that the inner life is no retreat from the outside world of history and politics but is constituted by it. With its extended analogy between Marlow's inner and geopolitical journeys and its confusion of inside and outside worlds, shells and kernels, *Heart of Darkness* seems to co-operate with this kind of reading just as much as it does with the New Critical view.

Deconstruction has a rather ambiguous place in this contest over the nature of modernism. In Chapter 3 I described the complex relations between modernism and Derrida's reading practices in relation to Joyce, but Derrida's readings are not really typical of what has come to be known as deconstruction: they tend towards parody more than allegoresis, imitating the text being read rather than construing it as an allegory for poststructuralist literary theory. In the previous chapter I claimed that the real proponents of this kind of theoretical allegoresis were de Man and Miller. To illustrate the slow accumulation of political and ideological perspective in narratology, I'd like to trace this process from deconstruction onwards, beginning with a transition represented by two readings published in 1985: J. Hillis Miller, whose reading of *Heart of Darkness* as an allegory of deconstruction itself seems now curiously confined to its formalist obsessions, and Christopher Miller, who shows that those formalist obsessions can be transformed into the vocabulary of ideological critique and employed to draw out the political and historical unconscious.

J. Hillis Miller's analysis, '*Heart of Darkness* Revisited', is intent on finding the themes of Derrida's reading of Saussure in Conrad's text. It begins from the well-trodden view of the narrative as modelled on the conventional 'grail quest', or a story in which the pursuit of a divine object gives the narrative its forward movement and its promise of some kind of ultimate revelation. In such a story the quest for the grail becomes a quest for the meaning of the story, where the discovery of the grail is the event which gives the whole narrative its significance. In *Heart of Darkness* the journey undertaken by Marlow towards Kurtz's inner station in the Congolese jungle is seen in just such terms, as the journey towards some revelation and towards the meaning of the narrative. The starting point of Miller's analysis is that this kind of journey towards revelation is the structure of a parable in which a reader reaches some obvious and detachable moral at the narrative's end such as 'crime doesn't pay' or 'honesty is the best policy'. What then interests him is the description that the external narrator gives of Marlow's method of storytelling:

> The yarns of seamen have a direct simplicity, the whole meaning of which lies within the shell of a cracked nut. But Marlow was not typical (if his propensity to spin yarns be excepted), and to him the meaning of an episode was not inside like a kernel but outside, enveloping the tale which brought it out only as a glow brings out a haze in the likeness of one of those misty halos that sometimes are made visible by the spectral illumination of moonshine. (*HD*, 1983, p. 8)

Miller finds in this commentary a theme closely related to Derrida's critique of the Saussurean sign, that the meaning of a sign is not really within it at all, but that it lies outside it in the structure to which it belongs. For Miller, a traditional parable, like the traditional yarns of seamen, advances a straightforward model of the relation of a tale to its meaning, where the story itself is 'the inedible shell which must be removed and discarded so the meaning of the story may be assimilated' (1989, pp. 211–2). Marlow's story, however, does not see meaning on this model of the story as a shell within which its meaning is contained like a kernel. The darkness which lies at the heart of Conrad's tale is also something that envelops it and that is metaphorically represented by the dark atmospheric conditions of Marlow's journey and by the dark clouds which hang above the Thames as Marlow narrates. The quest for meaning in Conrad's tale is a grailless quest in the sense that when we reach Kurtz all is not revealed – the meaning that we expect to discover at the heart of the narrative, the nature of the heart of darkness, the detachable moral towards which we think we are proceeding remain obscure. At the climax of the novel, in Kurtz's dying words 'The horror! the horror!', the expectation is dashed and we are left looking only at words whose meaning is, at best, left suspended, suggestively spread across the tale and its images of darkness which envelop Marlow's quest.

The Derridean themes are clear in this reading. The grailless quest for meaning in the narrative echoes the quest for presence of meaning in a sign – a quest that never comes to rest and never finds its grail in some kernel content. For Derrida, the desire for presence is a desire to escape from language as pure exteriority and identify an inner meaning, to reach beyond the signifier to the signified, or to find in the container a contained meaning. Thus Derrida saw writing, which is traditionally the external container of meaning, as the condition of all language or as the prison house from which no escape is possible. Conrad's text seems to advance the same model. To illustrate this, Miller points to the failure of Marlow's narrative not only to reveal its meaning through Kurtz, but also to support ideas of language which assume the presence of a signified content, like the communicative or referential functions of language. Marlow's narrative regularly falters in moments of fear that his words cannot convey his experience, and at such moments both the referential and the communicative models of language are explicitly questioned:

> He was just a word for me. I did not see the man in the name any more than you do. Do you see him? Do you see the story? Do you see anything? It seems to me I am trying to tell you a dream – making a vain attempt because no relation of a dream can convey the dream sensation... No, it is impossible; it is impossible to convey the life sensation of any given epoch of one's existence – that which makes its truth, its meaning – its subtle and penetrating essence. (*HD*, 1983, p. 39)

Both Marlow and the reader are stuck in the exteriority of language and in the impossibility of expression. Just as we cannot see Hyde's face, we cannot see Marlow or Kurtz through writing. We cannot penetrate the meaning of Kurtz's final words any more than Marlow can because ultimately our experience as readers is not visual but of written words and exterior signifiers. In this way any assumption of the transparency of language to fictional events is undermined by such reminders of its inescapable opacity.

As paraphrases go, this one has been a heresy, but my aim has been to communicate as quickly as possible that Miller's reading of *Heart of Darkness* proceeds along similar lines to the one I presented of *Dr Jekyll* in the previous chapter. The thrust of the reading is to demonstrate that the text is *about* the failure of language to reveal the truth. No doubt if we sat him down Miller would agree that at some level it is also *about* Africa, *about* colonial power, but his reading implies that this is not what it is *really about*. His reading perhaps belongs in a tradition of readings of *Heart of Darkness* which insist that it is really about something other than empires and which see either the inner self or narrative itself or a combination of the two as loftier themes. I would include some other admirable readings of *Heart of Darkness* in this tradition, such as Garrett Stewart's 'Lying as Dying in *Heart of Darkness*', an adequate précis of which can be found in the last sentence of my previous chapter, and Peter Brooks's *Reading for the Plot* which argues a case strikingly similar to Miller's, that the text's failure to deliver truth ultimately yields a kind of narratological darkness in which one layer of ineffability covers another in the relation between Marlow's story and Kurtz's. Brooks is typical of the tradition of political denial in that his disaffection with formalism leads him less towards a political than a psychoanalytic modification of formal narratology. Like Miller, Brooks is content to see narrative as a dynamic process rather than as a static structure, content to accommodate contradictions in narrative which the structuralists have tried to reduce:

> I am convinced that the study of narrative needs to move beyond the various formalist criticisms which have predominated in our time: formalisms that have taught us much, but which ultimately cannot deal with the dynamics of texts as actualised in the reading process. My own interests ... have more and more taken me to psychoanalysis and especially to the text of Freud: since psychoanalysis presents a dynamic model of psychic processes, it offers the hope of a model pertinent to the dynamics of texts. (Brooks, 1985, pp. 35–6)

While this might lead into a more dynamic analysis of narratives, it does nothing to break the reciprocity between narrative crisis and the human psyche which presided over modernism: in practice it leads into a criticism that is formalist about time, or that sees plot as a temporal organisation of experience, as the formal element of psychic processes, but still to the exclusion of political and geographical particularity.

I am in no way critical of this position, nor convinced that political particularity is a worthy goal for narrative criticism. But my job here is to chart the transition from structural to political formalism, and my interest in Brooks's reading of *Heart of Darkness* is that it is separated from the perspectives of subsequent card-carrying political critics such as post-colonialists and feminists by a whisker. It is always implicit in *Reading for the Plot* that the enquiry into plot is an enquiry into a collective psyche, a social desire for plotting and telling. Much of his discussion of the narrative's failure to adequately summarise the significance of darkness is organised around a psychoanalytic need to master death: the tradition of the 'panoramic vision of the dying' which compresses 'all wisdom and truth' into the final moment and the last opportunity for dying. But because Brooks sees Marlow's narrative primarily as a retelling of Kurtz's story, it is Marlow's final lie to Kurtz's Intended that represents the panoramic moment for his story and the ultimate failure of his story to represent Kurtz's. Brooks describes this moment in Marlow's narrative as if it were a response to a social demand for effability and communicative meaning:

> Language as a system of social communication and transmission, as the medium of official biographies and readable reports, has no place for the unspeakable; it is used rather to cover up the unnameable, to reweave the seamless web of signification. The cover up is accomplished by Marlow's substituting 'your name' – the name of the intended which we are never in fact given – for the nameless, as if to say that any proper name can be used according to the circumstance, to ward off the threat of a fall from language.   (1985, p. 252)

It is language seen as 'interlocutionary and therefore social system' which must exclude the unnameable, and this exclusion is represented by the intended's exclusion from the circle of listeners on board the Nellie.

Brooks doesn't make much of the gender difference between the intended and Marlow's interlocutors on the Nellie, or of the gendered nature of his loyalty to Kurtz and his official story. If his conclusion is more narratological than feminist, if it excludes that Foucauldian sense of exclusion and inclusion as aspects of political power which features so prominently in Said's dealings with Conrad, its sense of the social nature of interlocutions is weakened as a result. He highlights the narratological insight that 'the way stories are told, and what they mean, seems to depend as much on narratee and narrative situation as on narrator' (1985, p. 252) without analysing the division of male and female narratees. It seems like a very minor insertion into this narratological framework, and yet a very major change in emphasis, to interpret Marlow's oscillation between the need to lie and the possibility of telling the truth about Kurtz in the light of this gender division, as when Nina Pelikan Straus points out that Marlow's world is 'distinctly split into male and female realms – the first harbouring the possibility of "truth" and the second dedicated to the maintenance of delusion':

> Marlow speaks in *Heart of Darkness* to other men, and although he speaks *about* women, there is no indication that women might be included among his hearers, nor that his existence depends upon his 'hanging together' with a 'humanity' that includes the second sex. The contextuality of Conrad's tale, the deliberate use of a frame to include readers as hearers, suggests the secret nature of what is being told, a secrecy in which Conrad seems to join Marlow. The peculiar density and inaccessibility of *Heart of Darkness*

may be the result of its extremely masculine historical referentiality, its insistence on a male circle of readers.   (1992, p. 50)

One of the ways in which Straus's reading differs from the perhaps male narratological fascination with textual organisation is that it implicates Conrad and the external reader in that organisation, so that the circle of male listeners is seen as a key device for the interpellation of readers. The only real difference between this observation and the predominating commentaries on the text in the formalist and narratological traditions is the word *male*. But its insertion represents the deployment of narratological resources to analyse something real and political, something that is not only part of the text's formal organisation but a dynamic process which takes place between the text and its real readers without lumping them together. For Straus, the exclusion of the intended highlights what Spivak calls the 'autobiographical vulnerabilities' of its readers which will determine different responses of real readers to the ineffable secrets which the text encodes as darkness. If nothing else, this helps to explain the difference between the glow of initiation and the expressions of baffled exclusion that have marked the gender divide in my tutorials on Conrad's text, and therefore translate innocent narratological facts into social dynamics beyond the covers. Straus concludes from the maleness of Marlow's community of interlocutors that the 'privilege of conscious autobiographical dramatisation on a woman commentator's part must become less rare' (1992, p. 64) in order to expose the lie of narratological objectivity. This is undoubtedly one direction for narratology that it should articulate issues of narrative organisation with individual possibilities for identification and pleasure in the reading process, even if that means having to listen to personal tales of social exclusion and oppression.

My feeling is that the real value of this narratological inflection is not to be found in the opportunity it provides the critic for self-dramatisation but in the account it provides of the textual unconscious and the ideological importance it attaches to that which is excluded. The psychoanalytic contribution to socio-narratology is at its weakest when the issue of identification drags the critic's usually dull and invariably unreliable life story into the reading, like a past colleague of mine whose lectures on narrative used the concepts of positionality and identification as opportunities for long dissertations about himself. Psychoanalysis is at its best when it dismantles the privatised conception of the unconscious to see it as a socio-linguistic or collective form of repression. Criticism may be, as Straus claims, a covert form of autobiography in what it chooses to see and what it chooses to repress in a reading, but critical self-dramatisation, as we have learned from recent metafictions, will only succeed in specifying the distance between one's own metacommentary and that of another reader. I plainly do not need to know who Straus is, and even less so to know how she would represent herself, to absorb the political importance of the exclusion of the intended from the interlocutionary community in *Heart of Darkness*.

Nor do I need to know anything more about Christopher Miller's autobiographical vulnerabilities (is he white, is he black?) when he argues a similar case in *Blank Darkness: Africanist Discourse in French* about the exclusion of the word 'Africa'. If Straus saw the exclusion of the intended from the secret world of male heroism as a metaphor for the exclusion of gender as a narratological issue, Miller does the same thing when he argues that Africa, like the intended, is seen in the text as a void without a name. It is a kind of blank space waiting to be filled, as Marlow's early recollections of the map indicate, by the coloniser's act of mapping and naming. As such the text does not represent Africa as a particular place at all but abstracts it into a Western atavistic fantasy into which the traveller can escape the forward thrust of Western progress to journey backwards towards primitive origins. Following Ian Watt's reading in *Conrad in the Nineteenth Century*, Miller charts the process of erasing and suppressing specific references to the Congo Free State, to its sovereign King Leopold, to place names and to the name of Africa in general as a way of indicating the text's double project of reference to and the failure to refer to Africa as a real place. Like Said's analysis of the Western fantasy of the Orient in *Orientalism*, Miller claims that the text is a kind of parody of Africanist discourse and its failure to grasp the particularities of culture and place. It is a reading clearly informed, though perhaps indirectly through Said, by Derridean, Foucauldian and psychoanalytic perspectives, but whereas those readings tended towards the view of the narrative as a parodic failure in the ability of narrative to deliver truth, Miller sees the ineffable absence at the heart of darkness as Africa itself. What is ineffable for Miller is not truth in the abstract but the truth of Africa in its particularity, so that his insertion of Africa into the blank space implies that it is not just a self-referential narrative but an exposure of the political and cultural misunderstandings of Africanist discourse in general. Whereas the readings of J. Hillis Miller and Brooks never quite break out of their tradition, reading *Heart of Darkness* as the deconstruction of narratological knowledge, Christopher Miller's insertion of Africa as the incommunicable and ungraspable truth of the narrative no longer works within the terms of a facile choice between the formal and political:

> Is Africa 'repressed' in anything but name? The word is practically synonymous with absence in Western discourse . . . Now in a text where every detail points to Africa. 'Africa' alone is missing, encoded in a new phrase, 'heart of darkness'. That phrase can never be wholly identified as either a repressed, encoded real referent or a fictive pseudo referent, independent of the real world. *Heart of Darkness* is in fact deeply engaged in both projects at once. (1985, p. 92)

It is such a simple thing to say, but it is also a new kind of reading. It represents the new narratological world in which the critic can be deeply engaged in the projects of historicism and formalism at once. It is no longer necessary to say, as Ian Watt did in 1979, that '*Heart of Darkness* is not essentially a political work'. Like Straus's reading, Miller repeats many of the often recycled observations about narrative structure in *Heart of Darkness* but puts them to work in the service of an ideological argument, so that the view of the text as both political and formal is reflected in the way that the reading proceeds. It is as if formalist narratology has done all of the hard work of textual analysis over the years, but has stubbornly refused, until about 1985, to jump the last fence and insert political issues such as gender and place into the argument.

Christopher Miller does not really deserve the credit for this convergence of perspectives. His reading is too derivative – too full of echoes of Freud, Derrida, Foucault, Watt, Brooks – to be seen as an original moment of interdisciplinary connection. But perhaps this is the point about the new convergence of critical schools, that socio-narratology is built on this convergence, this derivativeness, this standardised salad of formal, historical, psychoanalytic and political thinkers, this canonic finitude of critical intertexts. The irony may be that there is a kind of imperialism at work in the critique of imperialism or in dissidence at large – a central bureau of narratological resistance. As J. Hillis Miller declared in his presidential address to the Modern Languages Association of America in 1986, literary criticism has become an American export: 'Although Literary Theory may have its origin in Europe, we export it in a new form all over the world – as we do many of our scientific and technological inventions, for example the atom bomb.' He may have been joking, but he points to a frightening shadowing of the shift of the imperial centre from Europe to the United States in postcolonial criticism. It is American university money after all that has canonised these critics and re-exported them in the digestible form of self-help guides to the postcolonial world. It is a condition not unlike the green revolution in agriculture, where self-help for the world's starving populations came in the form of American technical innovation which had to be bought, rendering the starving people of the world dependent on American agribusiness for any hope of improvement: selling postcolonialism to the third world is ideologically akin to selling a Massey Ferguson to the local agrarian capitalist – a monopolisation of resistance by the oppressor.

Oddly enough, when Said comes to read *Heart of Darkness* in his epic *Culture and Imperialism* in 1993, he leaves himself, and narrative criticism, off the list of complicitous acts of imperialist mastery: 'Conrad', he argues, 'wants us to see how Kurtz's great looting adventure, Marlow's journey up the river, and the narrative itself all share a common theme: Europeans performing acts of imperial mastery and will in (or about) Africa' (1994, p. 25). No doubt, in a gesture of autobiographical invulnerability, Said could dismiss the idea that he too was performing an act of imperial mastery in the export of postcolonial perspective with reference to his Palestinian origins and his sterling work to help the oppressed, those who, in his own words, 'require and beseech domination, as well as forms of knowledge affiliated with domination' (1994, p. 8). The main emphasis of Said's argument in *Culture and Imperialism* is that it is impossible to think about narrative (and culture in general) without also thinking about imperialism. To do so is to exclude part of the picture, the part that formalism has always systematically excluded. Like Jameson, Said tends towards the view that an awareness of the patterns of global imperialism have become necessary in the reading of nineteenth century and modernist novels and that the English village is no longer intelligible as a free-standing entity. The *contrapuntal reading*, for Said, is an 'understanding of what is involved when an author shows, for instance, that a colonial sugar plantation is seen as important to the process of maintaining a particular style of life in England' (1994, p. 78).

Said's reading is like Christopher Miller's in that it sustains an interest in both the formal aspects of the narrative and its imperial history, and works through the insertion of Africa into established narratological approaches, or substitution between what formal narratologists have traditionally called 'reality' and what he is calling 'imperialism':

> Recall once again that Conrad sets the story on the deck of a boat anchored in the Thames; as Marlow tells his story the sun sets, and by the end of

the narrative the heart of darkness has reappeared in England; outside the group of Marlow's listeners lies an undefined and unclear world. Conrad sometimes seems to want to fold that world into the imperial metropolitan discourse represented by Marlow, but by virtue of his own dislocated subjectivity he resists the effort and succeeds in doing so, I have always believed, largely through formal devices. Conrad's self-consciously circular narrative forms draw attention to themselves as artificial constructions, encouraging us to sense the potential of a reality that seemed inaccessible to imperialism, just beyond its control ... (1994, p. 32)

Said is reaching for a more integrated relationship between imperial themes and formal organisation by arguing that the self-consciousness of narrative is what distinguishes it from the orthodox imperialist narrative, forsaking the realist authority of narrative as an anti-imperialist gesture, a vision that points to the way out of official imperialist narratives. The narrative is janus-faced in that on the one hand the meticulous formal organisation of its framing devices and its circle of listeners seems to offer no way out of the imperial mentality, and we are dependent on the 'assertive authority of the sort of power that Kurtz wields as a white man in the jungle or that Marlow, another white man, wields as narrator' (1994, p. 26). But on the other hand the self-consciousness of the narrative is that of an outsider's ironic distance from the imperial mastery of narrating and colonising:

> Conrad's realisation is that if, like narrative, imperialism has monopolised the entire system of representation - which in the case of *Heart of Darkness* allowed it to speak for Africans as well as for Kurtz and the other adventurers, including Marlow and his audience - your self-consciousness as an outsider can allow you actively to comprehend how the machine works, given that you and it are fundamentally not in perfect synchrony or correspondence. (1994, p. 27)

If there is a more profound interweaving and overlapping here between form and content, it is brought about less by an analogy between narrative and political power than from the view of narrative as power. It derives from the conviction, restated throughout *Culture and Imperialism,* that issues of imperial power are 'reflected, contested and even for a while decided in narrative' (1994, p. xiii). This is a kind of narratology which no longer merely responds to the need to insert political issues into the formal analysis of narrative, one which no longer acknowledges the possibility of their separation and, in the case of *Heart of Darkness,* no longer entertains a choice between the particular and the universal. Words, stories and political power are effectively all the same thing:

> By accentuating the discrepancy between the official 'idea' of empire and the remarkably disorientating actuality of Africa, Marlow unsettles the reader's sense not only of the very idea of empire but of something more basic, reality itself. For if Conrad can show that all human activity depends on controlling a radically unstable reality to which words approximate only by will or convention, the same is true of empire, of venerating the idea, and so forth.   (1994, p. 33)

The ease with which Said passes from formal to political issues throughout his work is exemplary of the recent move away from those tedious demonstrations that a narrative exceeded the significance that any analytic model imposed on it. What I don't like about Said's reading is the reactionary emphasis it places on biographical identification between readers and authors. It often seems, when reading Said, that he reads texts as covert autobiographies and that the final horizon of reading is the positionality of the author. Hence his appeal to the self-consciousness of the outsider in Marlow's narration is underwritten by Conrad's own sense of alienation from Englishness, his 'residual sense of his own exilic marginality' which caused him to 'qualify Marlow's narrative with the provisionality that came from standing at the very juncture of this world with another' (1994, p. 27). It represents the return of biography in criticism which has gained new acceptability from the New Historicist idea that the relationship between an author's life and his fictional narratives is one of intertextuality and contextualism, and further impetus from the idea that we met a moment ago in Straus's essay, that the assumed neutrality of criticism should be subverted by making its covert autobiographical significance explicit in the gesture of self-dramatisation. It reduces narrative self-consciousness to the idea of a self-conscious narrator, which is in turn reduced to the conscious political intention of an author. This is confirmed by the definition of contrapuntal criticism I cited a moment ago which seems to understand the reading as a cooperative exegesis of what an author intended to show without leaving room for the reading to uncover that which is repressed. This is in evidence throughout the reading of *Heart of Darkness* in what I would see as an over-identification between Said and Conrad on the basis of shared biographical experiences of exile in a metropolitan imperial centre which reduces the reading to a passive reception of successfully communicated attitudes to international politics. It is as if all that good work, performed by Marxists and structuralists over the years to reverse the hierarchy between an individual and language, is undone every time Said calls Conrad a genius. There is an impression of deep narcissism, on the scale of Marlow's with Kurtz, in Said's relationship with Conrad, that the latter is a genius when his intentions seem to coincide with Said's own. Taken in conjunction with the mirror effect between his topic and the global dominion of postcolonialism as an export, it seems metaphorically if not meteorologically probable that dark clouds hung over Manhattan while Said said his bit.

8 Postmodern Narrative Theory Reading Postmodern Narrative: Coetzee's *Elizabeth Costello* and *Slow Man*

When postmodern critics read Victorian or modernist narratives like *Dr Jekyll and Mr Hyde*, or *Heart of Darkness*, the subject and the object, or the critic and the narrative, are separated by a significant historical and temporal gap. The postmodernism in those situations belongs to the critic and not the narrative, and all the conscious and unconscious assumptions of the contemporary epoch, its theories and ideas, its history and its ideology are brought to the narrative by the critic. But what happens when the temporal gap closes, when contemporary critics write about contemporary novels or when postmodern narrative theory takes postmodern narrative as its object? Given the general argument of this book, that narrative and narrative theory, literature and criticism, or the novel and the critic are increasingly inseparable in the postmodern age, what is the role of the critic in a world of theoretical fictions, self-conscious narratives and self-referential discourses?

There is a kind of writing about contemporary narrative, evident at every level from the student essay to the celebrity monograph, that views the relationship of postmodern critic and narrative, or postmodern theory and postmodern narrative, as one of felicitous reciprocity. There is a sense, in this kind of writing, that the postmodern novel, for example, produces or reproduces the themes, notions and claims of postmodern narrative theory or postmodern cultural theory. The key precepts of postmodern thought are identified, in this kind of writing, as the thematic content of novels, as part of a demonstration that these are, indeed, postmodern narratives. It is worth identifying two species of this kind of circular relation of narrative and theory. In the first place there is what might be called the circle of cultural content. According to this circle, the critic will identify key epochal characteristics in the cultural theory of postmodernism – perhaps Jameson's account of nostalgia, Harvey's time-space compression or Baudrillard's discussions of simulation – and proceed to identify those cultural characteristics in fictional representations of the world. This is a syndrome that applies particularly, for obvious reasons, to novels or other narratives that set their action in the contemporary world, so that the cultural-theoretical analysis of the contemporary world can apply equally to the narrative representation of that same world. 'Look', these critical acts will say, 'this narrative represents a world of simulation, or nostalgia, or of time-space compression'. But we should not be too surprised by this discovery that the represented world in a novel yields to the same analysis as the world outside of the novel, or demonstrates anything about the narrative other than the realism of its representation. Nor is it only in the case of realistic novels set in the contemporary world that this circle presents itself. The nostalgia of culture in general, or the self-consciousness of the contemporary world, can also be discovered as the thematic content of postmodernism's self-conscious historical novels. In the second place, there is the syndrome that might be called the circle of narrative theory, according to which the critic will make use of an influential account of postmodern narrative, like Hutcheon's notion of historiographic metafiction, and proceed to seek the defining characteristics of the notion in a given novel. 'Look', such a reading will declare, 'postmodern novels are historiographic metafictions. There is historiographic metafiction in this novel, therefore it is a postmodern novel.' In many cases the circle of narrative theory is embedded in the circle of cultural content, as in an argument that says that the postmodern world is all about looking back to the past, that the novelistic version of this is the historical novel, and therefore that this historical novel is a postmodern novel, very much of its time. Let me then restate the problem of the previous paragraph. In a world where the novel is increasingly self-analytical and theoretical, what can the critic or theorist do to avoid the mere restatement of the novel's own critical and theoretical knowledge, or to save the theory–fiction relationship from the narcissistic self-affirmation of these tautologies?

One way of thinking about the postmodern novel is that, like the self-conscious television advertisement, it is trying to anticipate an objection, or a resistance, from the reader to the strategies through which it constructs its world or advances its perspectives. Since Genette, the term 'prolepsis' has come to mean a moment of narrative flashforward, but originally, to the classical rhetorician, it meant a kind of anticipation that is often built into an argument, especially the anticipation of an objection to that argument. In this meaning, the function of prolepsis would often be to incorporate the answer to that anticipated objection into the argument itself, to head it off before it happens with a counter-argument. Sometimes the anticipation of an objection requires no counter-argument to have its effect since the very act of anticipation itself undermines the potential objection, detracting from its independence or pointing to its predictability. At other times the orator will flatter the objector and seek to incorporate all the cleverness of the objection into the oration, and so claim it for itself, as when a lecturer says, 'Now the clever ones among you will be thinking, hang on a minute....' Proleptic discourses can disarm or mollify an audience or a readership by articulating their objections in advance, and yet there is always room for the double clever ones to resist or object to the technique itself: 'now hang on a minute... this prolepsis is appropriating my objections, articulating them for me, and putting words in my mouth', and for the triple clever ones to recognise that that is what is happening right now, and object to it and so on. But I need to heed a warning from Peggy Kamuf here about the readability of academic writing:

> But why anticipate, why call up resistance? It's a familiar tactic; we've all used it many times – to respond in advance to imagined or anticipated objections, as if one could conquer the other's resistance before it has even had the chance to manifest itself. Many books are written almost entirely in this mode of preconquered resistance, which usually makes them quite unreadable.   (Derrida, 2002, p. 7)

We do not, in other words, have to look to Cicero for this kind of technique, and nor is it confined, in the contemporary world, to the most overt acts of persuasion such as the television advertisements we looked at in Chapter 5. Prolepsis of this kind structures discourses of all sorts, from everyday conversation to academic criticism, and represents another example of the temporal structure that has been discussed throughout this book as supplementarity, where a future possibility produces that to which it is said to be added on, or structures the moment from which it is supposed to follow. As a projection forward to the moment of reception, and particularly to the kind of resistance that a discourse will meet in its readership, this kind of supplementarity is characteristic of self-conscious discourses in general, which know themselves by anticipating such possibilities. This is one way of understanding the self-consciousness of the postmodern novel: that its self-knowledge is a kind of anticipation of a possibility from which the novel follows, or a relation of supplementarity between the literary object and its critical reception. If my suggestion in the previous paragraph is right, that there is a kind of circularity in much writing about the postmodern novel, it is not necessarily some narcissistic disorder on the part of the critic who seeks the affirmation of theory in the novel. There is a temporal loop here, an originary anticipation in the novel that renders the subsequent distanced analysis of a critic or theorist redundant in advance.

The opinions of Elizabeth Costello

The question of critical and theoretical knowledge could be regarded as a subset of the broader issues of opinion, statement, knowledge and belief in the novel that were explored in Chapter 1. Novelists must not preach, they say (as if it would be possible to separate literature from moral instruction), but they are prevented from doing so openly by two basic features of the novel: the fact that opinions, statements and beliefs are usually attributed to the voice of a character or narrator, and the novel's basic dialogicism or tendency to stage opinions and beliefs against, alongside or in dialogue with different views. Authors can hide their own opinions and beliefs, take no responsibility for them or test them out against opposite views. Sometimes it is clear that a novel is a form of hidden polemic, which allows for the advancement of opinions or arguments while offering the author the alibi of the ventriloquist – that these are not my thoughts, views or political opinions, but those of a fictional character or a narrator. There is, in fiction, a general problem of attribution or responsibility that allows at the same time the statement of belief and the disowning of belief, as well as a range of subtle and not so subtle techniques for the endorsement of one belief over another, or the manipulation of a reader's resistance. One way in which the old-fashioned kind of prolepsis (the anticipation of an objection) can work in the novel is by embodying a belief and the objection to that belief in the relationship between two characters, so that, in their interaction, two sets of ideas vie with each other for superiority, and a possible, external objection on the part of a reader can be internalised. It is true that, in the dramatisation of polemic, the novelist can take advantage of a huge range of possible methods for defeating the objection, from sophisticated polemical dialogue to the cheap manipulations of sympathy and moral insinuation, but it doesn't seem adequate to think of questions of knowledge and belief in the novel in these terms, as if the dramatisation of ideas were just some ploy through which an author subtly and implicitly advances arguments and opinions insidiously. The relationship between what an author thinks and the novel that author writes, between what an author intends and the actual performance of what he or she produces, has been central for postmodern criticism and theory, and for the postmodern novel itself. And as always, the complexity of the question is compounded when the opinions and beliefs in question are not about social inequality, war, the existence of God or the nature of love, but about the nature of a novel, about the relationship between a novel and a belief itself or about the novel's very mode of knowing and believing things. There is, in other words, a simple level on which questions of belief can be addressed, often to do with what characters think and how those thoughts relate to what authors think, and there is a complex level, often to do with the whole performance of the novel, which opens into the abysmal logic of the self-referential whenever the novel contemplates its own knowledge and itself. In Ian McEwan's *Saturday* (2005), for example, we learn a lot about the protagonist's views on the upcoming war in Iraq, not only because we have access to his thoughts, but because he debates the subject openly with his children. By spending a little time on the Internet, we can also confirm that many of these views have been publicly expressed by Ian McEwan himself, so that there is an unusual level of authorial ownership of the opinions and beliefs expressed by Perowne. This is the simplest level of opinion and belief in the novel, in which an identifiably authorial view is, as it were, embodied by a character, and debated internally and externally in the course of represented events. Something much less simple comes into view if we turn our attention to the question of literature. Perowne's rather shaky views in favour of the invasion of Iraq are dramatised within what might be called the realistic frame of the novel. They ask us to accept that these are plausible opinions in a man like this, on this day in history, and to recognise a more general historical context of anti-war opinion represented in the protests of 15 February 2003 in London. But Perowne also holds a set of views about literature, which take place plausibly within the realistic frame of the novel – isn't this what a man like this, at a moment like this, would think about the novel? – and at the same time open the abyss of self-reference as they bring that realistic frame into view. He finds the magical realism that his daughter Daisy has made him read childish; he marginally prefers fiction that represents a recognisable physical reality, but finds it workmanlike in its accumulation of detail; perhaps most significantly, he regards the efforts of the novel to explore, convey and represent consciousness as insufficient, a kind of dereliction of duty, compared to the quotidian engagement with the materiality of the mind in his own work as a neurosurgeon. We can see clearly here the different levels of complexity involved between a novel's representation of political opinions and beliefs and a novel's representation of ideas about the nature of fiction. While both can be read as realistic representations of what a character thinks, the latter set of issues form the basis of a performative contradiction between the level of character and the ontological frame for the existence of that character: whatever Perowne thinks about the insufficiencies of the novel for the representation of consciousness, his own consciousness is, at another level, an instance of the phenomenon he regards as insufficient. The performance of the novel above the level of character is, therefore, to ensure that his views on fiction entail their own objection.

This is, by virtue of its realistic frame, a relatively straightforward example of the aporetic possibilities of self-commentary in the novel. Aporia is contained in *Saturday* to an ironic undercurrent that never quite steps forward to demolish the referential illusion of its storyworld. No author steps impossibly into the fictional universe, and Perowne's fictionality is not openly declared from some ontological upstairs. Nevertheless, the inclusion of views on literature in the range of represented opinion and belief provides a basis for viewing the novel as a self-referential statement, bringing with it a smattering of the logical mayhem that seems to accompany self-referential statements in general. We can easily see the effect scaled up in a novel such as J.M. Coetzee's *Elizabeth Costello* (2004), which, in addition to representing a wide range of opinion and belief on vegetarianism, animals, the problem of evil, the nature of love and death, also takes the question of belief in literature, the role of the novelist and the relationship between novels and the opinions of novelists as its central topic. The central device for this dramatisation of ideas, about the world and about the novel, is the figure of the surrogate author – some figure within the fictional world who stands for the author – which in this instance is the most literal kind of surrogate author possible: the protagonist as novelist. A novel about a novelist has a more direct way of addressing questions about authorial belief than one about a neurosurgeon who has read the odd novel, and this one is particularly direct:

> Realism has never been comfortable with ideas. It could not be otherwise: realism is premised on the idea that ideas have no autonomous existence, can exist only in things. So when it needs to debate ideas, as here, realism is driven to invent situations – walks in the countryside,

> conversations – in which characters give voice to contending ideas and
> thereby in a certain sense embody them. The notion of *embodying* turns
> out to be pivotal. In such debates ideas do not and indeed cannot float free:
> they are tied to the speakers by whom they are enounced, and generated
> from the matrix of individual interests out of which their speakers act in
> the world – for instance, the son's concern that his mother not be treated as
> a Mickey Mouse post-colonial writer, or Wheatley's concern not to seem an
> old-fashioned absolutist.   (*EC*, 2004, p. 9)

This is, to recall Elizabeth Dipple's phrase, non-novelistic thinking, the
kind of writing we would expect to find in a work of criticism and not a
novel; but when a novel is about a novelist, when it is set in a series of situations in which the techniques, the intentions and the ethics of novels are
discussed with the novelist, such discourse becomes the stuff of the novel.
In itself, this does not create a different problem from the one discussed
in McEwan's novel above, which also contains discussions of realism that
function as critical ideas as well as self-commentary; but there is a different question here that McEwan's novel never generates: the question
of 'who speaks?'. The passage is 'about' the question of who speaks, in
the sense that it addresses directly, at a discursive level, the question of
embodiment, of the attribution of ideas to characters and of the artificial creation of situations for the purposes of debating those ideas, but it
is also an instance of that question, because we do not know for sure to
whom we should attribute the thesis it advances. This is a paragraph that
occurs in the first few pages of the novel, in a scene in which Elizabeth
Costello, a 66-year-old novelist, has travelled to the fictional Altona College in Pennsylvania to receive a literary award. Her acceptance speech for
the award is titled 'What Is Realism?', and for this reason alone we might
assume that the paragraph cited above is written in a mode of focalisation. Anyone who has read *Disgrace* or any other Coetzee novel will know
him as a master of focalisation, of having a natural ability to slip into the
mind style of a character, and to indicate to the reader whose mind we
are inside. But that is not what is happening here. To the question 'Who
speaks?' we cannot answer Elizabeth Costello, despite the proximity of
the paragraph's content to the topic of her acceptance speech. Costello
is not present in the scene in which this paragraph occurs, which represents an encounter between her son John, who has accompanied her
to the event, and Gordon Wheatley, the chairman of the jury who have
conferred the award. The contention of the passage is that when a realistic novel wants to represent ideas, it must invent situations in which

characters can embody those ideas. The 'as here' of that third sentence apparently represents the scene itself in which John and Wheatley are discussing the basis for the jury's decision – ideas that have nothing to do with realism, and seem to rule out focalisation (perhaps through John's mind) as an explanation for the passage. There is a more obvious answer to the question 'who speaks?', one that draws to some extent on knowledge of the structure of voices already advanced in the first few pages of the novel, namely, that this is the voice of an authorial narrator providing commentary on the fictionality of events as they unfold. The assumption, which I will back up further in a moment, that this is the voice of a narrator intruding with opinions about the nature of realism helps to focus the performative contradiction of the passage. At one level, 'as here' refers us to the embodiment of ideas in the preceding exchange between John and Wheatley and to the necessary invention of a situation for the purpose of debating those ideas. At a secondary level, it also points out that a set of ideas about ideas in realism are being expressed by someone who is not embodied at all, whose ideas do in fact float free, and that the performance of the narration at this point therefore contradicts the explicit statement it advances.

My interest in this example is partly for its ability to represent something we think of as characteristically postmodern in the novel, either for the apparent intrusion of an author into the fiction or for the contradiction it offers between what a narrative says and what it does. I said above that the principal device for the dramatisation of ideas about the novel in *Elizabeth Costello* is the creation of a surrogate author, but it now seems that we have two internal authors, one who is a character and the other who is a narrator, both of whom are opinionated on the subject of realism. The authorial narrator, the one who is more than just a focaliser of Costello's mind, is prominent only in the first chapter of the novel, and might be regarded as the primary voice. It is certainly the voice that comes first, in the opening sentences of the novel, before we have met Costello:

> THERE IS FIRST of all the problem of the opening, namely, how to get us from where we are, which is, as yet, nowhere, to the far bank. It is a simple bridging problem, a problem of knocking together a bridge. People solve such problems every day. They solve them, and having solved them push on.
>
> Let us assume that, however it may have been done, it is done. Let us take it that the bridge is built and crossed, that we can put it out of our mind.

> We have left behind the territory in which we were. We are in the far
> territory, where we want to be.   (*EC*, 2004, p. 1)

The preliminary relocation in time and space required of novel readers,
conventionally achieved by deictic words and introductions, is conducted
here as self-commentary upon the problem of the opening. It asks us to
relocate to new territory in an entirely abstract way, to assume that it has
been done, without any of the work through which such an imaginative
leap is normally earned having yet been done. The voice is not the invisible, absent narrator of *Disgrace*, but rather someone who, from the outset,
highlights the problems and conventions of realism. Like the passage on
realism above, the opening of the novel is both constative and performative, meaning that it makes a statement about something and at the same
time it does something; it is about openings while at the same time being
an opening, and again there is some tension, if not contradiction, between
the two. Though it would seem that the act of opening cannot coincide
with the statement about openings, that the actual imaginative relocation
requires some specifics of time, place and character, I would argue that the
abstract, generic discussion of the bridge is highly effective as an instance
of beginning, and that the naming of the problem goes some way to being
the solution to the problem. When the third paragraph begins with the
more conventional introduction of the protagonist – 'Elizabeth Costello
is a writer, born in 1928, which makes her sixty-six years old, going on
sixty-seven' – there is a feeling of comic minimalism that continues from
the authorial narrator's exposure of the artifice and drudgery of openings.
The interest of the opening, in other words, derives from the co-presence
of two authors, one conjured by the other, where one occupies the realistic referential frame of the novel while the other exposes the artifice of
that frame. The co-presence of these voices is sustained throughout this
opening chapter, as a series of clunky adjustments establish the realistic mode of the narrative in full view of the reader. There is an intrusive
comment on narrative tense as the narrator adjusts to the experiential
present at the start of the fifth paragraph: 'In the spring of 1995 Elizabeth
Costello travelled, or travels (present tense henceforth), to Williamstown,
Pennsylvania, to Altona College, to receive the Stowe award' (*EC*, 2004,
p. 2). We hear the voice again as the narrator begins to observe the relation between what is narrated and the events that actually take place. 'We
skip', the narrator starts to say when he can't be bothered to narrate all
the events, or considers them unworthy of narration: 'There is a scene in
the restaurant, mainly dialogue, which we will skip' (*EC*, 2004, p. 7). The

narrator will even weigh up in front of us the necessity and the danger of skipping for the realistic illusion:

> The presentation scene itself we skip. It is not a good idea to interrupt the narrative too often, since storytelling works by lulling the reader or listener into a dreamlike state in which the time and space of the real world fade away, superseded by the time and space of the fiction. Breaking into the dream draws attention to the constructedness of the story, and plays havoc with the realist illusion. However, unless certain scenes are skipped over we will be here all afternoon. The skips are not part of the text, they are part of the performance. (*EC*, 2004, p. 16)

The intrusion is a commentary upon and an instance of intrusion, and here we can see some of the proleptic rhetorical effect of self-commentary. How are we to object to intrusion, on the grounds that it interrupts the realist illusion, when the intrusion is itself an articulation of that complaint? To object is to agree. Perhaps more importantly, if we do find ourselves being interpellated by the intrusion into the objection it advances, we might also find ourselves duped by the narrator into the illusion that there are real events, scenes and dialogues taking place that the narrator must decide to represent or not, since the idea of skipping seems to uphold the referentiality of the narrated sequence as much as it exposes its artificiality.

The creation of a surrogate author will normally suffice for the purposes of novelistic self-contemplation, but the effects are compounded here by the inclusion of an intrusive authorial narrator openly discussing and highlighting familiar critical questions – the question 'who speaks?', the referential illusion, the problem of realism, the question of opinion, statement and belief in the novel. The debates about authorship in the twentieth century make us wary of saying anything about the real author, or of confusing an authorial narrator with an actual author, let alone an authorial character like Costello with an external author. The presence of two authors here is a mechanism that asks us to contemplate the relationship between Coetzee and Costello, even if we insist, like good structuralists, that the authorial narrator cannot be identified as Coetzee. The idea that Coetzee is playing with exactly these formalist pieties about the unavailability of the external author, or the dangers of identifying narrators with authors, is easily corroborated by a glance at his recent output. In *Summertime* (2009), for example, a biographer is writing a book about a writer, recently deceased, called John Coetzee from interviews with former lovers, friends, acquaintances and colleagues. The fictional memoir, a mode that Coetzee also employed in his earlier works *Boyhood* and *Youth*, draws constantly on the combination of factual and invented representations in a way that is not categorically separable from his fictional productions. The relationship of Coetzee and Costello is an elaborate version of this dynamic, and Coetzee has made use of the persona of Costello outside of this novel on several occasions. The chapter that we are discussing, in fact, began life as a lecture, delivered in 1996 at Bennington College, Vermont, in which Coetzee presented a fiction in the persona of Costello on the subject 'What Is Realism?'. Coetzee did the same thing when he was invited to give the Tanner Lectures in Princeton in 1997, delivering under the title 'The Lives of Animals' a fiction about Costello visiting Appleton College to deliver the Gates lecture on the lives of animals, which became Chapters 3 and 4 of *Elizabeth Costello*. A reading of the acknowledgements at the end of the novel gives some indication of the extent to which Coetzee has made use of the critical and philosophical material of the novel in other contexts, raising the question, in person, of who speaks, or to whom we attribute these opinions and arguments. A reading of the epilogue of Derek Attridge's book on Coetzee (Attridge, 2004) will give a much fuller understanding of the confusion that took place in these performances between Coetzee's and Costello's personae, and a reading of Stephen Mulhall's *The Wounded Animal* (2009) will provide an in-depth analysis of the novel and its origins in relation to questions about fictional and philosophical statement. But even if we confine ourselves to the relationship within the novel, the question of authorship is extended far beyond the usual effects of the surrogate author. One of the obvious differences between these real life performances by Coetzee and the novel is that the speaker of a lecture is embodied: if nothing else, the difference of gender between John Coetzee and his fictional author Elizabeth Costello is plain for all to see. This gives to the notion of embodying, that crucial concept for realism's dealings with ideas, a kind of tension generated in the difference between speech and writing. I may not assume, for example, that the authorial narrator I have been discussing in the novel is male as readily as I would in a lecture, in the physical presence of the author. The relationship between John Coetzee and Elizabeth Costello is marked by gender difference in both cases, but more visible in speech than in writing. Like everything else about the exploration of internal and external authors, gender difference is openly reflected upon in the novel as part of the question of the autobiographical basis of Elizabeth Costello's fiction. Asked by an interviewer if, in her novel *Fire and Ice*, she finds it easy to write as a man, Costello answers, 'Easy? No. If it were easy it wouldn't be worth doing. It is the otherness that is the challenge. Making up someone other than yourself. Making up a world for him to move in' (*EC*, 2004, p. 12). If gender difference seems at first to distinguish between Coetzee and Costello, the authorial challenge of otherness also unites them in the reciprocity between a male author inventing a woman and a woman author inventing a man, and in this way, the reflections of the surrogate author function as self-commentary on behalf of the act of external authorship. As Costello answers the questions of interviewers, talks at dinner, debates on the radio or argues with her Kafkaesque gatekeeper about the nature of novelistic belief in the last chapter of the novel, she articulates many of the author's own self-justifications in the face of a set of critical responses that are still to come.

Elizabeth Costello is not just an author, one who happens to have some well-developed opinions on the subject of realism, and not only an author who holds many of the philosophical positions that we know Coetzee to have advanced outside of the novel. She is a metafictional author. The novel with which she made her name, *The House on Eccles Street*, is about Joyce's *Ulysses*, and it takes Marion Bloom as its protagonist. It is one of those postmodern rewritings (not unlike Coetzee's own *Foe* (1987) which rewrites Daniel Defoe's *Robinson Crusoe*) that allows a fictional character to migrate from one novel to another, as if they had some reality beyond the confines of their original representation. Like the fictional author, the fictional novel is a device for extending Coetzee's self-discussion and it becomes a means of warning against, or mocking in advance, certain kinds of critical response to the novel. When her first interviewer, for example, asks her what she is saying in *Eccles Street*, and if, because Marion Bloom refuses to have sex with her husband, she is saying 'that until men have worked out a new post-patriarchal identity, women should hold themselves apart', Costello terminates the interview. The kind of work that readers and critics do to extract from novels some kernel statement of belief, some social theory or political programme is consistently held up to ridicule. When the final chapter puts her on trial in its reworking of Kafka's parable of the doorkeeper, she protests that as a writer, it is not her profession to believe:

> *I am a writer, a trader in fictions ... I maintain beliefs only provisionally: fixed beliefs would stand in my way. I change beliefs as I change my habitation or my clothes, according to me needs. On these grounds – professional, vocational – I request exemption from a rule of which I now hear for the first*

> *time, namely that every petitioner at the gate should hold to one or more*
> *beliefs.*   (*EC*, 2004, p. 195; original italics)

If, according to the logic of analogy that I have been sketching, we regard this as self-commentary on Coetzee's part, we face another paradox: applied to itself, this statement becomes an act of absolution from the responsibility of belief, and the view of the writer's profession becomes, in turn, an imitation of belief about literature. Thought of as self-commentary, it both does and does not absolve Coetzee from responsibility for the view of the writer it advances, since agreement with it entails the view that the writer does not hold to the belief: it advances the statement about the fiction at the same time as it retracts it, under the alibi of mere imitation.

Metalepsis in *Slow Man*

There is nothing impossible about *Elizabeth Costello*. For all its responsibility-evading sophistry, its self-cancelling self-knowledge about the nature of fiction, it remains a realistic novel about an author. It is difficult, as a critic, to say anything about it that it doesn't seem to be saying about itself; as Hillis Miller said of *Ulysses*, everything we can say about it has already been anticipated by it, and we feel constrained to a kind of paraphrase, a repetition in slightly different words of its statement and its performance. This is the predicament that I set out to analyse in this chapter: the circle, the tautology, of postmodern narrative and postmodern narrative theory. There is, however, a significant difference between the idea of a novel as a statement and the idea of a novel as a performance, between what it says and what it does, that can be used to rescue the critic from this condition of redundancy, of saying again less elegantly what a novel has already said. This distinction between the constative and the performative, the saying and the doing, comes into view more clearly when we move to a novel that does impossible things.

The end of *Elizabeth Costello* is not the end of Elizabeth Costello, for she reappears in Coetzee's next novel *Slow Man* (2006), a narrative about a man who loses a leg in an accident. Like John Fowles's *The French Lieutenant's Woman*, this is a novel that spends 12 chapters establishing a realistic story only for an author to step into the thirteenth apparently to announce that this is all just fiction. But whereas Fowles's act of illusion-breaking is simply an authorial intervention, Elizabeth Costello turns up at the door of the novel's protagonist, Paul Rayment, and shakes him by the hand. This is clearly the same Costello, an Australian novelist, born in 1928, author of *The House on Eccles Street*, and now clearly wandering impossibly across some ontological boundary between the author and the character. On arrival, she reads to him the opening sentences of *Slow Man*, the novel we are reading, thus identifying her, impossibly, as the author of the novel she has arrived in. It is tempting, of course, to groan at this most hackneyed of postmodern clichés, but in Coetzee's hands, there is something worthwhile to be found among the logical impossibilities it begets. This is what Genette called metalepsis, by which he meant 'any intrusion by the diegetic narrator or narratee into the diegetic universe... or the inverse' (*SM*, 2006, pp. 234–5). It is, as I suggested in the Introduction, one of the definitive characteristics of postmodern fiction, and has to be distinguished from the surrogate author, who is merely an analogous, authorial figure within the diegetic universe, on the grounds that the fictional illusion itself is at stake:

> The concept of metalepsis, which Genette uses to describe crossovers between narrative levels, has gained wide currency owing to its popularity in much postmodern writing. Basically, metalepsis is a narrative technique in which ontological axioms, e.g. that authorial narrators live in a different world from that of their characters, are undermined with the result of destroying one's impression that the narrated world is real.   (Fludernik, 2009, p. 100)

According to this ontological axiom, the boundary between the world of the author and the world of the character cannot be crossed if that narrator is extra-diegetic, in the sense of being an undramatised, external viewpoint. The idea of an uncrossable ontological boundary between narrative levels works better for some kinds of narrative voice than others, and this is why Fludernik takes the authorial narrator as her example, since authorial narrators function on the basis that they occupy the same ontological ground as the real author, external to the fictional world depicted. The clearest cases are those where the authorial narrator is in possession of impossible knowledge, that is, the kind of knowledge that no human could have of another human that we normally associate with omniscience. A narrator who knows everything about a character, about their past and their future, and is capable of entering into that character's thoughts, is an impossible person, a convention that we accept in fiction that has no correlative in life, unless by comparison with God. A novel that allows interaction between an omniscient authorial narrator and a character about whom the narrator holds this kind of knowledge necessarily draws attention to the inherent artificiality of that convention, or to the impossibility that the convention asks us to accept.

There are two aspects of this account of metalepsis that I want to explore in relation to *Slow Man*. The first is the notion of the uncross-ability of the ontological boundary between the author and the character, and the other is the idea that, between these narrative levels, there exists a kind of hierarchy analogous to the relation of human beings to God. When Costello arrives at Paul Rayment's home in the thirteenth chapter, she sits and recites the following words from the opening of the novel:

> *The blow catches him from the right, sharp and surprising and painful, like a bolt of electricity, lifting him up off the bicycle.* Relax! *He tells himself as he tumbles through the air,* and so forth.   (*SM*, 2006, p. 81; original italics)

If we assume what we are being asked to assume here, that these words belong to Costello (how else would she know them?) and not to Coetzee, we have to accept a certain kind of logical doubleness. The inference we are asked to make, perhaps by the 'and so forth', is that if we keep reading we will continue through the text of Coetzee's *Slow Man* as we have just read it, and work our way forward to this very point, where Costello arrives at Rayment's house. The doubleness we encounter here is partly that Costello, from this point forward, is both the teller and the told, the subject and the object of narration. How then are we to under-stand the unfolding scene? Has it been written already by Costello? Will she write it in the future? It is, after all, impossible for her participa-tion in the scene and her writing of it to coincide. Like the narratological shipwreck we explored in Dr Jekyll in Chapter 6, some kind of tempo-ral or spatial distance between the teller and the told is necessary to save this situation from the self-consuming logic of self-reference. We might, as Fludernik suggests, simply decide that the fictional illusion is, at this point, destroyed by the metaleptic crossing, and throw the book on the fire. The case for doing so is, in some ways, contained in those first sentences of the novel. The narrative mode here is that of free indi-rect discourse, with the voice of the third-person narrator clearly located inside Rayment's head, fully capable of reporting and conveying the most minute movements of his interiority. If Costello wrote those sentences, she is, it would seem, entirely responsible for the invention of Rayment's inner life, for the texture of his thought through which we have become so intimate with him over the previous 12 chapters. As she recites this opening, registering his reaction to a discourse of which he could know nothing, she splits him in two, between the person whose inner life is her own invention and the person who might now be reacting to her words, or to the condition of his own being as her fiction, as if she were both in control of him and not. If illusion-breaking contradiction seems to rear its head in multiple ways here, there are also ways in which a reader's more persistent sense-making efforts are rewarded. If we look carefully at the opening lines of the novel, there is some reason to doubt Costello's authorship:

> THE BLOW CATCHES him from the right, sharp and surprising and painful, like a bolt of electricity, lifting him up off the bicycle. *Relax!* he tells himself as he flies through the air . . .   (*SM*, 2006, p. 1)

Trivial as it might seem, the fact is that the words Costello recites are not exactly the words that open the novel. In Costello's version in Chapter 13, the word 'flies' has become the word 'tumbles', indicating to us that the text we are reading and the one for which she is apparently claiming responsibility are not identical. If they are not identical, if there is some gap between the text we are reading and the one Costello supposedly wrote, the most acute crises of self-reference, the ones that would come about with the arrival of Costello in her own novel, are not logically necessary: the transposition of 'tumbles' to 'flies', as a marker of difference between the internal and the actual novel, opens up a range of possibilities that avert the novel's self-consumption when the subject and the object of narration coincide. The first is that this is not properly thought of as metaleptic crossing at all, and that the representation of Costello is no more problematic than it was in *Elizabeth Costello*: she is an authorial figure who happens to have written a novel with an opening very close to, but not identical with, that of the novel we are reading; the realistic illusion is not itself endangered, since Costello is not really our external author, and so metalepsis has not taken place. We might similarly view the text we are reading to be a subsequent draft of the one whose composition is represented here, in progress, so that the 'and so forth' of her citation does not signify the identity of the two texts, or lead inexorably into self-cancellation. Alternatively, we can regard the difference between 'tumbles' and 'flies' as a marker of the difference between Costello's narrative, which is internal to the fictional universe, and Coetzee's, which is external, and real. According to this reading metalepsis brings the narrative levels into view for the reader, and both the illogicality of the situation in which Costello is the author of her own fictional universe and the impossibility of her stepping out of it expose her claim to authorship of the novel as delusion. It seems then that our efforts to make sense of the idea of

Costello's authorship of Paul are pushed in one of two directions, one which aims to preserve the fictional illusion through metalepsis denial, the other which abandons the illusion to wallow in the new impossibility of a novel about the interaction of a novelist and her character. Like many postmodern novels, the project of *Slow Man* is to sustain both positions, one which advances the diegetic world as a possibility and the other which dismantles it as ontological impossibility.

If the boundary between the character and the author is ontologically uncrossable, dramatisations of its crossing are not only adventures in impossibility but are also scenarios for the exploration of ontological hierarchy. This is, in part, what is at stake in the meeting between Costello and Rayment, since the interaction between them seems to entail some kind of equalisation. From the moment of meeting, the idea that Costello and Rayment occupy incommensurate realms of being is discounted: Costello declares her motive for the visit as a wish to 'explore for myself what kind of a being you are' and to be sure 'that our two bodies would not just pass through each other' (*SM*, 2006, p. 81). The reciprocity of Rayment's interaction with Costello is encoded in a number of ways, including the ambiguity of her recurring phrase 'You came to me': 'In certain respects I am not in command of what comes to me. You came, along with the pallor and the stoop and the crutches and the flat that you hold on to so doggedly and the photograph collection and all the rest' (*SM*, 2006, p. 81). The ambiguity here is between a literal and a metaphorical interpretation of 'came to me'. On literal grounds, Rayment contests who came to who ('*I* came to *you*? *You* came to *me*') while Costello refutes his argument with an alternative meaning of the idiom – 'You came to me. That is all I can say. You occurred to me – a man with a bad leg and no future and an unsuitable passion' (*SM*, 2006, p. 85). Rayment's existence, the nature of his being, is suspended between these two meanings, between the reality of Costello's arrival and the possibility that he exists only in her imagination, and his development in the novel is a steady realisation of the latter. If absolute power seems to lie on the side of the author, or with the creative imagination, in this relationship, there is a reciprocal movement in the novel that seeks to elevate Rayment from the condition of a character to the condition of an author. In the public library, reading Costello's novels, Rayment has a Copernican moment of realisation that there is 'a second world that exists side by side with the first' and that his existence is a kind of afterlife: 'Is this what it is like to be translated to what at present he can only call *the other side*. Is that what has happened to him? Is that what happens to everyone?' (*SM*, 2006, p. 122). The theological implications of his condition of being created by someone standing over him are never far away and these become the subject of discussion with Costello who insists that the relationship is mutual:

> *He finds her by the riverside, sitting on a bench, clustered around by ducks that she seems to be feeding* – it may be simple, as an account, its simplicity may even beguile one, but it is not good enough. It does not bring me to life. Bringing me to life may not be important to you, but it has the drawback of not bringing you to life either.   (*SM*, 2006, p. 159; original italics)

Like a Beckettian pair, the ontological condition here is that of *esse est percipe* (to be is to be perceived), so that Rayment's awareness of his own metalepsis, his translation to the other side, is an act of authorship as much as of being authored – of bringing to life as well as being brought into existence. The italicised words here, which belong to the second sentence of this twentieth chapter, identify the focalised representation of Costello as an act of authorship by which Costello herself is conjured by Rayment, so that the act of bringing to life, or creation, is distributed mutually between the author and the character. The effect of ontological equalisation in the second half of the novel, of placing the author and the character on the same ontological plane, and in a position of mutual dependence, is supported by a strand of suggestion throughout the novel that Costello is no more the author than Rayment himself. As in *Elizabeth Costello*, the idea is easily corroborated by information from outside of the novel, but in this case it is information that seems to link Coetzee not with Costello but with Rayment (The two men are about the same age, there is a physical resemblance between them, they live in the same place, Coetzee is known as a keen cyclist, a man with an interest in photography, etc.). It is as if his project is to invert the hierarchy of narrative levels between the author and the character as we found it in *Elizabeth Costello*. If, in that novel, the surrogate author is confined entirely to the diegetic universe, while Coetzee remains in God-like control over that universe, in *Slow Man*, the ontological hierarchy is inverted to the extent that the author has become the character, subject to the life-giving creativity of the internal author-God. The inversion is codified in the anagram GOD-DOG, which underlies the exploration of dogs in *Disgrace*, is rejected as 'too literary' at the end of *Elizabeth Costello* and which Rayment comes across in Costello's notebook in *Slow Man*, and acts as a starting point for his ontological realisations. The issue of the hierarchy of narrative levels, which has been deployed in the earlier novels as part of a thematic concern with the power relations of animals to humans, and for the discussion of authorship in general, is inflected in more obviously ontological ways, as a result of the metalepsis of *Slow Man* by questions of care, of being-in-the-world-with-others, and the struggle between fate and freedom. Authorial control, in this framework, may stand in the place of God, but it is a power to be renounced in order to distribute the authorial function more evenly across the cast of characters, or actants in the diegetic universe.

Omniscient authorial narrators normally know everything about a character including what is to become of them, but this is not Costello's condition in *Slow Man*. It is part of the novel's levelling project to put her in a position equivalent to Rayment's in terms of her knowledge of the future. Rayment is a man without a future, a man whose future has been taken from him by the accident at the novel's opening, and Costello is as uncertain about what he should do now as he is. She is an author without Olympian height, who has fallen into human time, and this is part of the demotion that metaleptic crossing entails for her. Deprived in this way of the privileged teleological perspective, the knowledge of outcomes and endings and of conventional omniscience, she is lowered to the level of participation in a universe with an unforeseeable future. In this way, the novel's metalepsis and its levelling of the author and the character construct a direct link between the temporalities of writing and acting. We are asked to understand Costello's arrival in the novel as a kind of authorial crisis resulting from the condition of not knowing what is going to happen next, and in this respect she shares the authorial function with the character of Rayment. In fact the distribution of the authorial function can be cast wider than that, once the border of writing and acting is breached. Even Drago, a minor character, the son of the nurse that Rayment has fallen in love with, is drawn into this analogy between what a man like Rayment should do in a situation like this and what a novelist like Costello should do with a novel like this:

> Mr Rayment has an accident as a result of which he loses a leg. He engages a nurse to look after him, and in no time he has fallen in love with her. He has intimations that a miraculous, love-born reflorescence of his youth might be around the corner; he even dreams of engendering a son (yes, it is true, a little half-brother to you). But can he trust these intimations? Are they not perhaps a dotard's fantasies? So the question to ponder, given the situation as I have described it, is: What does My Rayment, or someone like Mr Rayment, do next?   (*SM*, 2006, p. 138)

In this succinct plot summary, Costello appeals to Drago, with his 'looks of an angel of God', in the position of an authorial helper, and at the same time as a reader of a moral scenario, from which to hypothesise about good action. She is to be disappointed, because Drago will not hypothesise, beyond the suggestion that Rayment and Costello should split up, but we know that the consequence of that action is 'like tramps in Beckett', a state of non-existence. Drago's role here is authorial and readerly, in the sense that he is asked to help Costello to invent the future, but he also articulates a response on behalf of the ordinary reader: a pragmatic response that fails to address the ontological conditions that have been produced by metalepsis. In the dialogue between Drago and Costello, we see again the workings of rhetorical prolepsis, namely, the anticipation and defeat of an objection between an external author and an external reader dramatised as dialogue between characters.

The predicament of the postmodern reader

In novels like *Elizabeth Costello* and *Slow Man*, there is a feeling that the critical responses of a reader have been appropriated in advance by the novels' own interests in themselves. There isn't much that I can say about these novels that they don't already say about themselves, and my role, as a critic, can feel like mere paraphrase or illustration of the novel's own critical self-analysis. But it has also been clear, in this discussion, that there is something logically chaotic or aporetic about a discourse that refers to itself, and always something in the performance of self-referential statements that exceeds the statement itself. We have come up against the idea of the performative contradiction repeatedly in this discussion, but here we can give the notion a precise description, through the idea that a discourse, an utterance or a statement is often doing more than it is saying, and particularly in cases where the statement includes itself in the set of things to which it refers. The proposition 'All generalisations are false', for example, leaves one's head in a spin because, as a generalisation, it entails its own falsity, but if it is false, it appears also to be true. Like the liar paradox discussed in Chapter 6, it is both a statement about something (generalisations) and an instance of that something, and in such cases, the 'more' that is performed on top of the surface statement is to render undecidable the truth value of the proposition advanced. But the presence of a truth claim (x is true, x is false) in the sentence is not necessary for the production of undecidability itself, as Bertrand Russell demonstrated with his famous paradox about sets. In Russell's paradox the chaos is not caused by the question of truth, but by the question of belonging, or self-inclusion: it is clear that some sets belong to themselves (such as the set of all sets), but what happens when we think about the set of all sets that do not belong to themselves? Is this set a member of itself? Because if it is not a member of itself, it satisfies the basic condition of membership, meaning that it is a member of itself, but on the other hand if it is, then it isn't. In this case, the aporia results from an extreme case of the doubleness of naming a set and belonging to it, and as a predicament, this is far more common that it might first appear. If I use the word 'language', or the word 'word', I find myself in this predicament, of, on the one hand, advancing a name of a set and, on the other, an instance or member of that set: these are sets that are members of themselves. These examples don't seem to present any particular problem, but they do indicate that, at metalingistic moments, language will always find itself in this predicament, of being a statement about language and also being an instance of language. From this predicament, we only need to add in any element of negation, of language being untrue, being incapable of communication, being fictional or not being language, for the contradiction of the kind that we find writ large in metafiction to appear.

There are two significant observations that can be drawn from this predicament, and which prevent us from regarding it as puerile paradox-mongering. The first is that postmodern fiction is a very complicated example of the basic predicament, demonstrating as it does the three key elements of aporetic self-reference: the question of truth, the problem of self-belonging and the predicament of metalinguistic statements. The second observation is that we don't have to travel to some obscure corner of set theory to encounter this predicament. Postmodern narrative fiction may offer some particularly complicated examples of aporia, but they are examples that take their place in a world of self-contemplation and self-commentary, not only because metalepsis is rife on television or in the gaming industry, but also because the same kind of aporia is visible in the most familiar, local and natural metalinguistic moments, like the word 'word'. Taken together, these two observations form a case for the idea that the critical reading of postmodern fiction is one of the most sophisticated engagements available to us with a predicament that has established itself in every corner of modern life – the rigorous end of our engagement with cultural self-referentiality of a more general kind. But there is another way of making the case that paradoxes and contradictions should not be dismissed as trivial, which runs through the work of Derrida, Lacan, Butler and Zizek, but which finds particularly clear expression in the work of Alain Badiou, namely, that these questions of self-reference somehow lie at the centre of ontology, or questions of being. Throughout the discussion of Coetzee I have used the word 'ontological' to refer to issues that arise between narrative levels or to what Fludernik called the 'ontological axioms' of fiction. In the analysis, many of the issues of including authors in fiction, or of authors participating in their own fictional creations, led us directly into questions of self-commentary and the logic of self-inclusion, for which Russell's paradox offers a kind of mathematical formula. But it is worth looking at the way that Badiou discusses this question in *Being and Event* (2006), in the context of our search for some kind of space for the reader from which to resist, or avoid the mere repetition of, the strategies of postmodern fiction. For Badiou, Russell's set of all sets which are not members of themselves, being both a member of itself and not a member of itself, 'annihilates the logical consistency of the language' and its consequence (a price that no logician would be willing to pay) is that 'all mathematics is abolished' (Badiou, 2006, p. 41). Badiou calls this situation, after Cantor, an 'inconsistent multiplicity': a consistent multiplicity is a logically coherent unity containing no such member (such as the set itself) that will disrupt the set, whereas an inconsistent multiplicity contains within it an element that leads to contradiction, paradox or the failure of the count-as-one. Most logicians, faced with the inconsistent multiplicity, have resorted to a metaphor that I too have been using in this discussion: the metaphor of too-large-ness of something inside, or an excess of a set over the formal and deductive resources of the language from which it was inferred: the inconsistent multiplicity is too large 'to be counted as a set in the same way as the others' (Badiou, 2006, p. 41). Badiou points out that there is something onto-theological, that is, concerned with being and concerned with God, about the way Cantor discusses inconsistency because there 'where the count-as-one fails, stands God'. The inconsistent multiplicity, where we get those giddy feelings of illogicality, where our logical language leads us into contradiction, is a point where mathematics makes contact with a supreme infinite being or absolute being, where the simple being of a set, or the count-as-one, breaks down. This can seem an extravagant leap, from the breakdown of logical consistency to onto-theological questions, but it is, in a sense, an internal feature of ontological and theological thinking that logic fails as we attempt to think of the largest beings or unities. If we think of Anselm's formulation of the ontological argument for the existence of God (*id quo nihil maius cogitari posit*: that than which nothing greater can be thought), set theory's issues of scale and narrative theory's issues of ontological level are both visible.

It is worth noting that the argument that we have just sketched in Badiou's account of Cantor is very like the reading of Coetzee we have just proceeded through, to the extent that it moves from questions of the internal embedding of set within set, to the logical inconsistency of set theory resulting from self-referential sets and their contradictions, to onto-theological questions about being, just as we moved from questions of narrative level, to the breakdown of narrative levels into contradiction, and so to the onto-theological implications of authorial metalepsis. It is also worth noting that the authorial intervention from which our reading began, about the nature of realism and its discomfort with ideas, followed immediately from a conversation between Costello's son John and Gordon Wheatley:

> 'Without infinity we would have no mathematics' says Wheatley. 'But that doesn't mean that infinity exists. Infinity is just a construct, a human construct. Of course we are firm that Elizabeth Costello is the best. We just have to be clear in our minds what a statement like that means, in the context of our times.'   (*SM*, 2006, p. 8)

Wheatley seems to mean here that the foundations of mathematics are no more solid than the basis of literary value judgements, but to John, the analogy makes no sense, and he hopes Wheatley does not 'write as badly as he thinks'. Perhaps a stronger analogy pertains between the concept of infinity in set theory and the manipulations of narrative level that bring questions of authorship into contact with the onto-theological concepts when logical consistency breaks down. We might say then that the concept of infinity is working in two distinct ways in this example. It is an explicit topic of conversation, rather associatively linked to literary value by Wheatley as he makes a point about the foundations of mathematics, the objection to which is then articulated in John's thoughts. Infinity at this level is addressed as a topic, in the mode of a statement or argument attributable to a particular character. But it is also part of the performance of the text as a whole insofar as it emerges from the metacommentary on authorship that runs through the novel and that follows a similar course into logical inconsistency as Badiou's discussion of set theory. The mention of infinity at the level of content, in conversation between characters, seems trivial, and might pass unnoticed, unless its inclusion in the discussion points implicitly to something larger than itself, in the novel's performance, about the logic of narrative levels. In fact the concept of infinity occupies Badiou's attention for a considerable proportion of *Being and Event*, as he traces the idea from the infinite God of medieval

Christianity into modern mathematics, so that we might think there is some uncanny anticipation of, or even knowing connection between, the novel itself and the interests in mathematical ontology into which this reading has strayed. In this knot of the statement and the performance of the literary text, the argument of a philosophical work about the ontological dimensions of set theory and use I am making of that in my reading, we find ourselves facing the kind of circle identified at the start of this chapter. For it is not only the metacommentary, the critical reading, of the novels that is being addressed or appropriated by the novels in advance here, but also a body of philosophical argument understood here to be in some way performed by the novels at hand. If Badiou's discussion of Russell's paradox is in some way helpful for a reading of Coetzee, it has to be helpful beyond the level of explicating the novels' statements, or content, and has to operate with a logical connection stronger than the one that opens this paragraph – the relation of 'being very like' – which characterises the weak circle between fiction and theory, and the associative logic of much writing about postmodern narrative. The stronger logical connection comes from the idea that Badiou's discussion provides a kind of algebra for an understanding of self-reference and its relation to ontology. This is, in fact, much stronger than the conventional way of linking narrative form with ontology in narrative theory, which finds in the concept of metalepsis an ontological dimension entailed in the impossibility of crossing between real and fictional universes. It is not only in the construction of a chain of being, a hierarchy of universes embedded inside the real site of communication between an external author and an external reader, that ontology comes into play in fiction. The boundaries between reality and fiction, and the impossibility of crossing them, can seem ontologically trivial in comparison with the questions of being that inhere in inconsistent multiples. If we return for a moment to Badiou's account of Cantor, we find that the notion of impossibility is not some catastrophic meltdown for mathematical ontology, but rather a kind of doorway into its modern epoch:

> ... one could also argue that Cantor, in a brilliant anticipation, saw that the absolute point of being of the multiple is not its consistency ... but its inconsistency, a multiple-deployment that no unity gathers together.
>
> Cantor's thought thus wavers between onto-theology – for which the absolute is thought as a supreme infinite being ... and mathematical ontology, in which consistency provides a theory of inconsistency, in that what proves an obstacle to it (paradoxical multiplicity) is its point of

impossibility, and thus, quite simply, *is not*. Consequently it fixes a point of non-being from whence it can be established that there is a presentation of being.   (Badiou, 2006, p. 42; original italics)

In the terms of modern set theory that Badiou goes on to discuss, the point of impossibility is a kind of foundation for thinking about being, and not, as it first seemed, a point at which we declare the failure of logic, or the self-cancelling excess of paradoxical performances, in the way that much postmodern thinking is inclined to do. What we have been thinking of as self-cancelling excess, as the too-large interior space, or the contradictory performance that supplements the statement is no more a catastrophic ending for the novel than its original conditions of possibility. And that, in turn, is an over-complex way of saying that contradictions are inherent in fiction, whether novels point them out for themselves or not.

The portentous conclusion that offers itself here is that metaleptic fictions enact, according to the algebra of self-referential sets, allegories of the impossible foundations of being. In fact I am almost equally drawn to the comment of an Amazon.com reviewer who finds *Slow Man* unsatisfying and irritating: 'How could a stranger just move into his apartment and know all about him?' Between these two poles, and these two attitudes to illusion-breaking, lies an answer to the question from which we departed in this chapter, of what a critic or reader should do when faced with a postmodern narrative that seems to know it all about postmodern theory. We find, in the metacommentary of *Elizabeth Costello* and *Slow Man*, a comprehensive discussion of critical topics that relate to the dramatisations they present, discussions that are both internal to and commentaries upon the storyworlds they present. If the metalepsis of *Slow Man* seems to add a further layer to the discussion of fictional authors in *Elizabeth Costello*, something that happens at the level of performance rather than statement, there always remains a layer, or a further dimension, which cannot be fully appropriated by the self-conscious discourse itself, namely, the reaction of a given reader to that self-consciousness. *Slow Man* can add something performative to the explicit discussions and lesser performative contradictions of *Elizabeth Costello*, but it can never fully reflect on these additional reflections, or develop metacommentary on metacommentary without collapsing into nothing. There must always be a response, which cannot coincide with the thing responded to, and the range and nature of such responses cannot be appropriated or controlled. Gerald Prince formulates this succinctly in his discussion of metanarrative signs: 'if reading a narrative means adding to it a metanarrative commentary, not only do they [metanarrative signs] indicate what such a commentary may consist in and how it may intervene but they help to specify the distance between a text's own metacommentary and the metacommentary of a given reader' (Prince, 1982, p. 128). The possibility of this distance, between internal self-knowledge and external response to that self-knowledge, or between anticipated and actual response, inhabits any structure of discursive self-criticism. The two poles or attitudes above illustrate this, one of which seeks to articulate, and move on from, a logic that underlies the issues of self-belonging and self-inclusion, while the other rejects the nonsense of metalepsis. They are both forms of resistance to postmodernism. They are indifferent, at different levels of sophistication, to the apocalyptic melodrama of contradiction, and remind us that any effort to appropriate the response to narrative by narrative's self-knowledge, or to preclude resistance by anticipating its objections, will only modify that response and that resistance.

Annotated Bibliography

Barthes, Roland. *Image Music Text*. Ed. and Trans. S. Heath. London: Fontana, 1977.

Including Barthes's 'Introduction to the Structural Analysis of Narratives', an excellent statement of the case for the linguistic model in literary studies and the 'deductive' relationship between critical method and practice, this is a collection which also illustrates the application of semiotic analysis to non-literary narratives, particularly in photography. The collection also marks an interesting contrast between the structuralist Barthes and the poststructuralist phase in which he wrote 'Theory of the Text' (below).

Barthes, Roland. 'Theory of the Text'. *Untying the Text: A Post-structuralist Reader*. Ed. R. Young. London: Routledge and Kegan Paul, 1981.

The case against the deductive approach to narrative analysis as represented in his 'Introduction to the Structural Analysis of Narratives', and particularly good on the conception of critical writing as creative production. Though slightly over-dramatised, the essay is at its most interesting when it comes closest to the declaration that criticism has come to an end as a result of the collapsing distinction between criticism and theory. It therefore relates particularly well to the argument in Chapter 3 of this book.

Bird, J. et al. eds. *Mapping the Futures: Local Culture, Global Change*. London and New York: Routledge, 1993.

A stunning collection of cultural critical essays, most of which take David Harvey's *The Condition of Postmodernity* as a starting point. Ranging from theoretical generality to specific analyses of the politics of London's Docklands, the modern home and the shopping mall, these essays orbit around the topic of globalisation and its relationship to localities and regions: Mike Featherstone's essay 'Global and Local Cultures' provides a helpful theoretical background to Chapter 5 of this book. The collection represents the interdisciplinary diversification of narrative theory into political and economic issues, and the reciprocal influence of perspectives in cultural geography in the discussion of cultural forms.

Booth, Wayne. *The Rhetoric of Fiction*. Chicago: University of Chicago Press, 1961.

A classic of narrative criticism which represents the tendencies in New Critical analysis of prose towards formal approaches to questions of character and reference. Particularly good on the production of sympathy in fictional narrative and the aesthetic effects of unreliable narration, it makes a useful companion to Chapters 1 and 6 above. Also an excellent example of the value placed by formalist criticism on the objectivity of a metalanguage and the importance of aesthetic distance in the description of narrative technique.

Brooks, Peter. *Reading for the Plot: Design and Intention in Narrative*. New York: Vintage, 1985.

A very stimulating discussion of narrative theory and the need to move beyond formalism. Illustrative of the impact of psychoanalysis, particularly as it relates to the traditional notion of authorial intention. Excellent on plot as an organising principle for narrative, and including the reading of Conrad's *Heart of Darkness* referred to in Chapter 7 of this book.

Cohan, Steven, and Shires, Linda. *Telling Stories: A Theoretical Analysis of Narrative Fiction*. London and New York: Routledge, 1988.

An excellent discussion of new emphases on ideology and subjectivity in narrative criticism, which pursues examples from literature alongside narratives elsewhere in culture, such as television advertising. Makes an interesting contrast with the earlier title in the New Accents series, *Narrative Fiction* by Rimmon-Kenan (below), as illustration of the transition from formalist to political narratology. Attests to the general tendency in recent narrative theory to apply psychoanalytic theory as a political strategy.

Culler, Jonathan. *Structuralist Poetics: Structuralism, Linguistics and the Study of Literature*. London: Routledge and Kegan Paul, 1975.

The most comprehensive survey of the impact of structuralist thinking on literary studies including some of the movements 'beyond' structural analysis. Particularly clear on the work of Jakobson and Greimas and their place in the evolution of structuralism towards a poetics of the novel and a general semiotic science.

Currie, Mark ed. *Metafiction*. London and New York: Longman, 1995.

Though I say it myself, a very good collection of writings on the subject of self-consciousness in fiction and in criticism. The volume focuses on the breakdown of the border between criticism and fiction as part of the crisis in metalingual objectivity. It includes an introduction which charts the evolution of literary self-consciousness alongside issues in literary theory, particularly in the relationship between historiographic self-consciousness and the return to historical perspective in the new historical criticisms of the 1980s.

Currie, Mark. *About Time: Narrative, Fiction and the Philosophy of Time.* Edinburgh: Edinburgh University Press, 2007.

This book pursues the enquiry into time, especially issues of archive fever, supplementarity and narratological prolepsis from theoretical contexts into fictional examples. Good further reading for Chapter 5 above.

de Man, Paul. *Allegories of Reading: Figural Language in Rousseau, Nietzsche, Rilke and Proust.* New Haven: Yale University Press, 1979.

Slightly bossy, very complex and logically slippery, but a fascinating discussion of 'figural' language in literature and the way that it often yields knowledge of the difficulty (de Man says 'impossibility') of pinning language down with linguistic terminology. Part of the entertainment is trying to follow arguments that don't always seem to support the outrageous claims to which they lead about the collapse of referential meaning, and trying to connect the texts as we know them with the ones that de Man represents. Nevertheless, a stunning display of deconstruction as allegorical interpretation and a seminal text for narratology, particularly the chapter on Proust.

Dipple, Elizabeth. *The Unresolvable Plot: Reading Contemporary Fiction.* London and New York: Routledge, 1988.

A rich resource for any student of metafiction with studies of writers such as Borges, Calvino and Beckett. An excellent last chapter on the problems involved when a theorist writes a novel with reference to Eco's *The Name of the Rose.* Dipple's premise is that a work of fiction can achieve more than a work of theory: that Eco's novel has didactic power and has achieved insights which could not be conveyed in his theoretical writing. This chapter in particular is recommended as further reading to the themes of Chapter 3 in this book.

Eagleton, Terry. *Literary Theory: An Introduction.* Oxford: Blackwell, 1983.

Undoubtedly one of the turning points in literary theory despite doing little justice to some of the thoughts it represents, this is a thorough survey of the critical ideas which predominated before the resurgence of interest in history and politics. Very entertaining and instructive on the subjects of poststructuralism and psychoanalysis in literary theory.

Fludernik, Monica. *Towards a "Natural" Narratology*. London and New York: Routledge, 1996.

One of the most stimulating contributions to the development of narratology in its cognitive phase, offering a comprehensive survey of all aspects of contemporary narrative theory.

Fludernik, Monica. *An Introduction to Narratology*. London and New York: Routledge, 2009.

An excellent introduction to narratology for students, with an accessible summary of developments from structuralism to the present, and a helpful focus on the importance of narratology for the study of literature.

Harland, Richard. *Superstructuralism: The Philosophy of Structuralism and Poststructuralism*. London and New York: Methuen, 1987.

One of the most lucid discussions available of philosophical aspects of poststructuralism. I would say the best possible starting point for anyone attempting to come to terms with Derrida or Foucault, and a useful though (even) less detailed introduction to other thinkers such as Baudrillard and Deleuze. One of the many virtues of this book is the all-encompassing idea of 'superstructuralism' which links formal to political and ideological themes.

Harvey, David. *The Condition of Postmodernity*. Oxford: Blackwell, 1989.

Essential reading for the student of postmodern culture, especially those with an interest in the economic and political aspects of the age. Good further reading for Chapter 5 of this book, and an essential preamble for Bird et al. (eds.), *Mapping the Futures* (above).

Heise, Ursula. *Chronoschisms: Time, Narrative and Postmodernism*. Cambridge: Cambridge University Press, 1997.

A study of time and narrative in the postmodern novel, with an extremely useful introduction sketching changes in the experience of time in the contemporary context and their relevance for narrative form. An excellent follow-up for the themes of time and postmodernism discussed in Chapter 5.

Herman, David. *Story Logic: Problems and Possibilities of Narrative*. Lincoln: University of Nebraska Press, 2002.

A deep, scholarly account of the state of narrative theory, and a rich resource of material drawn from disparate traditions of linguistics, philosophy and the cognitive sciences. The book makes the distinct contribution of the notion of *storyworld* to cognitive narratology, as discussed in the Introduction. Excellent chapters on temporality in narrative, and a thorough account of the relation of the new cognitive narratologies to the classical, structuralist phase.

Herman, David. *Basic Elements of Narrative*. Oxford: Wiley-Blackwell, 2009.

An attempt to identify the basic elements of narrative as it occurs across a broad range of media, including film and the graphic novel. The most significant recent contribution to a broad socio-narratology, providing excellent substance and definition to claims for the ubiquity of narrative in the contemporary world. The book offers a clear account of the idea of a classical and a postclassical phase in narratology.

Holub, Robert. *Reception Theory: A Critical Introduction*. London: Methuen, 1984.

Reception Theory and Reader Response Theory have not been explicitly addressed in this book, though many of their perspectives have been incorporated. This guide is a useful introduction to the central emphases and to the work of Hans Robert Jauss, Wolfgang Iser and others who sought to explain the reading process from the point of view of the reader's active construction of the text.

Hutcheon, Linda. *A Poetics of Postmodernism: History, Theory, Fiction*. New York and London: Routledge, 1988.

A book that is mainly influential for having defined postmodernism in fiction through the concept of the historiographic metafiction. Whereas 'radical metafiction' is modernist for Hutcheon, the historiographic metafiction establishes the specifically postmodern interest in the relationship between literature and history. A rich and complex discussion with a very impressive range of literary reference.

Jameson, Fredric. *The Political Unconscious: Narrative as a Socially Symbolic Act.* London: Methuen, 1980.

An extremely persuasive argument that politics is the ultimate horizon for literature and criticism, and an early example of the new wave of critics who draw on psychoanalytic theory for political purposes. Though less glib than Eagleton's *Literary Theory,* there is a similar sense of impatience with the American critical obsession with language and form.

Jordan, Elaine ed. *Joseph Conrad. New Casebooks Series.* London: Macmillan, 1996.

A collection of readings of Conrad, including *Heart of Darkness,* which includes those by Ian Watt, Peter Brooks, Nina Pelikan Straus and Christopher Miller discussed in Chapter 7. The volume also has a good introduction which places Conrad studies in relation to developments in criticism.

King, Anthony ed. *Culture, Globalization and the World System*. London: Macmillan, 1991.

A collection of papers from a conference in 1989 dealing with globalisation. A good starting point for those in search of a babble-free discussion, and one of the first examples of the importance of cultural geography in postmodern theory. The essays have a sociological character and are particularly focused on questions of personal and collective identity. Stuart Hall's essays on new cosmopolitan identities are useful companions to my discussion in Chapter 5 on the importance of storytelling in the construction of identity.

Leech, Geoffrey, and Short, Michael. *Style in Fiction: A Linguistic Guide to English Fictional Prose*. London and New York: Longman, 1981.

An excellent summary of linguistic approaches to literary style and an indispensable guide to the close reading of prose. This is a text that reflects the Anglo-American tradition of literary linguistics before the influence of structuralism and semiotics, and seems systematic in its exclusion of those developments. Particularly good on forms of fictional focalisation and on the representation of speech and thought in the novel. Anyone interested in pursuing the issue of speech and thought representation can find an excellent essay in *Narrative in Culture* (ed. Nash, below) by Christine Brooke-Rose.

Lodge, David. *After Bakhtin: Essays on Fiction and Criticism*. London and New York: Routledge, 1990.

Some very entertaining material including a discussion of Imre Salusinski's volume of interviews *Criticism in Society* and an excellent first chapter, 'The Novel Now', which focuses on the reciprocal influence between fiction and criticism. To close the gap between what Lodge calls 'humanist' and 'poststructuralist' accounts of fictional meaning he turns to the work of Bakhtin, whose view of the novel as a composite of various discourses leads him into a third 'ideological' view of the novel as a form of political resistance.

Lyotard, Jean-Francois. *The Differend: Phrases in Dispute*. Trans. G. Van den Abbeele. Manchester: Manchester University Press, 1988.

Sometimes laughably vague, but a good text on which to base an investigation into Lyotard's attitude to narratives and to their political and ideological function in the world. The text is fragmented into numbered paragraphs, which makes it rather unlinear, but this is clearly part of the point.

Nash, Christopher ed. *Narrative in Culture: The Uses of Storytelling in the Sciences, Philosophy and Literature.* London and New York: Routledge, 1990.

The diversification of interest in narrative to areas such as economics, psychoanalysis, the law and the sciences is represented here rigorously. Originating in a Warwick University conference, this volume represents a significant shift for narratology out of departments of English.

Onega, Susana ed., *Narratology.* London and New York: Longman, 1997.

A collection of essays representing the evolution of narratology from its formalist and structuralist phases into more recent approaches, though the emphasis on political criticism is very soft.

Prince, Gerald. *Narratology.* Berlin, New York and Amsterdam: Mouton, 1982.

Another systematic narratological handbook, largely based on the work of Roman Jakobson, though also with reference to Booth, Genette and Todorov. Includes a dry but extremely accurate discussion of the 'metanarrative sign' and the way in which it assimilates critical perspective into the fiction.

Readings, Bill. *Introducing Lyotard: Art and Politics.* London and New York: Routledge, 1991.

Sometimes dense, but never dull, Readings gives a very Lyotardian account of Lyotard with particular reference to the importance of narrative and narratology to the thinking behind the concept of postmodernism. He always remains within the orbit of the political responsibility of the critic or the narratologist.

Rimmon-Kenan, Shlomith. *Narrative Fiction: Contemporary Poetics.* London and New York: Methuen/Routledge, 1983.

The textbook of narratology before politicisation, and a valuable companion to Leech and Short (above) as it includes perspectives that they exclude. Very clear on focalisation in narrative, though rather muddied on the theme of narrative time.

Ronen, Ruth. *Possible Worlds in Literary Theory.* Cambridge: Cambridge University Press, 1994.

The best place to go for an account of the importance of possible worlds semantics and philosophy for literary studies. The introduction and first chapter give an excellent overview, and are particularly good on the manner in which possible worlds theory addresses questions of reference in narrative of the kind discussed here in Chapter 2.

Said, Edward. *Culture and Imperialism* (1993). London: Vintage, 1994.

Theoretically thin but impressive in its range of reference. An example of the post-colonial school of criticism and its attempts to move beyond social class within nations as explanations of the political unconscious of narrative.

White, Hayden. *Metahistory: The Historical Imagination in Nineteenth Century Europe.* Baltimore: Johns Hopkins University Press, 1978.

The best place to look for the structuralist approach to historical discourse, an approach which emphasises its textuality and therefore led into many of the poststructuralist attitudes to history discussed in Chapters 3 and 4 here and the New Historicist emphasis on the discursivity of history.

Bibliography

Adorno, Theodor. *Negative Dialectics*. Trans. E. Ashton. London: Routledge and Kegan Paul, 1973.

Adorno, Theodor. *Aesthetic Theory*. Trans. C. Lenhardt. London: Routledge, 1984.

Althusser, Louis, *Lenin and Philosophy*. Trans. B. Brewster. London: New Left Books, 1977.

Althusser, Louis, and Balibar, Etienne. *Reading Capital*. Trans. B. Brewster. London: New Left Books, 1975.

Attridge, Derek, and Ferrer, Daniel. *Post-structuralist Joyce: Essays from the French*. Cambridge: Cambridge University Press, 1984.

Attridge, Derek. *J.M. Coetzee and the Ethics of Reading*. Chicago: Chicago University Press, 2004.

Attridge, Derek, et al., eds. *Post-structuralism and the Question of History*. Cambridge: Cambridge University Press, 1987.

Badiou, Alain. *Being and Event*. Trans. Oliver Feltham. London and New York: Continuum, 2006.

Bakhtin, Mikhail. *Marxism and the Philosophy of Language*. Trans. L. Matejka and I. Titunik. New York: Seminar Press, 1973.

Bakhtin, Mikhail. *The Dialogic Imagination*. Trans. C. Emerson. Austin: Texas University Press, 1981.

Bal, Mieke. *Narratology: Introduction to the Theory of Narrative*. Trans. van Boheemen. Toronto: Toronto University Press, 1985.

Barthes, Roland. *Image Music Text*. Ed. and Trans. S. Heath. London: Fontana, 1977.

Barthes, Roland. 'Theory of the Text'. *Untying the Text: A Post-structuralist Reader*. Ed. R. Young. London: Routledge and Kegan Paul, 1981, 31–47.

Baudrillard, Jean. *Simulations*. Trans. Foss et al. New York: Semiotext(e), 1983.

Baudrillard, Jean. *America*. Trans. C. Turner. London: Verso, 1988.

Benveniste, Emile. *Problems in General Linguistics*. Trans. M. Meek. Coral Gables: University of Miami Press, 1971.

Bhabha, H., ed. *Nation and Narration*. London and New York: Routledge, 1989.

Bird, J., et al., eds. *Mapping the Futures: Local Culture, Global Change*. London and New York: Routledge, 1993.

Booth, Wayne. *The Rhetoric of Fiction*. Chicago: University of Chicago Press, 1961.

Brooks, Peter. *Reading for the Plot: Design and Intention in Narrative*. New York: Vintage, 1985.

Brooker, Peter, ed. *Modernism/Postmodernism*. London and New York: Longman, 1992.

Coetzee, J.M. *Foe*. Harmondsworth: Penguin, 1987.

Coetzee, J.M. *Disgrace*. London: Vintage, 2000.

Coetzee, J.M. *Elizabeth Costello: Eight Lessons*. London: Vintage, 2004.

Coetzee, J.M. *Slow Man*. London: Vintage, 2006.

Coetzee, J.M. *Summertime*. London: Harvill Secker, 2009.

Cohan, Steven, and Shires, Linda, *Telling Stories: A Theoretical Analysis of Narrative Fiction*. London and New York: Routledge, 1988.

Connor, Steven. *Postmodernist Culture: An Introduction to Theories of the Contemporary*. Oxford: Blackwell, 1989.

Conrad, J. *Heart of Darkness* (1902), London: Penguin, 1983.

Coward, Rosalind, and Ellis, John. *Language and Materialism*. London: Routledge and Kegan Paul, 1977.

Culler, Jonathan. *Structuralist Poetics: Structuralism, Linguistics and the Study of Literature*. London: Routledge and Kegan Paul, 1975.

Culler, Jonathan. *On Deconstruction: Theory and Criticism after Structuralism*. London: Routledge and Kegan Paul, 1983.

Culler, Jonathan. *Framing the Sign*. Oxford: Blackwell, 1988.

Currie, Mark, ed. *Metafiction*. London and New York: Longman, 1995.

Currie, Mark. *Difference*. London and New York: Routledge, 2004.

Currie, Mark. *About Time: Narrative, Fiction and the Philosophy of Time*. Edinburgh: Edinburgh University Press, 2007.

de Lauretis, Theresa. *Alice Doesn't: Feminism, Semiotics Cinema*. London: Macmillan, 1984.

de Lauretis, Theresa. 'Gaudy Rose: Eco and Narcissism'. *Substance* 47 (1985): 13–29.

Deleuze, Gilles, and Guattari, Felix. *Anti-Oedipus: Capitalism and Schizophrenia*. Trans. R. Hurley et al. New York: Viking Press, 1977.

de Man, Paul. *Allegories of Reading: Figural Language in Rousseau, Nietzsche, Rilke and Proust*. New Haven: Yale University Press, 1979.

de Man, Paul. *Blindness and Insight: Essays in the Rhetoric of Contemporary Criticism,* second edition. London: Methuen, 1983.

de Man, Paul. *The Resistance to Theory.* Manchester: Manchester University Press, 1986.

Derrida, Jacques. *Speech and Phenomena and Other Essays on Husserl's Theory of Signs*. Trans. D. Allison. Evanston: Northwestern University Press, 1973.

Derrida, Jacques. *Of Grammatology*. Trans. G. Spivak. Baltimore: Johns Hopkins University Press, 1976.

Derrida, Jacques. 'Signature, Event, Context'. *Glyph* 1 (1977): 172–97.

Derrida, Jacques. *Writing and Difference.* Trans A. Bass. Chicago: University of Chicago Press, 1978.

Derrida, Jacques. *Positions.* Trans. A. Bass. London: Athlone, 1981.

Derrida, Jacques. *Mémoires, for Paul de Man.* New York: Columbia University Press, 1986.

Derrida, Jacques. 'Psyche: Inventions of the Other'. *Reading de Man Reading.* Ed. L. Waters and W. Godzich. Minneapolis: University of Minnesota Press, 1989.

Derrida, Jacques. 'Ulysses Gramophone: Hear Say Yes in Joyce'. *Acts of Literature.* Ed. D. Attridge. New York and London: Routledge, 1992, 253–310.

Derrida, J. *Without Alibi* trans. P. Kamuf. Stanford, CA: Stanford University Press, 2002.

Dipple, Elizabeth. *The Unresolvable Plot: Reading Contemporary Fiction.* London and New York: Routledge, 1988.

Eagleton, Terry. *Literary Theory: An Introduction.* Oxford: Blackwell, 1983.

Eco, Umberto. *The Role of the Reader: Explorations in the Semiotics of Texts.* Bloomington and London: Indiana University Press, 1979.

Eco, Umberto. *Reflections on the Name of the Rose.* Trans. W. Weaver. London: Secker and Warburg, 1985.

Featherstone, Mike. 'Global and Local Cultures'. *Mapping the Futures: Local Culture, Global Change.* Ed. J. Bird et al. London and New York: Routledge, 1993.

Fludernik, Monica. *Towards a "Natural" Narratology.* London and New York: Routledge, 1996.

Fludernik, Monica. *An Introduction to Narratology.* London and New York: Routledge, 2009.

Foucault, Michel. *The Archaeology of Knowledge.* Trans. A. M. Sheridan Smith. London: Tavistock, 1972.

Foucault, Michel. *Madness and Civilization: A History of Madness in the Age of Reason.* Trans. R. Howard. New York: Random House, 1973.

Foucault, Michel. *The History of Sexuality.* Trans. R. Hurley. London: Pantheon Books, 1978.

Foucault, Michel. 'My Body, This Paper, This Fire'. Trans. G. Bennington. *Oxford Literary Review* 4 (1979): 1.

Gasché, R. 'Deconstruction as Criticism'. *Glyph* 6 (1979): 177–216.

Gasché, R. 'Setzung and Ubersetzung: Notes on Paul de Man'. *Diacritics* Winter 11: 4 (1981): 36–57.

Gasché, R. *The Tain of the Mirror: Derrida and the Philosophy of Reflection.* Cambridge, Mass. and London: Harvard University Press, 1986.

Genette, Gérard. *Narrative Discourse: An Essay in Method* (1972). Trans. J. Lewin. Ithaca: Cornell University Press, 1980.

Greenblatt, Stephen. *Shakespearean Negotiations: The Circulation of Social Energy in Renaissance England.* Oxford: Oxford University Press, 1988.

Hall, Stuart. 'Old and New Identities, Old and New Ethnicities'. *Culture, Globalization and the World System.* Ed. Anthony King. London: Macmillan, 1991a, 41–6.

Hall, Stuart. 'The Local and the Global: Globalization and Ethnicity'. *Culture, Globalization and the World System.* Ed. Anthony King. London: Macmillan, 1991b, 19–40.

Harland, Richard. *Superstructuralism: The Philosophy of Structuralism and Post-structuralism.* London and New York: Methuen, 1987.

Hart, Kevin. *The Trespass of the Sign: Deconstruction, Theology and Philosophy.* Cambridge: Cambridge University Press, 1989.

Harvey, David. *The Condition of Postmodernity.* Oxford: Blackwell, 1989.

Hassan, Ihab. *The Dismemberment of Orpheus: Toward a Postmodern Literature.* New York and Oxford: Oxford University Press, 1979.

Hawkes, Terence. *Structuralism and Semiotics.* London: Methuen, 1977.

Heise, Ursula. *Chronoschisms: Time, Narrative and Postmodernism.* Cambridge: Cambridge University Press, 1997.

Herman, David. *Story Logic: Problems and Possibilities of Narrative.* Lincoln: University of Nebraska Press, 2002.

Herman, David. *Basic Elements of Narrative.* Oxford: Wiley-Blackwell, 2009.

Holub, Robert. *Reception Theory: A Critical Introduction.* London: Methuen, 1984.

Hutcheon, Linda. *Narcissistic Narrative: The Metafictional Paradox.* London: Methuen, 1980.

Hutcheon, Linda, *A Poetics of Postmodernism: History, Theory, Fiction.* New York and London: Routledge, 1988.

Iser, Wolfgang. *The Implied Reader: Patterns of Communication in Prose Fiction from Bunyan to Beckett.* Baltimore: Johns Hopkins University Press, 1974.

Iser, Wolfgang. *The Act of Reading: A Theory of Aesthetic Response.* London: Longman, 1978.

Jakobson, Roman. 'Closing Statement: Linguistics and Poetics'. *Style in Language.* Ed. T. Sebeok. Cambridge, M.A.: M.I.T. Press, 1960.

Jakobson, Roman. 'On Realism in Art'. *Readings in Russian Poetics.* Ed. L. Matejka et al. Ann Arbor: University of Michigan Press, 1978.

Jameson, Fredric. *The Prison House of Language: A Critical Account of Structuralism and Russian Formalism.* Princeton: Princeton University Press, 1972.

Jameson, Fredric. *The Political Unconscious: Narrative as a Socially Symbolic Act.* London: Methuen, 1980.

Jameson, Fredric. *Postmodernism, or the Cultural Logic of Late Capitalism.* London: Verso, 1991.

Jameson, Fredric. 'Postmodernism and Consumer Society'. *Modernism/Postmodernism*. Ed. P. Brooker. London and New York: Longman, 1992.

Jauss, Hans. 'Literary History as a Challenge to Literary Theory'. *New Literary History* 2: Autumn (1970): 1.

Jauss, Hans. *Towards an Aesthetic of Reception*. Trans. T. Bahti. Minneapolis: University of Minnesota Press, 1982.

Jordan, Elaine, ed. *Joseph Conrad. New Casebooks Series*. London: Macmillan, 1996.

King, Anthony, ed. *Culture, Globalization and the World System*. London: Macmillan, 1991.

Kristeva, Julia. *Nations without Nationalism*. Trans. L. Roudiez. New York: Columbia, 1993.

Kuhn, Thomas. A *Theory of Scientific Revolutions*. International Encyclopedia of Unified Science 2:2. Chicago: University of Chicago Press, 1962.

Lacan, Jacques. *Ecrits: A Selection*. London: Tavistock, 1977.

LaCapra, Dominic. *History and Criticism*. Ithaca and London: Cornell University Press, 1985.

Lawson, Hilary. *Reflexivity: The Post-modern Predicament*. London: Hutchinson, 1985.

Leech, Geoffrey, and Short, Michael. *Style in Fiction: A Linguistic Guide to English Fictional Prose*. London and New York: Longman, 1981.

Lentricchia, Frank. *After the New Criticism*. London: Methuen, 1980.

Lentricchia, Frank. *Criticism and Social Change*. Chicago: Chicago University Press, 1983.

Llewelyn, John. *Derrida on the Threshold of Sense*. London: Macmillan, 1986.

Lodge, David. *After Bakhtin: Essays on Fiction and Criticism*. London and New York: Routledge, 1990.

Lyotard, Jean-François. *The Postmodern Condition*. Trans. G. Bennington and B. Massumi. Manchester: Manchester University Press, 1983.

Lyotard, Jean-François. *The Differend: Phrases in Dispute*. Trans. G. Van den Abbeele. Manchester: Manchester University Press, 1988.

McHale, Brian. *Postmodernist Fiction*. New York and London: Methuen, 1987.

Macherey, Pierre. A *Theory of Literary Production*. Trans. G. Wall. London: Routledge and Kegan Paul, 1978.

McEwan, Ian. *Saturday*. London: Vintage, 2005.

Maitre, Doreen. *Literature and Possible Worlds*. London: Middlesex Polytechnic Press, 1983.

Melville, Stephen. *Philosophy Beside Itself on Deconstruction and Modernism*. Minneapolis: University of Minnesota Press, 1986.

Miller, Christopher. *Blank Darkness: Africanist Discourse in French*. Chicago: University of Chicago Press, 1985.

Miller, J. Hillis. 'Stevens' Rock and Criticism as Cure', Part 2. *Georgia Review* 30 (1976): 5–33.

Miller, J. Hillis. *Fiction and Repetition: Seven English Novels.* Oxford: Basil Blackwell, 1982a.

Miller, J. Hillis. 'From Joyce to Narrative Theory and from Narrative Theory to Joyce'. *The Seventh of Joyce.* Ed. B. Benstock. Bloomington and London: Indiana University Press/Harvester Press, 1982b, 3–4.

Miller, J. Hillis. '*Heart of Darkness* Revisited' (1985). *Heart of Darkness: A Case Study in Contemporary Criticism.* Ed. R. Murfin. New York: St Martin's Press, 1989.

Mitchell, W.J.T., ed. *On Narrative.* Chicago: Chicago University Press, 1981.

Mitchell, W.J.T. *The Politics of Interpretation.* Chicago: Chicago University Press, 1982.

Mulhall, Stephen. *The Wounded Animal: J.M.Coetzee and the Difficulty of Reality in Literature and Philosophy.* Princeton: Princeton University Press, 2009.

Mulvey, Laura. 'Afterthoughts on "Visual Pleasure and Narrative Cinema" Inspired by *Duel in the Sun*' (1981). *Contemporary Film Theory.* Ed. A. Easthope. London and New York: Longman, 1996a.

Mulvey, Laura. 'Visual Pleasure and Narrative Cinema' (1975). *Contemporary Film Theory.* Ed. A. Easthope. London and New York: Longman, 1996b.

Nash, Christopher, ed. *Narrative in Culture: The Uses of Storytelling in the Sciences, Philosophy and Literature.* London and New York: Routledge, 1990.

Nuttall, A.D. *The New Mimesis: Shakespeare and the Representation of Reality.* London: Methuen, 1983.

Onega, Susana, ed. *Narratology.* London and New York: Longman, 1997.

Pavel, Thomas. *Fictional Worlds.* Cambridge, M.A. and London: Harvard University Press, 1986.

Prince, Gerald. *Narratology.* Berlin, New York and Amsterdam: Mouton, 1982.

Readings, Bill. 'The Deconstruction of Politics'. *Reading de Man Reading.* Ed. L. Waters and W. Godzich. Minneapolis: University of Minnesota Press, 1989.

Readings, Bill. *Introducing Lyotard: Art and Politics.* London and New York: Routledge, 1991.

Ricoeur, Paul. 'Narrative Time'. *Critical Inquiry* 7, Autumn (1980): 169–190.

Ricoeur, Paul. *Time and Narrative.* Trans. K. McLaughlin and D. Pellauer. Chicago: University of Chicago Press, 1984.

Riffaterre, Michael. *Fictional Truth.* Baltimore and London: Johns Hopkins University Press, 1990.

Rimmon-Kenan, Shlomith. *Narrative Fiction: Contemporary Poetics.* London and New York: Methuen/Routledge, 1983.

Roe, Emery. *Narrative Policy Analysis*. Durham and London: Duke University Press, 1994.

Ronen, Ruth. *Possible Worlds in Literary Theory*. Cambridge: Cambridge University Press, 1994.

Rousseau, Jacques. *Essays on the Origin of Language*. Trans. J. Moran. New York: Ungar, 1966.

Ryan, Marie-Laure. *Possible Worlds, Artificial Intelligence and Narrative Theory*. Bloomington and Indianapolis: Indiana University Press, 1991.

Said, Edward. *Orientalism*. Harmondsworth: Penguin, 1978a.

Said, Edward. 'The Problem of Textuality: Two Exemplary Positions'. *Critical Inquiry* 4 (1978b): 4, 673–714.

Said, Edward. *The World, the Text and the Critic*. Cambridge, M.A: Harvard University Press, 1983.

Said, Edward. *Culture and Imperialism* (1993). London: Vintage, 1994.

Salusinski, Imre. *Criticism in Society: Interviews with Jacques Derrida, Northrop Frye, Harold Bloom, Geoffrey Hartmen, Frank Kermode, Edward Said, Barbara Johnson, Frank Lentricchia and J. Hillis Miller*. New York and London: Methuen, 1987.

Sapir, Edward. *Language*. New York: Harcourt Brace, 1921.

Sarup, Madan. *An Introductory Guide to Post-structuralism and Postmodernism*. London: Harvester Wheatsheaf, 1988.

Saussure, Ferdinand de. *Course in General Linguistics*. Trans. R. Harris. London: Duckworth, 1972.

Stevenson, R.L. *Dr Jekyll and Mr Hyde and Other Stories* (1886). London: Penguin, 1979.

Stewart, G. 'Lying as Dying in *Heart of Darkness*'. *Publications of Modern Language Association* 95 (1980): 3.

Straus, Nina P. 'The Exclusion of the Intended from Secret Sharing' (1992). *Joseph Conrad*. Ed. Elaine Jordan. London: Macmillan, 1996.

Todorov, Tzvetan. *Introduction to Poetics*. Brighton: Harvester Press, 1981.

Updike, John. *Self-consciousness*. London: Penguin, 1989.

Veeser, H. Aram, ed. *The New Historicism*. London: Routledge, 1989.

Veeser, H. Aram. *The New Historicism Reader*. London: Routledge, 1994.

Watt, Ian. *Conrad in the Nineteenth Century*. Berkeley: University of California Press, 1979.

Waugh, Patricia. *Metafiction: The Theory and Practice of Self-conscious Fiction*. London and New York: Methuen, 1984.

Weber, Samuel. 'Capitalizing History: Notes on *The Political Unconscious*'. *Diacritics,* Summer 13 (1983): 14–28.

White, Hayden. *Metahistory: The Historical Imagination in Nineteenth Century Europe*. Baltimore: Johns Hopkins University Press, 1978.

White, Hayden. 'The Value of Narrativity in the Representation of Reality'. *On Narrative*. Ed. W.I.T. Mitchell. Chicago: University of Chicago Press, 1981, 1–24.

Whorf, Benjamin. *Language, Thought and Reality*. Ed. J. Carroll. New York: M.I.T. Press, 1956.

Williams, Raymond. *Culture and Society*. London: Chatto and Windus, 1958.

Williams, Raymond. *The Long Revolution*. London: Chatto and Windus, 1961.

Williams, Raymond. *The City and the Country*. London: Chatto and Windus, 1973.

Wood, David. *The Deconstruction of Time*. Atlantic Highlands: Humanities Press, 1989.

Young, Robert, ed. *Untying the Text: A Post-structuralist Reader*. London: Routledge, 1981.

Index